Emma Speaks

*A Journey into the Soul
of an Animal Friend*

DIANA ST. JAMES

Prologue

This book describes the intimacy I developed with my extraordinary horse, Emma, and the role that telepathic animal communication had in increasing not only the depth of my connection to her, but to other animals as well.

I invite those of you, who are new to telepathic animal communication to join me in my discovery, my initial doubts and my realization that animals have a voice. You, who already believe in the sentience of animals and their communication abilities, may enjoy learning about a horse like none other in her special powers. Due to her astounding sensitivity, Emma was far more aware and attuned to worlds beyond our senses than most humans or other animals.

It may be a stretch to believe everything I describe. If it didn't happen to me, I may wonder as well. But it did. I've changed nothing about the animal characters, what they did or their dialogue. Human characters, including my veterinarians, employers, Elaine and Nina, have been combined, their names changed and descriptions altered.

I understand that what I have written is unusual. You may find the events I describe push your understanding of the world and you may find yourself needing to suspend belief, but acknowledge the source and accept it for the gift it is.

A glossary of terms for people unfamiliar with horses and dressage is provided at the end of the book.

Acknowledgments

I approached writing this book as I did other jobs I wasn't prepared to do – such as when I, who had no teaching education or experience, audaciously assumed a classroom of high energy middle school children. I vowed to survive and then thrive.

Fortunately my energy is driven by my passions - passions that marshal my resources and direct my focus. My passion this time was to write the remarkable story of the birth of intimacy between my horse Emma and me.

First and foremost I must thank, Emma, for teaching me to perceive with more than the traditional five senses. Thank you Mathilda, Gussey, Spunky and all the others for relationships rich in their fullness of humor, joy and love.

Thank you to those who taught me to write, especially Camille Minichino who not only is a teacher par excellence, but has gifts of intelligence, patience and energy. Thank you to Deborah Medvick who critiqued my efforts chapter by chapter and Carol Barrett who corrected my grammar. And for the invaluable advice and support from the California Writers Club Mt. Diablo Chapter, the Published Writers of Rossmoor and Ann Damaschino.

Thank you most of all to Carol and all other telepathic animal communicators for expanding the boundaries of my perception. And I must acknowledge Hafiz and St. Francis, ultimate animal communicators.

Chapter 1

This morning started as any other with the earth yawning and stretching awake - so predictable in its routine that it lulled me into believing this would be a normal day. Complacent in my habits, I brewed my Earl Grey tea and gazed out the bay window in my kitchen. The phone interrupted my contemplation of squirrels skittering in the tulip magnolia on my front lawn. I followed the squirrels' antics, tails twitching, and wondered what the world looked like to them as I roused myself to answer the phone.

"Diana! I'm on my way over to pick you up," Nina's tone left no room for discussion. "It's about time you met my new horse, Henry. I'll be there in ten minutes."

I plopped back down, squished the tea bag and pursed my lips to blow across the surface, momentarily fascinated by the miniature tempest I created. The tips of my fingers traced circles on the rim of the porcelain cup, tickling my ears with the high-pitched vibration. My eyes drifted up to a wisp of a cloud as it sauntered across the mid-summer sky. The squirrels sprinted across the street and disappeared into the shadows of the sycamore leaving me with a pang of loneliness.

How could I know that on this day I would chance upon a horse who would transform the way I related to all animals? A horse who would stretch my beliefs and lead me to experience worlds I didn't know existed?

Sure enough in a few minutes the hum of a car motor disturbed the quiet and I spotted Nina's brand new 1990 white Honda bop into my driveway. With a frame nearly six feet tall and carrying extra pounds Nina seemed to fill the interior of her car. I waved and hurried for the front door.

I bounded by my entry table, snatched my blue denim baseball cap with the galloping horse embroidered on the front panel and tugged a scrunchie tight to contain my thick shoulder-length blonde hair at the nape of my neck. I launched over the four steps on my porch, alighted on my toes and affirmed that although I might be a middle aged woman, I hadn't slowed down yet. I laughed at myself. The prospect of meeting Nina's horse had certainly put an extra spring in my step.

My 130 pounds of mostly muscle settled into the passenger seat. One of Nina's kids must have been the last to ride in the car so I adjusted the chair back. Although I was of average height, most of it came from my legs. Long legs, long arms, short waist, decent shape. Not much on my chest filled out my blouse, an attribute which didn't bother me. God help the attempt of the big-breasted equestrienne to look elegant at the sitting trot.

Nina looked all horsewoman in her dark brown breeches and newly polished black paddock boots. Her pressed white blouse looked too vulnerable to make a trip to the barn. Dirt, dust, horse snot, drool, hay, bedding. I found it nearly impossible to stay clean. My faded jeans and dark camp shirt would survive and if I was lucky, I wouldn't have to change for the rest of the day.

"So have you started looking for another horse yet?" Nina asked, her big blue eyes twinkling.

"No," I said, being snapped back to an emotion I had been mired in for weeks. "I'm still grieving for Fortune. Eight years of training is a long time to partner with a horse. The longest relationship I've had.

Retiring him was hard. If my riding instructor hadn't insisted it was time to get a more capable horse, I don't think I would have had the courage to part with him. Just last week I visited him to make sure he wasn't losing weight in his new home."

"I have a video of Swedish warmbloods for sale that you might want to look at," Nina offered. "They make great show horses. There's a really nicely built grey..."

"I'm not ready to get a new horse," I said, interrupting her sentence and swiveling my head to look out the side window.

"For goodness sakes, it has been about three months since you've been without a horse," Nina said, swiping her blunt-cut bangs to one side of her forehead.

The car veered off the highway onto the narrow road that led into the low hills that stood between us and the San Francisco Bay. Who would have thought that Contra Costa County, a mere half hour drive east from the city, had one of the highest populations of horses per capita in the nation? And all kinds of open space to ride in. Briones, Shell Ridge, Mt. Diablo.

"A new mare arrived at my barn. She's in training to be sold." Nina inclined her head towards me. "I have to tell you about her. You've never seen anything like this. Not even close."

"What do you mean?" I asked, intrigued by her words. "In looks or performance?"

Nina extended a leather gloved hand over to punch a button on the radio to flip stations. The resulting breeze sent eau de leather my way. I never understood why she put her riding gloves on at home. She adjusted the air conditioning vent away from her face and onto mine. I guess she assumed I wanted the smell blowing my way.

"Attitude and temperament that is off the chart," she said. "And the mare is actually not bad looking. She appears quite athletic and is a lovely mover." Nina closed the moon roof.

"What does she do?" My fingers slid over the armrest to open my side window a crack.

Nina slowed to make a right turn onto Bear Creek Road. "She does nearly everything a horse can do to be dangerous," she said. "She frets, bolts, rears and bucks. Seems to resist any attempts at control. You would think she was a wild horse from some Bureau of Land Management program and never knew domestication. But she was born nearby in Livermore. I have to agree with my friends at the barn. She is one mentally unbalanced horse."

"Once I saw a horse get really mad," I said. The memory seized my gut with disgust. "His rider, a professional instructor, was being unfair and abusive in demands for performance. Every time the horse offered the wrong behavior, the whip came crashing down on his flank. The horse got frustrated. You know that expression 'blood in the eye?' Well, that horse had it. He was ready to explode when the rider finally let up."

"This mare doesn't seem to need a reason to act out," Nina said. "The trainer is quite competent and fair."

Nina rammed her index finger into the on/off switch of the radio when the news came on. I was relieved. The media tended to dwell on the negative.

"Oh, I've been meaning to ask, how is work going?" Nina cocked an eyebrow my way.

"I found out that my boss uses drugs," I said, my thigh muscles involuntarily twitching as if I was preparing to flee. "That could explain her mood swings and irrational behavior. A peer in a service center told me she buys her drugs from one of our direct mail vendors. She's been at the company forever and is in tight with her upper management. Last week, on the way to the vending machines, I asked her if she wanted a coke and she replied, 'not the kind that comes in a can.'"

"So what are you doing to do?" Nina asked, clicking on her car blinker.

"Keep my head down and do the best job I can," I said, wiping dust off my sunglasses. "I found out that I'm not alone in being miserable working for her. One of the guys in the loan operations center told me that the previous marketing managers didn't last long. To get how extreme it is, he told me that a predecessor couldn't stand her and quit after two weeks. The rest either resigned or were driven out in short order."

"Who wants to go to a job like that?" Nina said, throwing up her hands in a gesture of commiseration. "Can't you find another one?"

"I would," I said, shaking my head, "if openings for heads of marketing departments for major financial institutions weren't so scarce."

Nina made a right turn onto a driveway and took the immediate fork to the left. Her car crow hopped over the ruts gouged during a wetter season – the pot holes barely covered by a miserly sprinkling of gravel. Towering, blue-green eucalyptus trees framed the road, lacing their branches overhead. After a bend to the left, three rectangular buildings with high peaked roofs appeared on the bit of flat ground that resisted the incline of the steep hillside. The slowly moving tires of the car stirred up dust and I could smell the earth as it baked in the heat of the unadorned sun.

The car slackened to a stop. A whiff of grass hay and fresh pine shavings made my nostrils quiver. My breath thickened in my throat, my limbic system flashed my brain with images of other barns I'd known. I ached with how much I'd missed that smell. Three months without a horse felt as if time was measured in years. I shook off the feeling and compelled my mind back to the now.

Strolling over to the middle barn, we gushed back and forth in boisterous exclamations of our shared experience of horses, eventually halting in front of a stall on the right. With a whoosh and a creak, Nina rolled open the wooden door with iron bars on the top half. Her smile broadened when her horse gave her a low nicker and pushed his nose into her hand.

"Well, here is my bouncing baby boy," Nina said as she snapped the cobalt-blue nylon lead to his equally blue halter. "Diana, meet Henry." She led him outside, secured him to the blanket rack on his door and unlocked the lid of her burnished wood tack box.

I slid over to him, giving him time to get used to me. Henry's well-proportioned and heavily-muscled body suggested he had been kept in good condition. The dark chocolate brown of his coat gleamed with health. I offered my hand for him to sniff and then ran my fingers along the crest of his neck. The muscles felt as hard and lean as they looked, but the shiny coat that glistened in natural oils felt surprisingly coarse. My heart warmed to his open, kind expression. He turned his neck to get a better view of me, his dark brown eyes moist and doe-like. Anyone would admire this horse.

I looked over to Nina as she bent down to retrieve a boar-bristled brush. Fine, blonde hair framed her round face. She was heavier than I'd ever seen her. Hashimoto's disease had slowed her down and she had stopped fighting the new pounds that seemed to pad her frame each year. Good for her to continue riding.

"He's lovely. What a soft, gentle eye." I eased my hand out to Henry's forehead and traced the white blaze with my fingertips. "And a beautiful head, too."

"I was concerned," Nina said, gliding the brush over his coat and raising motes of dust, "he might look too similar to Fortune."

"He does remind me of Fortune, but I'm okay."

Fortune. I hadn't thought about him for at least ten minutes. Was he happy in his new home? Did he miss me as much as I missed him? I used the back of my hand to swipe away the moisture that was pooling in the corners of my eyes.

"So, how are Henry's gaits?" I tipped my baseball cap up and stood back to get a better view of the angles of his joints and bone structure. His neck, although a little thick and set on low, matched his well-developed hind end. Henry was a pretty horse, but could he move?

At the other end of the barn a woman approached us, her arm outstretched and insisting that the slender, bay horse keep a distance from her. I didn't pay her or the horse much attention at first, waiting for Nina's reply. Then, at the very moment the woman passed by, some strange and overpowering feelings hurtled through my body. What felt like a bolt of laser-sharp light leapt from the horse's chest to my heart, delivering a strong jolt of energy.

I didn't feel any pain. My body didn't hurt. But I felt dazed.

"Something happened, didn't it?" Nina scrutinized me. Her brush thudded when she dropped it into her tack box.

I managed to nod. I watched the retreating horse, my head bobbing in rhythm to her swinging hips, her hooves barely touching the ground.

"It was that horse, wasn't it?" Nina said, her eyes unblinking and her forehead creased.

"I really don't know what happened," I said, leaning against the stall door for support. "I feel a bit disoriented."

"That was the horse I was telling you about," Nina said, eyebrows arched. "The crazy one."

"The crazy one?" My eyes widened and I leaned towards her, trying to mitigate the conflict those words made me feel. "Really? No, really? I don't know what to say. I can't help myself. Something very peculiar happened. I have to check this out." I felt tightness in my chest and the acceleration of my heartbeat.

"You've always welcomed a challenge." Nina said, shaking her head. She picked up the metal-toothed mane comb and worked on the tangles in Henry's forelock.

I shrugged my shoulders and whipped around to pursue the horse. That is, I intended to whip around, but instead moved as though my body was suspended in molasses. I couldn't believe what I was feeling. For goodness sakes I was forty-four and way too old for infatuations.

As I crept around the corner, I saw the mare being hosed off in the wash stall a few yards ahead. The deep, rich brown of her coat glistened reminiscent of highly polished mahogany. The sun's rays reflected highlights that glittered like the gold confetti that cascades from the refiner's cauldron.

"Do you have a couple of minutes to tell me about this horse?" I asked the thin woman dressed in well-worn leather chaps and sporting a ready smile. I took solace that my voice managed to sound okay and not emit some high-pitched, throat-clenching screech. My body was out of control and I wasn't sure what to expect.

"Sure, I'd be happy to," the woman said as she examined me from cap to sneakers. She stepped forward and thrust out her hand. "My name is Debra. This mare is for sale and has been in training with me for about two weeks. She's a five and a half year old thoroughbred. Her breeder and her current owner both raised sporthorses. Hasn't had much done with her, though. I've never encountered anything similar to this. I can't seem to find a way to reach her, to relate to her."

My gaze wandered over the sleek, wet body of the mare. What I saw confirmed she was a thoroughbred, the greyhound of the horse world. Long bones, lean muscles and a sculpted elegance. A long, sloping shoulder promised length of stride. The hip descended to a well-muscled hind end. Strength and speed. She was well built, a precision athlete.

A braided cotton lead rope tied her to the pipe fence with a quick release knot giving her about two feet of freedom. She strained at the tether trying to escape the spray of water from the hose.

"I need to be honest with you," Debra said, splashing water over the mare's legs. She paused a moment to appraise my face. "She might not bond with humans. I'm not sure she'll come around."

I swallowed. Those were strong words of warning. They swirled around and then submerged in my mind. Somehow, I didn't believe them. I didn't know why, but I knew enough to trust my intuition.

The mare pranced about the wet concrete slab, her hooves clicking a nervous cadence. Horses didn't always appreciate a cool bath, after getting sweaty, but they didn't usually fuss this much. Despite the short lead, the mare managed to keep in motion. She took a couple of steps back and forth, then sideways and threw in the occasional head toss. I had a lot of excess physical energy at times so I knew about fidgeting.

The sun, not far from its zenith, spilled light and warmth all around us. The ricocheting drops of water danced and glittered in the light and then released the fragrance of wet horse when it evaporated from the warmed ground. The mare's head and neck, right out of an antique English print, were classically beautiful. An intelligent face bore a prominent white star. Large, clear brown eyes were vibrant, aware and promised a fully conscious being was at home. Her neck arched in a graceful curve from the poll at the top of her head to her withers, the ridge between her shoulder blades. A thick black tail rippled in the breeze resembling a curtain of shimmering velvet. Her astonishing beauty held my eyes hostage.

"What has been done with the mare?" I asked, approaching closer to stroke her neck.

"The owner believed in starting her horses late so she wasn't pulled out of pasture until she was five, never raced. She went to a hunter/jumper barn for a couple of months, but for some reason that didn't work out. She went back to pasture until I was given her to sell."

"What's her breeding?" I asked.

"She's the daughter of a successful show horse, Alissando, and a mare off the race track, Coming Up Clover, a Bold Ruler granddaughter," Debra said as she coiled the sloppy hose to one side. "I call her Mel because her registered name is Melissanda."

"The looks of this horse appeal to me," I said, my gaze wandering over her body from muzzle to dock, looking for imperfections in conformation. I particularly liked the slant of her hip. "She is athletically built and I'm interested in a dressage prospect. I was wondering if I might come back and try her out."

"You want to ride her?" Debra asked, her surprise evidenced in her face and body language.

"How about next Saturday?" I asked, my heart beat rising again.

"You understand she may not make a decent riding horse, might not warm up to humans," Debra stepped closer to me, squinting her eyes against the sun.

"I appreciate what you're saying," I said, holding her gaze. "How about 2:00 p.m.?"

"If you really want to," she said, upturning her palms.

I regretted having to leave the mare and pivoted in a small-stepped semi-circle before dragging my feet to rejoin Nina. As I was about to enter the barn, my head swung left to get a last glimpse of the mare and to imprint the scene in my mind.

"I've watched her move, she's powerful for having a slight build," Nina said as she led Henry back into his stall. Emerging out into the aisle, she smiled and said, "I didn't think it would be this easy to get you interested in a horse again."

"I didn't think it was possible, but there's just something about her," I said, rubbing the vertical cords of neck muscle flanking my spine.

"Remember to go slow," Nina warned. "It's going to take some time to work through her issues. You did wonders with Fortune and he had some real problems you had to overcome."

"I'll be careful," I said, kicking at a couple of loose flakes of sawdust with my sneaker. "I'll know more after I ride her." My eyes avoided Nina. I wasn't sure I knew what I was feeling and didn't want to struggle with answers to any questions.

Based on what people were saying, this horse might be carrying some psychological baggage. That was a risk. But something had happened between that horse and me and I had to understand what it meant.

I hadn't felt anything comparable to this before. Feelings hadn't been the primary driver for the choice of my other show horses. Conformation, movement and demeanor were the most important selection criteria. I knew that love would follow.

Yes, the horse looked as if she could do the work of a show horse, but there was something much more. Despite the trainer's admonition, my mind surrendered to what had happened to my heart. What else could such a horse do to my life?

Chapter 2

My father was born in a small village in Croatia on a peninsula in the Adriatic Sea. His home was a one room stone hut with a dirt floor and no windows. His mother abandoned him when he was four, banished with her lover to Argentina to start a new life. At one point he was left with relatives who abused him so badly he nearly died. A remarriage by my grandfather resulted in a new wife who fed her own children first giving my father what was left, if anything. The family eked out a living from harvesting wine grapes in the valley and tilling the rocky slopes for the few vegetables that would grow.

Just twenty-one years old, with a borrowed pair of overalls, a fifth grade education, not knowing English and hopes for a better life, my father bribed an immigration official and boarded a ship to the United States. After he departed Ellis Island, his destination was the oyster beds in Louisiana where other Croatians had settled. Work was hard and the company store consumed his wages. A move to New York City found him working on the docks. Wanting a less risky trade and one less encumbered with unions and politics, he hired on at a restaurant and got the idea to apprentice in the business so that he could open his own establishment.

A first marriage didn't last long with his bride divorcing him and moving back to live with her parents and to birth the baby she was carrying. His path to his second marriage began in a New York City Slavic dance hall where he met my mother and they wed several months later. Believing that California was the land of opportunity, my father put funds aside and five years later moved his wife and their two daughters (my older sister and me) to San Francisco to open his own restaurant with two Croatian partners. His hours were long and he was rarely home.

Born in Boston to poor, uneducated, immigrant Lithuanians my mother felt pride in being one step up from the Poles. Her mother died when she was a young girl and her father followed a few years later. Orphaned she was forced to leave high school and her sister, fourteen years older, took her in. Taking up her sister's trade, my mother learned the skills of the professional seamstress. Wanting a more independent life, she moved to New York City to work in the sweatshops and due to her speed did well at piece work. When she met my father, she had been deeply disappointed in love and viewed him as her last chance to marry and start a family.

My full sister was born into the family three and a half years before me. She came into the world full of fear and would scream at any noise. Adding to her innate terrors, she lived through the legacy of the first born – in an especially repressive environment. Instead of baby-proofing the apartment, my stay-at-home mom believed that my toddler sister should exert self-control and not touch anything that wasn't hers, which was just about everything. My parents took her to a dentist that didn't believe in Novocain. By the time my teeth needed work, he had retired and I escaped the torture.

The family moved to San Francisco when I was eighteen months old, leaving the few family friends behind. My first memories are of my mother sitting in an old wooden chair, her arms wrapped snug around her chest, rocking back and forth weeping. My mother told me that the landlord wouldn't rent to families with children, so my sister and I weren't allowed to play in our cramped flat. That meant no running, no noise. Stay still. We weren't even allowed to look out the window in case someone reported us to the landlord. We evolved into living mummies.

My parents had just enough to pay the rent and eat. No radio or television. No spinning mobiles or colorful posters cheered up the place. No board games or interactive toys provided stimulation. No plant to watch grow or goldfish to feed.

My father was mostly absent and his presence, when he did show up, terrified us. I don't remember being hit as much as my sister. My father would rage when he came home from work and drag my sister into the bathroom where her buttocks were laced with belt marks. My mother would drop her arms to her sides, her pinched face looking helpless. I would run and hide in a corner, trembling with each of my sister's screams. My happiest memory was being left alone in my crib to suckle on a bottle and finally get warm when the afternoon sun peaked through the fog and blazed into the room with a west face.

At four years of age I got lucky during a rare visit to some Croatians in Mountain View. One of the adults asked if I wanted to go along with her to pick up her daughter from a horseback riding lesson. Although shy, I was hungry for any experience and went along.

The riding instructor must have seen the wonder in my face and asked if I wanted to ride. As soon as I sat on the horse, ecstasy enveloped me. Movement became an expression of joy. I realized I could negotiate space without punishment. I felt the power of the horse, and learned that strength was not always accompanied by repression and pain. I was exquisitely free and more importantly, felt safe.

From that day forward every nickel and dime I was given for an ice cream cone or payment earned from doing chores for others went into my savings account. I was obsessed with horses. Books, pictures, small plastic toys, anything I could get my hands on. I wanted to feel that way again.

My daytime obsession with horses spilled over to my sleep world. Shortly after that first meeting, I had a dream that recurred regularly throughout my childhood. The dream always started with my romping among a herd of horses grazing in a meadow. One invited me to ride him. His brown coat, burnished with copper highlights, was shiny and slick, his muscles rounded, full of health. I leapt onto his back and he sprung forward at an energetic trot with abandon and joy. No matter how hard I tried, I could only cling to his back for a couple of strides. In every dream I slipped off his rear end and tumbled down in the grass only to get up and witness the small herd gambol and cavort out of sight.

I was left alone in the pasture, miserably alone. The sunshine, colorful butterflies, other flitting insects and song birds couldn't alter my despair. I felt empty. In the morning, awake, I mourned my loss and felt worse. Having what I wanted for only a few moments exacerbated the excruciating ache in my heart. That dream only strengthened my longing to own a horse, to ride a horse and to fill my emptiness. I made a pledge to myself that I would live long enough to have my own. One that I could hold on to. One that wouldn't leave me. I could not have been more focused on a goal.

Eventually my parents moved to a suburb of San Francisco into our own home. I started kindergarten and continued through high school in that residence. Fortunately I had been gifted a quick mind and was a natural student. I knew how to sit still, cooperate and pay attention. The outside world thought I came from a happy, well-adjusted home life. I never let on.

My father's rages continued. His vocabulary expanded to calling me names that reflected his mistrust of women. He threw out any friends who came over to play or do homework and refused to let me go to their homes. His paranoia of women drove him to keep my mother close to him. Despite her resistance, he forced her to work in his restaurant and forbade her from making any friends.

Siblings often support each other, but my sister and I didn't share the same values. I loved animals and tried to make anything that was alive a pet. I even tried to capture and farm ants. My sister, on the other hand, could be found in the garden pulling the legs off of spiders one at a time, watching them writhe. One day when I came home during my first year in high school she grabbed me and pinned me on the floor while her boyfriend tried to rape me. My screams and struggles worked. She released me just as he was about to pull off my pants. Despite how careful I was when he was around, he still managed to trap me and put his hands on my body where they didn't belong. My sister watched…mute. I told my mother, but she did nothing.

My mother seemed to be unaffected by my pleas for any kind of help so I knew better than to complain about the pain in my feet. Once when we went to a shoe store, I noticed the grimace of the shoe salesman when he informed her that the shoes she had me in were two and a half sizes too small.

Escape into a fantasy world was my relief. I kept my dream of horses alive by reading every horse book that I could find. Will James became my favorite author followed by Walter Farley. After reading the *Black Stallion* series, I was determined to get an Arabian horse.

The first family pet that my parents would allow was a parakeet. My parents claimed him as their own, especially my father. The bird was an extraordinary character who loved butter in any form and dive bombed our dinner plates whenever they were filled with buttered noodles. He landed and with his cylindrical tongue poised to lick off the butter as quickly as he could before we shooed him off. Thus we named him Noodles. I loved this bird and played with him for hours at a time. I marveled at how this little animal, weighing in at a few ounces, could enforce his boundaries with my parents. He would not be petted.

I tried keeping turtles but they died on me. I did better with hamsters until my mother drowned them one day when I was away at school. I didn't get any more pets after that.

My sister tried running away from home a couple of times. The futility convinced me to stay put and get an education as my way out. Occasionally a short, after-school visit in the homes of one of my high school friends provided me a reprieve from my father's rages and the oppression I felt at home.

Good grades in high school gave me entrance to my choice of campuses in the University of California system. I shunned the Berkeley campus with its history of violence and chose the Davis campus with its rural atmosphere and, more importantly, its horse barn.

My first courses were in math, physics and chemistry. My long blonde hair attracted a lot of attention from the male engineering and science students, but I didn't seem to have much interest, although I dated occasionally. I thought about becoming a vet, but after a stint dehorning calves with a hot iron and seeing plastic discs inserted into the side of cows to allow the study of digestion, I decided that viewing animals as economic entities didn't work for me.

A couple of years before I graduated I dated a physics graduate student, Larry. Romantic relationships got past my barriers to being touched. I found that I enjoyed the affection of my boyfriend and was hungry for it. But I rebuffed my friends' hugs and I wouldn't let my family come anywhere near me. My physical space extended at least three feet and I felt uneasy whenever someone encroached on it.

Through a college volunteer organization Larry introduced me to working with mentally disabled adults who were employed in the sheltered workshop at the Sacramento Association for Retarded Children. A couple of times a week a group of college students headed into Sacramento to supervise and run a recreation program.

At my first meeting I watched our clients beam out their smiles and come running, scuffing and limping to greet us. I thought I would faint when they embraced the other volunteers. The first to reach me was a four and a half foot Down syndrome woman, Shirley. She threw her arms around my waist and buried her head on my chest. A grinning, freckled face with a front tooth missing beamed up at me and helped me endure my first affectionate hug. It took a long time to break through my emotional shell but after several months I actually looked forward to their impulses of fondness.

For all of their issues, my parents appreciated the advantages of education and funded my start. With work at the psychology department and the Crocker Research Nuclear Laboratory, I managed to pay for my last three years of college. As soon as my course work in mathematics was completed, I picked up psychology as a second major. Psycholinguistics – the study of how we acquire and use language – caught my attention. When it came time to choose graduate schools, my advisor recommended the Massachusetts Institute of Technology as the best in the world in that field. My advisor and I were both surprised when a professor at MIT called me to insist I accept their offer of admission and a grant for both tuition and living expenses. My excellent grades in psychology, background in math and science as well as high-percentile test scores on the standardized post-graduate examinations appealed to their admissions board.

In 1970, after a few months at MIT, I got a German shepherd to protect me when attending evening classes in the industrial area of Cambridge and I married Larry. I believed that I loved him, but I was emotionally immature at twenty-three. At that time I didn't know what the word "love" meant and with hindsight I realized that marrying him was an option dictated by survival. I needed emotional stability. I soon grasped that long distance relationships posed their own challenges. Despite the hurt I caused myself in giving up my path to a PhD, after my second year of graduate school I decided to leave the graduate program and try and save our marriage. Larry had finished his degree, entered the army and was assigned to a hospital in Washington, D.C. I joined him in Maryland, a state known for its horse country.

I took lessons at the Potomac Horse Center, responded to an ad on a bulletin board there and shared board on a horse to get more experience in riding. A late evening encounter with a fellow equestrienne landed me a job teaching mathematics at a private school. Finally I had the funds to maintain and care for a horse. My student savings account had grown to $750 since I had put my first nickel aside and this treasure trove would be used to buy my first horse. Knowing I would entertain nothing other than a purebred Arabian, a friend I'd met when riding made an appointment at Al Marah Arabians in the Maryland countryside.

Excited beyond anything I had ever felt, I walked the aisles of the stately barns with horses stabled on both sides, and sucked in the moist air flavored with hay and hide. The Arabian's classic, dish-faced heads with the delicate pointed ears and the large, expressive, wide-set eyes, peered out of their stalls curious to know who I was. It didn't take long before my heart was abducted by a spectacular black gelding. His eyes sparked with life and love when he nuzzled my hand, his expression changing from curiosity to gentle exploration. His cascading mane, falling to the middle of his shoulder, undulated in waves down his neck. He could have been straight out of one of my books. The barn manager confirmed my good taste and beamed forth the horse's multitude of accomplishments as well as the $55,000 sale price. Crushed, I learned that no horse on their farm was within reach.

I lowered my sights and consulted the classified section of local newspapers. Three months later I found Foxy, an energetic four year old, half-Arabian, half-quarter horse gelding, a brilliant chestnut with lots of chrome (white blaze and white stockings). He wasn't a carefully bred pure-blooded Arabian with a show history so his price was affordable. Here, two decades later, my dream was to be realized.

Six weeks after Foxy was mine, he went incurably lame. A local pony club took him in and would use him with children on soft ground for as long as they could. I was inconsolable until a second horse was given to me by a kind woman who boarded her horses at the same stable where I had Foxy. To both her and my horror her gift horse went lame from a pre-existing condition three months after I got him and had to be destroyed. My tears and anguish more than doubled.

Shattered, but determined to give horses another try, I borrowed money from anyone who would lend it to me. My riding instructor helped me find my next horse, a young mare, bred by Anheuser Busch, Jr. in St. Louis and who would jump over any obstacle, agile as a mountain sheep. My instructor had gotten me hooked on three-day eventing as my equine sport of choice. Nothing was as intoxicating as the adrenalin rush of galloping over cross-country fences, hooves pounding the turf and wind ripping my hair.

With the increase in my love of riding, the harmony in my marriage decreased even though I was careful not to visit the horse when my husband was home. He seemed to be jealous not only of the need I had to be with horses, but also the love I had for my dog. The dissolution of my marriage was inevitable when my husband suggested that I choose between him and the horse. I packed my belongings and my German shepherd into my brand new 1974 AMC Gremlin, and retreated to a rented room in a fellow teacher's house.

Free of the restrictions of my husband I could spend every day with horses. I tagged along with my riding instructor to enjoy watching the weekend horse shows. After viewing a rather catastrophic three-day event where three riders were thrown and one taken away in an ambulance, my riding instructor took me to the Potomac Horse Center in Maryland to see a dressage show – a change in pace she kept secret until we arrived.

The indoor arena was open to the air by a bank of evenly spaced windows. As a rider passed down the long side, the openings acted like a strobe. Each frame captured the horse and rider moving in slow motion as if they were on a carousel just starting up. The rider rose in the air, seemed to pause and then slowly descended only to start the cycle again. I watched spellbound by the elegance and beauty of horse and rider moving in perfect harmony with breath-taking moments of suspension as if they were unaffected by the natural laws of gravity. My instructor explained that I had just seen an Olympic horse execute the passage, a trot with tremendous suspension, a movement in the Grand Prix test which is the highest level in dressage.

A huge passion had been unleashed and I vowed that somewhere, somehow I was going to have a horse that could do those movements. Meanwhile I had a lot to learn about riding and horse management.

At this time one of my riding buddies, self-named the Jewish Dale Evans, introduced me to transactional analysis and teamed me up with a therapist who for a minimal fee would treat me while she completed her studies and got her license. What a gift. This work jump-started my recovery. I was determined that guilt and shame were not going to be my script for that much longer. I worked hard to eliminate sabotaging myself into self-condemnation. The therapist wisely counseled me to concentrate on the feeling and not a particular action. As I eliminated the more obvious behaviors, I got more clever. I was always punctual. And then one day I wasn't. What a great pay-off for feeling shame. The gap closed between realization of the feeling I had unconsciously created and the action that I had done to get there. The glorious day arrived when I was able to stop the behavior before it happened. I rejoiced. That was the first time I had control over my self-inflicted universe of contrition.

My teaching was a source of joy and I was vitalized by the process of opening the minds of children, giving them confidence in themselves and the courage to solve problems of all kinds. And I loved the children. Middle school may be avoided by others, but I flourished with the kids who challenged, confronted, protested and disputed everything. During a math class, a fifth grade girl demanded to know why there was no girls' athletic program – especially basketball which she loved. And thus I was recruited to coach even though I had never played basketball. I had refused to play when I was young because girls were restricted to two bounces before they had to pass the ball and I thought that was dumb. Fortunately what library books taught me about the lay-up and zone defense and the boys' coach about picks helped me lead the girls to an undefeated season against teams who had played in leagues for years.

After three years of teaching, I knew I had to leave the area. The East Coast didn't feel comfortable, it wasn't home. Besides, the salary of a private school teacher wouldn't pay for a horse and my own home and I wanted more financial independence.

In 1977 I sent my horse ahead and moved back to the San Francisco Bay Area. A college friend put me up until I found a job and could afford a little in-law cottage. By now my riding sport had fully evolved from eventing to dressage. Good thing because the clay soil of the East Bay - glue in winter and concrete in summer – didn't lend itself to the endurance work that the sport of three-day eventing required. I sold my mare who had carted me around fences safely but had little talent on the flat and purchased a thoroughbred with more promising movement.

In the job scene I lucked out. It only took six weeks to land a job at Lucky Stores Corporate headquarters. My position as a business analyst developing major data processing systems afforded me an overview of the business world. The four years that I was there taught me that making the business decisions seemed as if it would be a lot more interesting than building systems that supported the business operations.

To keep progressing with my career I worked for Integral Systems Incorporated, the predecessor to People Soft, and then Bechtel while going to night school to get my MBA. After graduation a short stint at a consulting firm landed me a job offer in a major bank's new product development and marketing department.

The work was interesting and I was inspired to learn all I could about marketing. It also helped pay the mortgage on a small ranch house I had managed to buy with almost nothing down. The house, a fixer upper, on a quarter acre in the suburbs was my sanctuary. My horse was boarded a close half-mile away.

At this time a couple of fellow employees introduced me to Sufism Reoriented, a spiritual order that follows the teachings of

Meher Baba, an Indian spiritual leader, who wrote their charter. In 1987 I took a trip with members of the order to Meher Baba's tomb in India. Although I started life as an atheist, while I was in India, my beliefs changed. I could not deny the spiritual intensity of the experience and the direct knowledge I had of God. I had one particularly life-changing, emotionally intimate encounter with a member of the order. Emerging from a cave where several holy men had mediated over the ages, a fellow traveler put her arms around me and enveloped me in a powerful love. For the first time in my life I learned how it felt to receive a mother's love – an all-inclusive and unconditional love. I felt my chest rend and a crack formed in the husk encasing my heart. The love reached a place that had been untouched. Back in California, I made the decision to make Sufism Reoriented my life, became a follower of Meher Baba and committed to living a spiritual lifestyle.

A spiritual perspective taught me to love my parents and sister and to be kind to them despite how they treated me. Unfortunately, for my own mental health I had to keep some distance. My therapist felt that their criticism, lying and manipulations would slow my recovery work. She likened my childhood to the experience of those in the Holocaust. Even so, getting through the holidays was especially tough - I still loved my family. To that my therapist stated, "Abused kids cling even tighter with hope for what they never had."

John Bradshaw's video of *Homecoming* and his book about the family system explained the issues that I needed to resolve - abandonment, damaged inner child and self-criticism. During some of my hardest times, I saw my therapist twice a week. My relationship to my horse and my riding helped keep me grounded and moving forward through the gut-wrenching work of therapy. Any day I didn't see my horse I was out of sorts.

My thoroughbred horse kept coming up lame even after trying everything my vet suggested, including surgery. I found him a home and bought Fortune, a five-year-old gelding that looked akin to one of the European sporthorses with more bone and substance than our American thoroughbreds. He had a big, energetic trot that covered ground, but needed development in the walk and canter gaits. His personality was a big challenge - refusing out of the blue to do something he had been doing all along such as getting in a trailer or canter half-pass. After eight years of hard work and making it to fourth level in dressage, Fortune didn't want to perform at the higher levels any more. I couldn't give up my yearning for dressage so I gave him to a woman who promised to keep him through his natural life.

Although I loved my job, the long commute into the city seemed to affect my health so when I got a call from an employment recruiter, I jumped at the chance to take a job just a couple of miles from my home.

The new job revealed all too soon I had been hired by a difficult manager. And I didn't have a horse.

Chapter 3

Saturday brought with it a temperate sun whose prodding woke me with gentle strokes of warmth. Once conscious the anticipation of seeing the mare again catapulted me into activity. My mind cautioned me to slow down; it was too soon to get excited and invested with feelings. Too many unknowns. Yet, I felt a draw as steady and as palpable as gravity. The need for horses in my life was tempered by my practical nature which took over in the sales process. The horse had to be ridden and had to pass the vet examination. Only with the purchase and safe delivery to my barn could I fully invest in the bonding process. The singular emotional response I had to this horse was new territory for me and I was a little frightened by it.

Off to the barn. Henry was alone in his stall when I walked by to say hello. No surprise that Nina wasn't there; she was off on another trip with the kids.

In the aisle of the third barn, the trainer was tacking up Mel. My breath stopped on seeing her. Perhaps she would be my horse. What would she be like to ride?

"Can I help?" I said, walking up to Debra.

"No thanks, I'm just about finished." She picked up a pair of nylon web side reins and snapped them to the rings of the snaffle bit, securing the ends to the girth leathers on either side of the saddle.

I wasn't fond of side reins. Little forgiveness. Despite the rubber donut, they created more of a barrier than an elastic boundary. Any mistake of the unschooled young horse would meet with punishment. The stainless steel bit would be unyielding to the soft, fleshy mouth of the horse. Her lips would be pulled back and the center joint would dig into her palate. Hot pizza had burned my palate often enough to educate me on how sensitive that area of mouth was. Besides I had seen too many horses with over bent necks that were the result of being schooled in side reins.

Debra picked up a pair of draw reins and draped them over her shoulder.

"Why do you need draw reins?" I turned to face Debra.

"I need the control," she said, keeping her eyes on the mare. She uttered her statement with such finality that I knew the discussion was over.

Debra adjusted her high-density foam vest, used to protect the ribs and core during a fall. She tightened the thick leather chin strap of her helmet. Good gracious, I thought, she isn't riding a bucking bull.

She reached down and pulled out a brass stud chain from her tack box. Snapping it to one side of the bit, she ran the chain over the mare's soft muzzle. I wrinkled my nose.

"I need the control to lead her over to the indoor arena." She pulled the chain snug. The mare flinched. My mind said maybe she has a reason for it. My heart revolted.

A boarder entered the aisle leading his horse, saw us and then turned around and left. A few minutes later, the same thing happened at the other end of the aisle with a different boarder. That's strange. Are they avoiding this mare? I wondered what they saw that I didn't.

The trainer lifted the saddle flap and tightened the girth a couple of holes. She checked her tack, turned and led the mare with a determined stride down the aisle. She sped up even more as soon as we were outside. I lengthened my stride to keep up with her. Good thing for long legs or I'd be jogging.

"This mare needs to be taken directly to the indoor arena," she said, turning her head over her shoulder to make sure I heard. "I wouldn't ride her outside. She's uncontrollable. Trail rides are out of the question."

She didn't slow her pace until the gate of the indoor arena snapped shut.

Uncontrollable? What did she mean? Our definitions were most likely out of synch. The mare fidgeted when she was being hosed off outside, but I chalked that up to the agitation of a horse unaccustomed to regular handling. I wasn't going to be dumb. I'd stay in close contact with what my gut was feeling. It never failed me. I would know if a problem was on its way.

"I let her loose once in the outdoor arena," Debra said, holding tight to the stud chain. "The mare ran and screamed until her sides were heaving. Her neck and chest were covered in froth."

I heard the words, tried to imagine what she described and then dismissed them as hyperbole. This mare probably lived her life at this point going from an interior stall with no windows to an indoor arena, briefly seeing the sky and touching the earth's dirt for a few seconds. That kind of life would be enough to make me act out. Why did people ask horses to live that way? Just because it was an accepted practice didn't mean it was a good choice.

Two riders were schooling their horses when we entered the arena.

"Are you going to work that mare here for awhile?" one shouted out.

"Yes, I'm going to longe her." Debra led the mare to one end of the arena.

Both riders dismounted and headed straight for the exit gate.

What strange behavior. Why did they have to clear the arena? I'd seen riders get uncomfortable when an unschooled horse showed up. Especially if handled by a green rider. Cautious, yes. But leave? This was a large arena that gave everyone plenty of room. And Debra was a trainer, not a beginner.

Debra removed the stud chain, shortened the side reins, hooked the longe line to the mare's bridle and released her hold. The mare shot off at brisk trot. Her head, evading the action of the bit, was over bent, well behind the vertical. As she gained speed, she dropped her hindquarters, bent her hocks, brought her hind legs under her belly and lightened her front end. She did naturally what it took me years to strengthen and train Fortune to do. She was clearly a capable athlete. The trainer circled her a couple of times in both directions and then pulled her to a halt.

"Do you want to ride?" she said, turning to me.

"No, that's okay," I said, "you go first." As much as my heart said to ride the horse, my mind knew better. Nina's cautionary words were playing softly in the background noise of my thoughts. If trouble was brewing, better to be watching it, than having it.

Debra removed the side reins and added draw reins, walked over to the corner of the arena and crept up the mounting block while keeping her eye on the horse. She froze for a moment on the top step, flashed a look up to the roof and seemed to mouth a silent prayer. Once seated, she asked the horse to trot, first left, then right. She cranked the reins tight before asking for the right lead canter. After a couple of strides, she brought the horse to an abrupt stop. "I have trouble getting her left lead," she said, jumping off after riding for no more than five minutes, if that. The duo made an uncomfortable pairing, not a partnership.

"Are you still interested in trying out the horse?"

She surveyed my face. In these circumstances, I presented an expressionless countenance. If I had to do any price negotiation, I didn't want anyone to know how strongly I felt about this horse.

"It's time to get on her back." I sighed and stepped forward to take the reins. I could feel the tempo of my heart beat increase.

Debra flipped up a stiff arm and raised her palm to stop me. "Please, won't you put on this hard hat and safety vest?" She pulled at the top snap on her vest.

"I hate hard hats," I said, waving her away, "and have never used a vest."

She didn't budge, so I obliged her only with the hat. As soon as she relinquished the reins, I unsnapped the draw reins and removed them. The mare stretched out her neck and twisted it, as though working out a cramp.

"Are you sure you really want to do that?" Debra said, her forehead pulled up in inquiry. "You're giving up a lot of leverage."

"Yes, I know I'm giving up some restraint," I said without taking my eyes off of the mare.

"Well, at least keep her on a tight rein." She turned and walked to a corner of the arena. "Don't give her her head."

I smiled and nodded, as if I agreed.

My feet pressed against the top step of the mounting block. Getting on the horse from this height was easier on the horse's back and less risky for the rider. I took a breath, held it and slipped my foot into the stirrup. My leg swung over the mare's back. I eased my weight down. All my senses were sparking with electricity and open full bore for the slightest indication of what the mare was communicating. Her back muscles were stiff and unyielding. I gently pressed my calves to her sides to ask her to walk on. With her first tentative steps I let the reins slip through my fingers a few inches. She stretched her neck down and forward, her stride slowing and getting slightly longer. Debra gasped when I dropped the reins and gave freedom to the mare's head.

I stroked her neck and told her she was okay, speaking in a low, soft tone. Her back muscles softened. I urged her into a trot and she moved off in a wavy line – typical of an unschooled horse. I trotted her in both directions and attempted some circles that ended up resembling the shape of potatoes. Despite her being uncertain as to what I wanted, she seemed willing to please. Every time I asked her to do something, she offered a response. Her awkwardness didn't diminish that her effort was a good sign.

I needed to feel her canter. My mind dusted off my deep space radar equipment. My abdominal muscles tightened. I knew the canter could be an explosive gait. I'd seen too many horses who were behaved at the trot suddenly buck and cavort when asked to canter. With her head unrestrained, this mare could put in some mighty big bucks and I would be defenseless until I gathered up the reins. I checked in with my gut. Cantering was safe.

My legs signaled for a more energetic trot. I slid my left leg behind the girth and pushed with my inside seat bone. The mare struck off in a well-balanced, pure, three-beat gait. Her long stride was easy to sit. No rushing, just an honest, forward canter. Then I brought her back to the trot and tried the left lead. She picked it up without hesitation. It was as lovely in this direction. I did a few more trot-walk-trot transitions. That was all I needed. I guided the mare towards Debra, eased to a halt, weighted my left stirrup and in slow motion slid to the ground.

"What do you think?" Debra said, leaving the corner and walking straight towards me. Her eyes penetrated any shell I might have.

"It's time to call the vet and set up an appointment for a pre-purchase examination." I loosened the girth. My mechanical assessment mode switched off since I no longer needed to determine the capabilities of the horse. Mel turned her head to look at me. I looked into her eyes. Another blast of some kind of energy washed over me.

"I've had a hard time getting her left lead canter, but you didn't. She struck right off," Debra said coming to a stop beside me. "You seem to get along with her."

I nodded. My relationship with the horse seemed natural and familiar.

Two days later, I headed back to where Mel was boarded for the appointment I'd made with my vet, John Taylor.

I tapped my fingers on the steering wheel as the car jounced up and down on the twisty two lane road and swung from side to side, up and down and around hair pin turns. The buttons on the radio got a good workout. No music calmed my twitchy stomach. I kept flipping the car's sun visor up and down. What was that Carly Simon song . . . "Anticipation"?

At last I made it to the barn. I wedged my periwinkle AMC Gremlin into a tight spot between a three-quarter ton truck and a dualie. I spotted Debra holding Mel near the outdoor arena. There was my horse, the horse who made my heart do acrobatics.

"Right on time," Debra said, extending her arm in a hand shake. "I'm glad you agreed to meet before your vet arrives." Debra led the mare into the outdoor arena. "I want you to see her aberrant behavior when she isn't confined. You may change your mind."

"I appreciate your honesty." I leaned against the fence for a better view. Wow, I never knew any trainer to go to this extent to point out the flaws of her client's horse. I had to respect her effort to make sure this would be a good fit.

Debra unbuckled the halter and jumped back outside the gate taking care to secure the lock. The mare lowered her shoulders, spun and zoomed across the arena with her nose pointed skyward and her tail arched and spread out like a streaming flag. Near the fence she skidded, did a quarter pirouette and faced me. Her forelock swept to the side and showcased her large, expressive eyes which seemed to be discharging sparks of energy. I felt as if I had just been X-rayed. Her stare penetrated my body and pierced my heart as if she were sounding its depths.

She rose up, her body vertical, front legs striking out high into the air. She towered above us, her vitality magnificent. Her front feet plummeted back to earth and she sprung off into a proud extended trot. She seemed to be suspended in the air, breathtaking in her animation. She covered enormous lengths of ground with each stride, barely touching the earth. She seemed to be living above the ground and not on it. A prima ballerina leaping across the stage on point could not move with more grace or fluidity.

On the next pass across the arena, the mare stirred the dust and created a whirlwind in her wake. I laughed to myself.

"My God, she's showing off," Debra whispered, shaking her head in amazement.

As soon as I replied, "You're right," the mare wheeled and charged towards me. A rush of wind preceded her arrival. She sat on her hind quarters and threw out stiff front legs, plowing furrows in the dirt and stopping inches from where I stood. I froze at the suddenness of her display. What was she going to do next? She thrust her head over the fence and pressed her forehead against my chest with a pressure so gentle it barely penetrated my shirt.

I felt as if I'd been lightly kissed. The touch so light it resembled the first tentative gesture from a shy child. The rising currents from the warmth of her body lifted the earthy scent of horse to my nose. Peace enveloped me. My hand slid up the front of her face, my fingertips tracing the fine bone structure of her forehead. Her soft silky hair was smooth and slick to the touch. My palm rolled to the side and stroked her cheek with the tenderness I'd use to touch the wings of a butterfly. The mare exhaled a sigh so deep it felt as if she was releasing a lifetime of burdens. My knees almost buckled.

Disbelief stretched across Debra's face. "You have to buy her." She sidled up within a half foot of me as if she needed to get a better view of what she'd just witnessed. "She's clearly your horse. You have to have her."

The mare's breath caressed my palm, both tickling and warming me. This time she nestled her forehead deeper against my heart, between my breasts.

"I'm feeling that too," I stammered. Warmth spilled from my chest down my abdomen, through my feet and into the earth. I scrunched my toes as if grabbing hold of something solid. I felt a film of tears misting my eyes.

The sound of a truck engine punctured my consciousness and ripped me back. It took concentrated force to rotate my head to face the parking lot and refocus my attention. John Taylor's white pick-up truck outfitted with compartments to house his veterinary equipment rolled into a parking space. I swallowed and filled my lungs with a deep breath. Debra haltered the mare and escorted her back towards the barn. I stomped my feet jamming them into the dirt in an attempt to get better grounded as I headed over to John.

"I think I've found my horse," I literally bubbled, smiling at him through the open window of his truck. His blond hair, bleached platinum from the sun, reflected dazzling white light.

"Good to see you too," he said, laughing. "Hey, with all of your heartache with Fortune I wanted to check up on this mare. You know how easy it is to mask issues. I called this barn's manager to find out if the mare had any history of unsoundness. She said as far as she knew the horse was physically sound, but had a severe screw loose." His truck door creaked and scraped open, its hinges the victim of endless miles on dust-filled roads. His six feet of lean muscle landed lightly on the dirt, his boots barely disturbing the fine silt underfoot.

"I've heard those stories, too." I moved over closer to him and got a whiff of his perspiration, a healthy smell of honest work. "But, I'm glad to hear she's been sound."

"The barn manager hoped you would buy the horse and take her away from here." His smile sagged into straight lips. "She thinks the mare is a liability – trouble waiting to happen."

My heart sank. What if John didn't pass the mare? Even though he might determine she was physically sound, he could flunk her for unsuitability of purpose. I trusted John. I wouldn't ignore his recommendation.

"Everyone seems to be spooked about this horse," I said, guiding him to the far barn. "But I haven't seen anything to worry about."

We found Debra in the barn aisle, holding the halter of the mare who fidgeted, tapping her feet back and forth in short staccato steps. Debra rocked her weight from one leg to the other looking as if she were a barefoot sun bather negotiating sun-scorched sand.

"You're going to tranquilize her, aren't you?" she said to John.

Wow, I thought, some greeting. She must be really anxious that this mare might act out.

"Let's wait and see." John walked up to the mare and looked into her eyes. He cocked his head and glanced at me, his eyes twinkling - their Nordic blue dappled with crystals of light. He nodded at Debra, and with the grace of a dance movement took the lead rope from her and handed it to me. He must have compared her jerky movements and nervous twitches with my quieter stance and grounded energy. As soon as the rope touched my hand, goose bumps raced over my skin. A simple thing. Hold the lead rope. But the lead rope felt alive. Electricity raced between us. The nerve endings of my hand were tingling as if I'd just hit my crazy bone.

With slow, deliberate movements John ran his hands over the mare's muscles, joints and tendons. First the left front leg, then the others. By the time he finished inspecting her entire body, the mare stood still, responding to John's soothing touch. The trainer stood nervously on the side.

John directed me to lead the mare outside so he could observe her gaits on the hard-packed gravel road in front of the barn. A few trips back and forth satisfied John that her strides were even and without any evidence of soreness. He motioned me to take her back inside, where he examined her eyes, teeth and performed all the other inspections that are part of a pre-purchase examination. The mare was compliant and responded to everything we asked of her, including standing quietly on plates of film. She even stood still while John re-positioned the black box, his portable X-ray machine, next to her hooves.

"So what do you think of her personality?" I asked when we walked back to his truck and were out of Debra's earshot. "Especially given what the barn manager told you?"

"She's a young, inexperienced horse," he said, flicking his hand at the wrist, "in need of some TLC." His eyes shone as he opened the truck door and jumped in. "For a horse recently out of pasture, I think she's just fine. I wouldn't worry about her reputation."

"What a relief." My stomach settled down in mid-flip.

"She's a very handsome horse," John started his truck. "I'll call you in a couple of days when I get the results of the X-rays back."

Fortunately I had my job to distract me while I waited for the X-ray results. Except for my boss, my work was enjoyable. Creating communication pieces that clearly conveyed the benefits of the product and that had meaningful appeal to our customers let me use my common sense. Advertising was fun and working with different vendors and creative groups let me meet new people. The job title was impressive – Group Vice President of Marketing and Product Development. Too bad the salary didn't tend to match it. But it was enough to let me afford my own home, show horse and truck and trailer. I still drove my old AMC Gremlin, but who cared. I didn't have much to complain about.

Fortunately the week was full of projects nearing completion and the mania we engaged in for next year's budget process fully employed my mind. The job was new enough that I worked long hours to get up to speed on the products and corporate culture.

Meanwhile, my heart was held in a wicked kind of limbo. Would John Taylor's X-rays expose some pernicious disease? My breath caught each time the phone rang and I ended the calls as quickly as I could. I wanted to hear John's gravelly voice and at last one evening I did.

"Her X-rays looked good. She does have a slight club foot on her left front, but it doesn't mean anything. I'm happy to pass the mare."

"What do you mean club foot?" I asked.

"There is a slight rotation in the bone," John said. "It's so slight that you don't have to worry about it. I've examined grand prix jumpers who had more rotation than she does. For all practical purposes she is a normal horse."

"Okay John, for better or worse she'll be mine." I felt light-headed.

I hung up the phone and whirled around my family room, a spinning top out of control. I felt as if my body would go airborne. Echoes from squeals of delight reverberated off the walls and tile floors.

Confident that Mel would pass the pre-purchase examination, Debra had said that she could deliver the horse on the weekend. I was glad that I had found a boarding facility only about twenty minutes from my home.

I sat down and wrote a check for the mare. Debra had told me that Mel's price had started much higher given her brother had sold for quite a bit, but she had talked the owner into dropping the price nearly in half given the mare's temperament. The amount was reasonable and I wasn't going to bargain. I found it curious, though, that the price was the exact amount that I had set aside to replace my leaking roof. The amount was too close to be a coincidence. The footprints of fate kept showing up with this horse.

At last my goal to have a top level show horse was to be fulfilled.

Chapter 4

My new mare needed a new name. Her registered name was too long and her nickname, Mel, did nothing for me.

Names were not my forte, so I slept on it, hoping for inspiration. In the morning, my body leapt from deep sleep into full wakefulness. I sat up in bed as if someone had tapped me on the shoulder. I heard a voice in my head say, "Emissary. Emma, the Emmisary!"

Wow, a voice in my head that wasn't my own conscious thoughts. I had strong intuitions, but usually not such a clear and definite voice in my mind. Perplexed, but mostly excited, I whisked into my office and snagged the dictionary to look up emissary. I reread it several times. What I read made me smile.

1. One sent on a mission for another.

2. A secret agent.

Emma would be her stable name, short and feminine sounding. Emissary would be her show name, sort of philosophical. The definition for emissary had some mystery to it. What kind of secret agent? What kind of mission?

I was lucky that I was buying a horse at the end of summer and not late fall when all of the boarding stables were full with horses brought in for the winter. Pine Knoll Equestrian Center rested at the end of a rural two-lane road near an entrance to Diablo State Park with its miles of trails. Although I'd never boarded there before, the place had always intrigued me when I rode Fortune by it on the way to the trail head. The spacious indoor arena, a real luxury, offered shelter from winter storms and a dry place to ride and school.

Antsy to greet my new horse, I showed up a good hour before Debra was scheduled to arrive. Saturday morning was a good time for the delivery. I'd have the rest of the day and all day Sunday to be with the mare. I also had plenty of time to get acquainted with the other amenities of the stable. The wash stall with its hot water connection was a benefit for horses.

The crunching of tires on gravel grabbed my attention and spurred me to run to the front of the barn. Debra's truck and trailer eased into the side parking lot. She hopped out of her truck, shot a greeting my way and went directly to the tail gate of her trailer, wide-bodied and tall enough for the 17-hand horses. My back shivered when the ramp dropped and thudded to the ground. Is this what it felt like when the church doors swung open to the bridal procession?

Once all four hooves had backed off the rubber-coated exit ramp, the mare, rather Emma, stared straight into my eyes. Emma . . . the sound fell comfortably on my ears. The name fit her.

Here at last she was at the stable I had chosen for her. I whistled through taut lips when the trainer handed me the cotton lead rope. Feeling the weight of the rope in my hand brought it all home.

My horse, a new boarding stable, a new beginning. I felt as if I had made a commitment as binding as a marriage vow. Not quite as drastic as a mail order bride. I'd seen her before, even ridden her once. But how well did I know her? Our relationship was at the beginning. What discoveries lay ahead?

"Welcome to your new life and your new home, Pine Knoll Equestrian Center," I said, insinuating myself next to Emma's shoulder to rest my hand on her neck. "I'll do my best to make you happy."

Emma looked around with a regal air as if she were assuming command. I followed her gaze out to the hills across the street. A small metal gate stood ready to provide admittance to trails for both Shell Ridge and Mt. Diablo State Park. The gnarled limbs of the native oaks on the hillside cut jagged puzzle pieces against the blonde dried grasses. The buckeye and laurel provided shade and an artist's delight in variations of green. The trails beckoned.

By the time I looked back, Debra had already secured her trailer and was heading to her truck. I waved and watched the truck blast off down the road leaving meteors of gravel catapulting behind her.

Alone with my horse, I exhaled and led her inside the main building that housed most of the horses and the arena. It must have covered a small city block. Two rows of stalls, homes to a variety of horse breeds framed the aisles on the long sides of the indoor arena. The fine silt generated by a well-used barn covered the slats of the wooden stall doors. Roof beams overhanging the arena provided roosting for a few pigeons who cooed and flapped, sending puffs of feathers, fluttering into the breeze. Emma's stall was in a far corner away from the pigeons' droppings. And away from where the other boarders tended to congregate. I appreciated my privacy. Good for both of us.

We were lucky. The one available stall had a window looking out to the east at the grassy foothills behind the barn. Although no paddock was attached to the stall, this arrangement was a step up from the mare's previous home with no windows and no way to hang her head out in the barn aisle. To provide relief from being stall bound, Emma would be turned out in a small, outdoor paddock for a couple of hours, most days of the week. Tom, an instructor at Pine Knoll, performed this service for a nominal fee. Even if I came out every day to ride her, she needed some hang time in the sun. Confining a horse to a stall twenty-four hours a day felt like an insane punishment. I always thought that big animals need more space.

Debra had warned me that the mare shouldn't be taken on trail rides, but I knew covering ground over different terrains was the best way to bond with a new horse and establish a partnership. So on the first day after Emma's arrival, I planned to head out, through the gate and into the hills, to ride alone. Other riders would distract me from staying in tune with my horse. I didn't need someone on hand to baby-sit me or call an ambulance. My gut said the horse would be fine. I would walk mostly and maybe trot a little. Get to know each other.

Emma embarked on her first excursion into the hills as if she had been whisked into Wonderland. So much to see. She reacted with more awe than fright. Her first sighting of a four foot boulder slumbering to one side of the trail worried her. It was a perfectly innocuous rock, not even covered with lichen or moss, just grey and smooth and very inert. Horses had their own private, idiosyncratic demons. I urged her to brave up, pressing and releasing my calves against her side with increasing pressure. After one hesitant step, she extended her nose and sniffed. Then relaxed and moved on. Perfect response. A half hour out and a half hour return or more often a little faster home since most horses tended to speed up when headed to safety and food.

On the way back, I sucked a deep breath into my lungs and reveled in the clean aroma of the sunbaked adobe earth mixed with the occasional spice of pine needles. No muni bus or car fumes here. The meditative rhythm of Emma's four beat walk loosened the muscles along my spine. A couple of sparrows twittered in an oak tree whose twisted limbs angled off from the main trunk, mistletoe clinging to the top branches. Cattle grazed on the crest of a distant hill, red-brown dots against an azure sky. How awesome. I was excited to be back on a horse. I was excited to have this young horse so full of potential.

More outings followed. Emma's trust in me budded and burgeoned. Even though she would occasionally startle at a nearby sound or the sudden appearance of a cow, I could coax her through it. Everything about Emma's behavior, from her good sense in dealing with new situations around the barn to her willingness to learn how to move with a new rider on her back, seemed to demonstrate that she was acclimating to her new life.

During the week, there was still enough light after work to manage an hour trail ride before dark. Our sojourns into the countryside were longer on weekends. Emma was progressing so well that I had to stop and count the days. Her confidence had improved dramatically with only two weeks of trail rides. Wow. That's impressive. I wouldn't have to be on high alert anymore. Emma's experiences were making her trail wise.

On the third Saturday after getting Emma, I headed out to the barn with a sack of carrots and apples. Emma deserved her treats. Work that week had been more than a little challenging. One of my staff put the wrong telephone number on a direct response piece that we had mailed out for a product promotion. A mistake, even with our triple checks, but with little impact since over 99.5% of the responses came back by mail and we put a message on the phone line directing any callers to the correct number. My boss, nevertheless, used the opportunity to ensure I understood the depth of my incompetence. I needed to be the buffer between her and my team. That meant I absorbed a lot. Riding would calm me down and help me to de-stress.

Astride my horse and eager to tread on kinder paths, I choose a well-shaded trail that bordered a creek. Several creek crossings provided a good opportunity to practice going through water. Each time, Emma splashed through the gurgling creek picking her way among the rocks tumbled by many winter seasons of rain runoff whose eagerness to rejoin the sea provided the polishing power. Lining the path, wind-sculpted sandstone offered a rich display of red, ochre and mauve. Bird watchers, the only other users of this part of the park, stood in awe to one side of the road with binoculars in hand, silently gesturing in the direction of a new spotting. The croaking from the creek's inhabitants soothed my ears. I sighed letting the warmth of the day soften my muscles.

Hot tubs held nothing compared to this form of surrender to joy and peace. I yielded to the motion of the horse. Her movement became a massage whose waves worked loose taut sinews and cramped joints. My muscles oozed into the saddle. Emma and I had taken another important step towards merging.

We strolled for about a half hour and took breaks to enjoy the natural beauty of the park before I turned around. The late afternoon sun burnished the air a light gold. The rays filtered through the leaves and danced in shimmering patterns on the ground. I sighed. This is what it's all about. This is why I ride. This is why I'm inextricably linked to horses.

My deep meditative state broke when Emma tossed her head with a firm shake. My mind slowly descended back into my body. What was that about? No flies or other irritating bugs were hanging around. I wanted her to keep walking quietly. I wanted to return to that sweet place I had been where thoughts are banned and one just is. Emma tightened her muscles to spring forward. Whoops. Time to get organized. I wasn't worried. Sometimes young horses, when first headed back to the barn, got a little too eager. I sat quietly and vibrated the bit to soften her mouth and get the kink out of her neck.

Within a hoof beat, I felt her emotions escalate from impatience to annoyance to anger. Emma bunched her muscles. I could feel her preparations to bolt through the saddle. Her anger increased to rage. The speed of change surprised me. What surprised me more was that her rage seemed directed at me. There was nothing in the environment to provoke her. I didn't know how I knew, but I knew that I was the object of her anger. Although I had ridden horses that were excited to get back, not one had ever turned their emotions against me.

She threw her head and tried to grab the bit. Her body tensed. I felt as if she was going to erupt into a tantrum of bucking and charging. I took the left rein and pulled it hard. I clutched both reins, prepared for battle. I was too old to be tossed off a horse and injured. I swore to myself she'd met her match.

Her neck and body were bowed around my left leg. This position forced her to become unbalanced and throw her weight onto her right shoulder. To stay upright she had to take a step to the right. I changed the bend as soon as I felt her figuring out how to counterattack. I pulled the right rein and wrapped her body around my right leg. I changed either her angle of movement on the road or the amount of bend in her body. I kept her in a constant state of change and unbalanced. I wanted her to worry about staying on her feet rather than how she was going to unseat me. Each time I changed her bend I held my breath. The split second that her neck was straight left me vulnerable to her acting out. Every nerve ending in my body was activated to keep her from taking control. If anyone was going to get hurt on the trip home, it wasn't going to be me.

"You ungrateful horse," I sputtered through my teeth. I was furious she'd threatened me. No horse I'd ever ridden, much less owned, had ever done that. "Not only have I given you a good home, I've offered you love and treated you with respect. You have no reason to act out. I have no room in my life for an animal that wants to harm me." I repeated this monologue as a mantra.

Each adjustment I made was gauged to get her to comply without inflaming her. Even with my keeping her unbalanced she managed to throw up her head and jump a few feet to one side. Each time she jerked I pulled hard on the reins to keep her neck bowed in a U shape. As soon as I sensed any indication of her letting up, I released the pressure on the reins and worked the bit to soften her mouth and neck. I kept waiting for her to give in. She didn't. Her maneuvers were non-stop. I had never experienced a fight this long.

She thrashed about and the unpredictability of her behavior made me insecure. I kept my seat firmly in the saddle and managed to cling to a secure balance point. I had no experience with this kind of behavior. Not knowing what she might suddenly do kept me in a state of high anxiety. I didn't know her well enough to know what she was capable of. Horses were known to suddenly flip over backwards on their rider. My fear only made me more determined.

I needed all twenty years of my experience in horsemanship to keep me on her and pilot her back to the barn. The hour it took left me emotionally and physically exhausted. My legs wobbled when I dismounted. The trembling in my arms made it a struggle to get the saddle off. All I wanted to do was get her back in her stall so I could regroup. I was beyond annoyed. Her behavior was totally unacceptable. All of the force of my being was focused into that thought.

If she didn't need to put on weight, I probably wouldn't have given her her grain. I closed her stall door and stared into her eyes piercing any protective layer she might have.

"Think about what you did," I spat out with a stinging fury. I really didn't care if she didn't understand a word I was saying. "Your behavior is totally unacceptable."

The following day I wondered what I would find when I arrived back at Pine Knoll and went to Emma's stall. Would I have to face another fight? I'd never run into a reaction this strong and focused before – not even close. If my force of will could conquer then I was prepared. I felt as if rebar had taken root on either side of my back bone. My riding boots could have been military boots with the mind-set I was holding. I marched up to her stall.

I didn't glimpse her at first. In the few weeks that I had her, she always waited for me at her stall door, eager to get out. This day, I surveyed her stall, letting my eyes adjust to the dim light.

Emma stood against the back wall with her head lowered, facing the corner. I couldn't resist a modest inner chuckle. The image that rushed into my mind was of a school child banished to the back of the room for a time-out. I slid open the stall door and poked in. Not an ear flick or a tail swish broke her silhouette. I ran my fingers over her shoulder. It was more of a ping saying I'm here, than a caress.

I wasn't feeling particularly affectionate at the moment. She lowered her head even further.

"Emma," I whispered.

She turned her neck to look at me keeping her head inches above the pine shavings. Her eyes half closed and her muscles sagged. Her body language read apology. I put on her halter. On the way out of her stall I noticed that she hadn't eaten her grain. That's unusual. Horses love grain.

I tied her up in the grooming stall. Her expression was soft and present, if not a bit chagrined. My intuition said she'd be fine, but my mind wondered how long that might last.

Chapter 5

S aturday mornings were the best – sunshine and anticipation. How exciting to be once again on a training program that would lead to a competitive show ring performance. I felt fabulous when I mounted Emma in the arena. In the few months I had her, she worked brilliantly. A cooperative disposition, athletic physique and a mind capable of staying focused made training a delight.

Today I'd polish up a couple of her skills, before heading out to the trail. I closed my calves, the signal to walk briskly. She responded with slow, dragging steps. What was that about? I tapped her with the whip to urge her to put a little more energy into it. No response. I tapped again. Still nothing. She was less energetic than I'd ever seen her. Was she sick? But she looked fine. My good mood oozed into the ground.

I took Emma to the outdoor arena to see if the open air would perk her up. It didn't. I finally gave up on my ride. I put her back in her stall and figured, just like us, she might be having a bad day. Not riding was disappointing. My energy needed an outlet. Vacuuming waited for me at home. Yeah, right.

My mind rehearsed my history with Emma on the ride home. Emma and I seemed to be getting along just fine. Whatever had caused her to rage at me that day on the trail a few months ago had vanished. Horses, when new to a rider, sometimes act out in strange ways. I reasoned her behavior was due to some form of neuronal burp. In fact, since that trail ride Emma hadn't shown the slightest hint of being naughty. Quite the opposite. Instead of dumping me when she needed to buck, she walked around the arena stiff legged, her way of letting me know that I'd better get off so she could blow off steam. Other horses weren't so mannered and sent their riders crashing into the dirt.

The months of mostly trail rides had provided us quality time to bond. Steep hills had strengthened Emma's hind end and back. The definition of her muscles rippling under her glossy coat told me that Emma had the conditioning to commence her dressage work in earnest. No more restricting to light, ring work.

Her schooling had gone extraordinarily well. She was able to do her walk-trot and trot-canter transitions without losing balance and tossing her head. Her response to my leg was quick and energetic. Leg yields from the quarter line were effortless, gliding sideways to the rail. Her halts were square in front and occasionally square behind. Total fun.

It had been going well until today. Oh well, one bad day isn't much.

The next day Emma was fine. She was on the bit consistently, bending her neck in that lovely arc, softly mouthing the bit, and pushing off from behind into my hands. Such a lovely feel. Her progress was so excellent that I worked on lengthening her stride in frame.

It went well for more than a week until she showed up listless and distracted again. She acted as if she didn't remember her training. Then the next day she was fine, but that didn't last. The lack of pattern to her behavior suggested something beyond my understanding. Now I was getting worried. Nothing logical about this. I didn't know what to do, so when I got home I called my vet, John, for an appointment.

Two days later at the barn, I greeted John in the parking lot. I always felt better when he was around. His brilliant, toothy smile radiated happiness and his easy-going demeanor calmed me down. I led him to Emma's stall. He listened patiently while I described each exasperating ride.

"All right, already," he said, putting his hand up to stop me. "You know mares can be real slugs."

"After my first mare, I swore I'd never get another one." I shook my head and shrugged my shoulders. "They're moody. Their energy level is all over the place. What puzzles me is Emma's variations in energy don't coincide with her estrus cycle – the heat part of her reproductive periods. I can't figure it out."

"That's odd," John said. He pushed Emma's stall door to the side and greeted her when she faced him. "She looks great. What's her temperature?"

"Normal," I grabbed Emma's halter from her stall door. "Tom has been turning her out regularly so she isn't cooped up in her stall. I don't think she's sour."

"Is she sound?" he asked, rubbing the back of his neck.

"Yes, no bobbing of the head or off loading of weight anywhere." I slipped Emma's halter over her head. "It's all about her lack of energy. Her lack of consistency."

I could almost see the wheels turning behind those blue eyes. John walked over to a corner of her stall leaving indents of pine shavings in his path.

"Where is she in her training?" he asked, looking down at a pile of fresh manure.

I always found it comical how we horse people were preoccupied with horse dung. Every time my horse dropped a load I would check it out. Manure could tell me a lot about the health of my horse. Was it too wet, too dry? Was the grain undigested? What was the color? Any strange odor? Whenever I heard a plop, plop, I'd see the owner's head turn. I did it too.

"The usual novice stuff for dressage," I responded. I lowered my head and scanned the poop to see if any answers would magically appear.

"What do you see in that sport?" he said, raising his head. "It seems so stuffy."

I looked at his worn blue jeans, plaid cowboy shirt with snaps for buttons and heavily tooled leather boots. No one would mistake him for anything but a western rider. I thought about the sparkling white breeches and top hat that upper level dressage riders wore at shows. Wearing white around horses didn't compute. One good sneeze from my horse and I was covered with black, dirt-encrusted snot. And the clothes on top were worse. The formal coat with tails and vest peeking out made the riders look more like a butler out of a British comedy than a serious equestrienne. Besides some dressage riders (we called them "dressage queens" or DQ's) thought dressage was the only true equestrienne sport. No wonder he felt that way.

"How do I even begin?" I said. A deep breath fueled my explanation. "Dressage has been my passion for the last fifteen years. It's something I have to do. The beautiful choreographed movements make me feel as if I'm gliding across the arena with an accomplished dance partner. It's similar to ballroom dancing, figure skating or ballet. To create the precision of the movement really connects you to your horse. Go and try and ride a perfect circle or a perfectly straight line or strike off at a canter at an exact spot. You need a partnership."

Even though sharing the depth of the love and the strength of my feelings had always been difficult for me, I had to explain dressage to so many people over the years that my answers seemed rote. Just as we need to breathe I needed to ride dressage. It was that basic.

"Square dancing is more my thing," he said, his lips pulling back to a grin.

"Color me surprised," I said and smiled back. "Dressage is addicting. I've never experienced a finer high than when I merge with another being to create beauty through movement. I'm hooked."

"I get my highs in other ways," he said looking at the tiny spoon attached to his key ring. John's allusion to his drug use made me blanch. What was it with vets? Other riders told me about another vet who showed up with blood shot eyes and alcohol on his breath. At least John's use wasn't during his work hours. Or so I assumed.

I took Emma's halter off and followed John out of the stall. I sat down on a bale of hay along the wall. He joined me.

"This is giving me a headache." I rubbed my forehead. "I've gone over it in my mind time after time. I've talked to my friends. The other boarders here. They don't get it either."

"If it'll make you happy, I'll run some tests," he said. He stood up and reached down into his bag and pulled out a syringe. "I'll look for anemia or a low-grade infection. Then I'll let you know. But I'll bet you dollars to donuts she isn't sick."

John called me at home a few days later in the early evening. The phone rang as I was about to head out the door to the barn.

"I can't find a physiologic basis for Emma's behavior," he said. "Remember she's a mare. They're the best and the worst. Their sensitivity makes them unpredictable."

"A real double edged sword," I said, sinking into the kitchen chair.

"Have you kept a calendar of her heat cycles?" he asked.

"Her inconsistency doesn't match her cycle," I said, remembering the entries in the notebook I kept in my locker at the barn.

"Sorry," he commiserated, "I have no idea how to help you."

Emma's increasing sluggishness became the standard. Each day I grew more and more disappointed. Everything I tried made no difference. A training program was impossible to maintain. My visions of upper level dressage dimmed, as if the projector's light bulb lost power. One day after work I had a hard time even getting Emma to trot.

That night at home, I sought my favorite chair for comfort. I slid into a whirlpool of self pity. Why is it so hard to get a horse that can do dressage? Is it this hard for other riders? Or am I special? I felt my back stiffen in determination for a change. I wasn't someone to indulge moaning for very long.

The early morning sun streamed through my kitchen window and glinted off the surface of my tea cup as I stirred in a heap of honey. I shook my head hoping that when my mind settled some brilliant thought would emerge. What might be causing Emma's inconsistency was chewing up a lot of my relaxation time. Way too much of my time. In terms of my priorities it had landed on the top of my list.

I got an idea. Emma seemed to enjoy being outside. Tom had told me that on several occasions he witnessed Emma prancing and playing in her turnout paddock. Perhaps a change in her stall might help. I knew other horses who bloomed after a change in location. Even though Tom had fallen in love with Emma and turned her out for more hours than her share, maybe she needed more outside time than she was getting. Tom had told me that Emma was quite enterprising in her efforts to entertain herself and managed to somehow get on the ground, reach under the lowest rail of the fence and pull a garden hose into her paddock to play with. Her tug on the hose must have broken the water spigot which then flooded the area. He found her grunting and squealing as she rolled in the mud. Toys and space. Maybe that will do it.

Some tricky negotiations with the barn manager and a lot of hard work landed Emma in a better housing arrangement with a large outside paddock. I paid to have a site prepared in an undeveloped area of the ranch, a shelter built and new fencing erected. My bank account balance plunged, but if that meant a happy horse and improved performance, then I'd give Emma more space.

The construction was completed late one Friday night. As I led Emma from the main barn, the beams from the halogen lamp on the back outside wall lit our way past the near end of the outdoor arena. About half way down the gravel aisle that bordered the arena, the light abruptly dropped off leaving me to feel our way to her paddock. I was disappointed. Her new space was too dark for me to see her reaction. I caressed her nose, unbuckled her halter and watched her fade into the darkness. Driving home I was ever hopeful that this improvement would fix the problem.

The next morning I couldn't wait to get out to see how Emma had settled in. "New and improved," just like we promoted on our marketing copy for the bank's products, is what I wanted to see. Lightness had returned to my step. When I got to the barn, I practically skipped down the aisle bordering the outdoor arena that led to Emma's paddock at the far end of the property. She spotted me.

"Good morning, Emma," I called out framing the greeting with a sunny smile.

She caught my gaze, turned away and marched up the slope. I froze. Each step she took put more distance between us. She was using the extra space to get away from me. I felt as if she'd slapped my face. It felt as if the world had served up another abandonment. She never nuzzled me or showed other signs of affection. Now she was avoiding me. I was hurt. Each day this horse had less going for her and in response I noticed that my feelings towards her had changed. The strong emotions that had attracted me to her were slowly dissolving like a sugar cube in hot tea - the strong crystalline structure full of sparkle and light mushing into a blob at the bottom.

But then again, for my purposes, Emma didn't have to be fond of me although that would be a bonus. I'd seen some pretty fancy show horses lay their ears back when their riders approached. Feelings aside, she had to do the work. I purchased her to be my dressage show horse, after all. I'd give this new situation a try before I cried out in desperation. An honest, fair trial.

Four months later I couldn't avoid the conclusion. Emma was no better. On the few days that we connected, she was brilliant, but more often she was distracted and lethargic. I was a couple thousand dollars poorer. What a lousy stalemate.

I was ready to go home after a rather dull ride and nurse my misery with a glass of cabernet when I spotted my good friend, Elaine, in the parking lot. She must have come out to ride a friend's horse. Her red hair shone with extraordinary vibrancy, not one grey hair to admit her age. She looked young and her abundant energy fooled people to think she was still in her thirties. Her designer sunglasses, perfect make-up and coordinated clothes fit with her modeling occupation.

Several of the boarders at Pine Knoll knew Elaine and sometimes asked her to ride their horses for them while they were out of town or when they were too busy to get out. Elaine and I often visited at the barn or when she didn't have a horse to ride, we made plans to meet at a local restaurant.

"Perfect timing," I called out and walked with her into the barn. "I need to talk something over with you."

"You never cease to amuse me," Elaine teased, capturing me with her engaging smile.

"Emma continues to frustrate me. The new stabling arrangement that I told you about doesn't seem to have made a difference in her commitment to work. She can be totally apathetic. What do you think?"

Seeing Elaine always made me feel better. I valued our friendship. We had met at a boarding stable when I first moved back to California. Over the years she proved herself to be kind, sensible and a very dear friend.

"I've watched you ride Emma when we've been out here at the same time," Elaine said, dropping a five pound sack of carrots into her storage bin. "I agree. She doesn't seem any better since you moved her to the outside paddock. Some days what I see is breathtakingly beautiful and other days she seems unresponsive. It is very strange. It has been a tough couple of years for you."

"She is such an athlete," I said. "I just don't understand what's going on."

"Diana, your life is dressage," Elaine said, straightening her button-front shirt with notched collar into her jodhpurs. "You worked hard with Fortune and with Rapport before him. You deserve a good horse that can take you to the top. Sell Emma."

My stomach lurched. Elaine wasn't usually this blunt. I hadn't thought about a new horse.

"Coming out here has been harder and harder," I confessed, strolling alongside Elaine over to her tack locker. "I've been getting a heavy feeling. I'm not getting what I want from this horse. My good rides aren't happening often enough. But for goodness sakes, I hate to sell a horse."

"That may be why I ride other people's horses and don't have my own," Elaine said. She unlocked a tack locker and pulled out a bridle and saddle soap.

"I've thought about how unfair this is." I filled a bowl of water from a nearby hose. "Dog and cat owners don't have to sell their family pets, if they don't perform well. And why do horses have to cost the equivalent of a small monthly mortgage to maintain?"

"They are very expensive pets," Elaine said, dipping her sponge into the bowl.

"We have fewer options." I held the bridle for Elaine. The open jar of saddle soap permeated the air with the clean smell of glycerin. "So, do I give up what I love and take up bowling, or do I get a new partner?"

"No contest. Breeches are so much more elegant than bowling shirts," Elaine said, laughing. She took the bridle from me and lathered it with saddle soap. "Tomorrow I'll bring out my camera and we can take pictures of Emma for sales posters."

My throat closed. That felt so final. Maybe Elaine was seeing what I was afraid to admit. What else could I do?

"Thanks Elaine," I said, turning to go to Emma's paddock. "I'll bring the film. It's good to have the pictures, but I have to give this more thought."

I brushed Emma's coat raising the natural oils from her skin. If she was going to have her picture taken tomorrow, I wanted her to look her best. I enjoyed the brilliance of the sun sparkling off of every inch, but I couldn't look her in the eye.

The next day I drove out to the barn with mixed feelings. I grabbed the box of 35mm film from the passenger seat of my car and padded over to Emma's paddock.

What I saw startled me. Emma's facial muscles were pulled so taut the bones of her skull were outlined under her skin. The whites of her eyes showed. I'd seen that haunted look before in horses who were in excruciating pain from an injury. Even as I scanned every inch of her body, I knew she wasn't injured. I could sense her emotions. She was distraught. I could barely look at her. Her discomfort made me miserable. All I knew was I couldn't stand her being in this kind of emotional pain, never mind try and sell a horse looking this bad. I was in agony over what to do. Why did I get so close to this horse?

Chapter 6

Thank God for my early morning revelations. The thought was as clear as a crystal day in the high desert. Ask Nina for help. Absolutely. She would know what to do. Whenever I had been challenged with an offbeat or really tricky problem, Nina seemed to have the key to the solution. She had a way of getting to the core of an issue - sometimes with surprising and life changing consequences. Late tonight, I'll call. She'll be home.

Nina didn't suffer fools. I skipped the opening pleasantries and went right to my situation with Emma. I finished what must have been a scatter-brained ranting and tried to sum it up.

"I love dressage," I said, looking at the elegant picture of a show horse on the cover of the *Dressage and CT* magazine resting on my side table. "I have an inner need to express my creativity and artistic side through that sport. Emma doesn't seem to be working out. What should I do?"

"I'm sorry that the new outdoor paddock didn't work out," she said with a serious note in her voice.

I reminded her how helpful she had been in the past with a whole variety of strange and remote problems. Isn't she the one who diagnosed my PTSD? Isn't she the one who knew me better than myself and insisted I trade in the AMC Gremlin that had been carting me around for eighteen years for the hot 5.0 Mustang convertible?

"I'm as stumped as you are," Nina said.

My breath caught. "What?" I stammered. I wanted a different reply. If this was all she could offer, I would be bereft, beyond verklempt. The sound of a quiet knock came over the phone line and then a muffled voice.

"Oh, it's my sister Carol," Nina said, putting down the receiver. I heard the latch on the front door and then a subdued chatter before Nina returned.

"What a surprise at this hour," Nina exclaimed. "My sister recently moved here from Texas. That's why you've never met her. I've an idea. I'm going to let you talk to her. Maybe she can help you."

Although puzzled at this abrupt shift, I trusted Nina. Following a brief introduction I explained to Carol my problems with Emma. From her questions I could tell that she wasn't too familiar with horses.

"I don't know if I can help you," Carol said in her Texas drawl. "I've only recently started using my ability to telepathically communicate with other people's animals."

"Like Dr. Doolittle?" I didn't quite believe her.

"Sort of," Carol said, letting out a couple of chuckles. "I talk to animals to have a better understanding of what's going on in their mind."

"Could you always do this?" I asked. She had my full attention.

"I had the ability in my childhood," Carol explained, "but I suppressed it because of the reactions I received. Whenever I tried to tell adults what I heard an animal say, they insisted I was talking nonsense. I lost trust in what I knew."

"Kids are so in tune." I nodded my head in agreement even though she couldn't see me.

"When I was in Texas," Carol said, "I befriended an animal communicator, and she helped me regain my confidence. At first I practiced by talking to my own pets. I haven't been doing this professionally or for very long, so I can't make any promises. I've communicated with dogs and cats and other small animals, but never a horse."

"How do you do it?" I asked. The scientist in me wanted to know specifics.

"Telepathically," Carol said. "I don't always need to meet the animal, but it seems to be much better if I do."

"What do you mean by telepathic?" I asked.

"When I ask a question, the response appears in my mind," she said. "The animal doesn't have to be present, but I hear better and get more information when I'm face to face. Especially in the beginning, when I don't know the animal. It's similar to the difference between talking on the phone and talking in person."

"What kind of responses do you get?" I asked. This was incredible.

"Feelings, images, concepts and words," Carol said. "The communication is very rich. I'd be willing to try to help you."

"Wow," was all I could manage to say. I heard the word "help." That definitely was going in the right direction. My chest expelled the breath I was holding. "I'm desperate. A part of me really loves this horse, but any future with her as my dressage mount seems bleak. I can't sell her the way she is. I'm stuck. How about next Saturday?" When Carol agreed, I gave her directions to the barn.

I hung up the phone and fingered the pictures that Elaine had taken. I was lucky. Emma had a good day. While under saddle, Emma's expression was focused on her work, none of the dejection showing. A prospective buyer would respond to the picture, but what would happen when she showed up and saw Emma standing in her paddock looking as if she had lost her last friend.

Something deep inside assured me that I needed to meet Carol. At the same time my dubious mind let loose all sorts of doubts that careened through my brain and looked for a place to land. Fortunately, my actions were driven by my intuition and heart.

My mind charged ahead. My background is in the sciences. I'm well schooled in good research practices and the fundamentals of the scientific method. I'm an independent thinker who believes in what I experience directly through my senses or intuition. My mind can figure this out. It knows how to test and question. Carol will have to prove what she claims in a way I understand.

My heart piped in. I can't forget that I've had some pretty unusual experiences in my life. Didn't I sometimes know things before they happened? Didn't I sometimes startle people by knowing what they were thinking? Didn't my transpersonal psychology class in college teach me about ESP and other phenomena? Some pretty unusual things happened when I went to India. But that was God. This is a horse. Animals only talk in the movies.

Although I'd never heard of animal communication before, the idea was way too intriguing to pass up. Nina had never steered me wrong, so it was hard to dismiss her sister as a quack.

But, what if it's true, can animals really talk?

Saturday arrived, offering a hazy sky, mild sun and gentle temperatures. Carol would meet Emma in her paddock away from the main barn and with a better chance to avoid any people who might overhear what was sure to be a strange conversation. I could picture the scene - Carol and I standing in front of Emma talking into what appeared to be thin air. People would be looking for Harvey, the six foot white rabbit.

Driving out to the barn, I anticipated Carol's visit with a mix of apprehension and excitement. I had no idea what was going to happen. I felt like a kid who was about to open a birthday gift from the classroom prankster.

I walked towards Emma's paddock with a sack of carrots in hand. A couple of riders were schooling their horses in the outdoor arena. A tall, well-built woman yanked on the reins of her horse. I shuddered. I could almost feel the metal gouge into the soft pink gums of the poor animal. How useless. In response, the horse threw his head straight up forcing the action of the bit to shift to his lips. The spectacle made me feel helpless.

"You idiot," the rider said, yanking even harder on the reins, "put your head down."

You're the idiot, I wanted to tell her. I never knew why people thought brute force would work on a horse. Horses, who could feel a fly land on their skin. Horses, who would change direction by the weight of a rein. The horse wasn't doing battle. He just didn't know what was being asked of him.

Too often it seemed as if people worked out their own issues on their horses. One instructor set up her horse to fail so that she could rage at him. You could almost map out the family system of the riders by the way they treated their horses. That's why recovery work was so important – don't pass on the cycle of abuse. That's why I spent so many years in therapy.

The horse opened his mouth wide to lessen the effect of the bit. The rider's face turned a deep purple-red. She raised her whip. I looked away. Watching would only make me sick. I had learned to be quiet. The most unconscious riders seemed to be the ones least open to suggestions.

Images of my father raising his hand to me hurtled through my mind. I needed to get away or my disposition would sour. I turned and retreated into the main barn. Elaine was tacking up a horse in the middle of the barn aisle.

"Hey, Diana, come on over here." Elaine called out.

Walking up to Elaine, I examined the horse she was saddling. Nice conformation. Elaine had moved up the responsibility ladder. Instead of helping people by exercising their horses for them when they were away she now shared board on one of Tom's horses. I hoped one day she might afford her own. No comparison. The intimate bond that grew between a horse and her person was hard to describe. Yeah, I got the heartaches associated with ownership, but I got the rewards, too.

"I've wanted to say something to you for a while now," she said, lowering her voice to a whisper. "Boy, I don't know how to say this." She lowered the saddle skirt and edged closer to me.

"Elaine, you know me. Spit it out." I watched her squirm. "Direct works really well." I wondered what she needed to say. How hard could it be to tell me for goodness sakes?

"A few of the boarders have been saying things about you." She bent over to straighten the brushes in her tack box. She rose and her eyes slowly crept up the front of my shirt. "You seem, well, aloof. Mysterious."

I laughed to myself. All that fuss for nothing. "And I care because?" I handed Elaine's horse a carrot from the bag I was holding.

"They don't understand you." She straightened and faced me. "Aren't you interested in going out on trail rides with any of them? They say they've asked you."

"No," I replied, looking down at my watch.

"They aren't that bad." Elaine laughed.

"Glad you like them," I said, smiling. "You and Tom are my barn friends. That's enough for me." Elaine liked everyone. I liked few. That's one of the drawbacks of living in a world where you feel what people are really saying instead of believing what's coming out of their mouths. Double messages confused me, made me tongue tied. I couldn't train myself to respond to the spoken word when I had received an entirely different message through the ether. Maybe that's why I seemed to get along better with animals than people.

"You're hopeless," Elaine said, throwing her arms around me in a warm and delicious embrace. I hugged her back. Elaine was honest. Tom was gentle and kind. Calling them both friends was easy.

"Got to go," I said and hurried out to the parking lot to wait for my visitor.

Carol showed up on time. She turned into the parking lot behind the wheel of her light blue, older model Toyota. The dust on the car looked as if it brought half of Texas along. The driver's side door opened with a rasping creak when Carol stepped out. Blue jeans, framed with a funky blue sweatshirt above and scruffy tennis shoes below, spelled casual. Fine, straight, brown hair was pulled behind her ears. Twinkling blue eyes hinted at a sense of humor. She's clearly younger than Nina, probably in her early thirties. Nothing about her spoke of some gorked out sixties hippie. No huge dangling earrings and head scarves to make her resemble a gypsy. She looked entirely normal, probably passed for one at her job. What was I expecting? Someone from outer space?

I almost started giggling when I heard her speak. Her Texas accent lightly punctuated her lilting voice. I had a hard time reconciling the idea that someone from Texas would purport to speak to animals. Wasn't that some kind of oxymoron? If she came from California, that would make more sense. She didn't have any strange foreign accent or peculiar affectation. I wondered when the chanting might begin and when the incense, candles and bells might appear.

"Hi Carol," I responded with as much warmth as I could offer someone I didn't know.

She locked her car door and walked towards me. She was a lot shorter than Nina, shorter than me.

"Thanks so much for coming," I said, conscious of the platitude I offered, but not knowing what else to say when I felt so awkward.

"My pleasure," she replied, shaking my hand. "Where's Emma?"

"Over there." I nodded my head towards the back of the barn and motioned for her to follow.

The riders in the outdoor arena had left for their trail ride. No one was within a city block. We'd be alone. Perfect.

We approached Emma's paddock, the one farthest from the main barn and farthest from where riders tended to congregate. Emma stood at the gate with her head and neck leaning over the top rail. That was strange. She usually walked up the hill away from me whenever she saw me. It didn't matter whether I had company or not. I couldn't figure out what was different today.

"Do you want to go inside the paddock with Emma?" I reached for Emma's halter.

"No, this is fine." Carol planted her feet.

"How should we start?" I looped the halter back to the fencepost.

"Well, polite society usually begins with introductions." Carol's broad grin crinkled the skin beneath her eyes.

"Huh?" I said, confusion tiptoeing across my face.

"And this is?" Carol gestured her hand towards Emma.

"Oh. Okay. Carol, this is Emma. Emma, this is Carol." I said, making an exaggerated sweeping curtsey.

"Hello Emma," Carol said. "I'm very pleased to meet you. You're very beautiful and . . . very big." Carol's gaze traveled from Emma's hooves to her forelock on top of her head.

Emma, most certainly looking for a treat, extended her nose towards Carol. When Emma leaned forward a few inches more, Carol leapt back. Her face looked anxious. I don't think she knew the difference between a threat and a greeting.

I could understand Carol's reluctance to get close to Emma if she wasn't accustomed to being around horses. Not only did Emma's shoulder rise above the top of Carol's head, but at nearly twelve hundred pounds she was about ten times larger than Carol.

"Diana, she speaks very clearly and very loudly." Carol stretched out a tentative hand towards Emma's nose with the tips of her fingers, stopping a good two inches short. "She agrees she's beautiful, and she's well aware of her size and strength."

Yeah, so. The horse is big, certainly compared to Texas quarter horses, and handsome. Anyone could see that. No magic here. I needed to get answers.

"I want to know if it's true she can't eat alfalfa hay." I said and reached up to Emma's neck to straighten a knot in her mane. "A woman here at the barn suggested she's allergic to it. Since I switched to grass hay, she seems to be picking up weight. But finding good grass hay is inconvenient. And it provides fewer calories and protein than alfalfa."

"Well, Emma, Diana wants to know if you can eat alfalfa hay." Carol's arm withdrew to her side, further out of Emma's reach.

Carol looked at Emma. Emma stared back. I couldn't see anything happen. A clod of dirt dislodged from my boot when I tapped it against the fence post. I wondered how long this was going to take. Patience, my heart pleaded. Not one of my virtues, my mind responded.

"Alfalfa makes her sick." Carol's voice interrupted my thoughts. "Let me think about that for a minute."

Carol inclined her torso and laid her palms across her belly. Between the pained expression on her face and her posture, she looked as if she were having stomach cramps. What was wrong with her? Food poisoning?

"Whew, ow," Carol said, standing upright. Her expression of pain faded. "It gives Emma gas. She bloats and then can't eat. So I guess she's allergic to it. But she says alfalfa is the best tasting food in the whole world. It's sweet ambrosia, and not having any is a big sacrifice. But she doesn't want to be sick, so uncomfortable."

"How do you know all that?" I asked. That was a whole lot of information she was attributing to my horse. I didn't see anything happen between them. At least she wasn't bent over anymore.

"Emma sent me the feelings," she said. "I felt her stomach bloating, as if it were my own. I felt the gas pains she experiences. I also felt the pleasure she gets when she eats alfalfa. Then I put what I felt into words. I'm just the translator."

Wait a minute. Carol's stomach felt bloated. She felt Emma's pleasure in eating alfalfa? How could she do that? Reading minds was one thing. Getting someone else's feelings? Rather, getting a horse's feelings. Getting the horse's intestinal discomfort in her own body?

But, Emma loved alfalfa hay. She dove at it if she saw even the tiniest speck on the ground. Hmmm. How would Carol know how much Emma loved alfalfa? Could Carol really feel what Emma was feeling?

"That's incredible," I said, trying to act normal while feeling skeptical. "Was she fed alfalfa when she was young?" That was a trick question. I knew the answer was yes, absolutely. Closed-ended yes/no questions meant she had a fifty percent chance of getting it right. In the future I'd need to be more clever.

"Yes," Carol said quickly. "But Emma says no one was there to see she was sick. She was left alone all those years."

Oh, my gosh. Carol gave me more than just a "yes" answer. How did Carol know that Emma was left alone? This was getting spooky. Could she really hear my horse?

"So, did she send you those feelings?" I asked.

"No," Carol said. "This time, she sent me the concept of sick and a picture of her alone in the pasture. She also sends words."

Wait another minute. Now the horse is sending pictures and words. Feelings, pictures and words that Carol is receiving in her own body? How far is this going to go?

But, Carol answered more than "yes." I knew that Emma had been turned out in a large field. The natural grasses had been supplemented with alfalfa hay. How did Carol know to use the word "pasture?" Emma's owner didn't visit her very often and when she did she told me that she saw Emma standing by herself, away from the other horses. Carol's translation seemed to be much more than good guesses. All of my senses focused. I felt tingly all over my body. Something was going on here that I couldn't dismiss.

"Ever since I moved Emma to this large outdoor paddock, she leaves her stall and walks up the hill as soon as she sees me coming," I said, pointing to the crest of her paddock. "All my other horses were pleased to see me. They would nicker or come running, often as soon as they heard my car. It hurts my feelings. I'm not sure she thinks much of me. Or the work we're doing together."

Little furrows formed between Carol's eyebrows. She squinted. I looked over to Emma. She seemed to be hanging out, enjoying the sun. I saw nothing happen.

"This is so adorable," Carol said, her narrowed lips morphing into a broad smile. "You ARE the high point of her day. You are so important to her she's overwhelmed. She has to pull away. Partly because she wants to extend the joy and partly because she doesn't know how to handle the pleasure."

"Huh?" I asked, looking to Carol for more. I wasn't quite getting the explanation.

"She's like a grade-school girl who has a crush on the captain of the high school football team and bumps into him unexpectedly. After the initial ecstatic joy, the girl shrinks back and blushes. Emma is shy."

I understood shy. Most people never suspected it, but I was quite shy and often preferred being alone than in groups.

I didn't think Emma had any feelings for me. What if she did? That would change how I felt towards her. That would make selling her harder. Maybe Carol was making this up. The feelings Carol described that Emma had for me felt complex. Not something I would think an animal might feel.

"When she walks away from you," Carol continued, "she says she continues watching you. Is that true?"

"Yeah. She's always cocked her head slightly to one side so she could see me." I said. "Wherever she went, she still managed to keep me in view. I didn't think it was significant, but I get it now. If she went up the hill to get away from me, once she was at a distance, she'd go about her business. She'd concentrate on something else."

How would Carol know that she kept watching me? These statements had to be based on something. Where was she getting that information? No one in the world would notice that but me. I was the only person during the weekday lunch hour at this end of the property. While I ate my sandwich in the car, Emma would always position herself so that she could see me. What if Carol was really talking to my horse? My mind logged a very big check mark in the column headed "Proof of Animal Communication."

Carol's stare pulled me back from my thoughts. I guessed she was waiting for another question.

"Please ask her why she looks so miserable," I said, a nervous sweat dampening my lower back. "She looks horribly depressed."

"You don't have to address your questions to me," Carol said, inclining her face towards Emma. "She understands everything you say. Simply ask her. I'll translate her response."

I let out a shallow burst of air. How silly is this going to get?

"Trust me," Carol said, straightening her back and expecting no less. Her immobility suggested she was waiting for my acknowledgment.

She might not be very tall, but it was clear you simply didn't mess around with Carol. I looked over to Emma. This question prompted the whole interview. It had to be asked and answered. I would feel stupid, but giving in was easier.

Sighing, I shuffled over to Emma and asked, "Why are you so unhappy and distracted? Please tell me, Emma." I held my breath, not having any idea what she might say.

Carol's face showed deep concentration. She stood still, looking down at the ground as if she was pouring her soul into the dirt. Her face scrunched, turning her eyes into slits. She must have seen my concern when she looked up at me.

"She's sharing with me how she feels," Carol said. Her expression softened and then looked serious again. "She's very distressed at the prospect of you selling her. It's terribly frightening. She loves you with all her heart. She doesn't want to leave you."

"We haven't been together that long," I said. "Just two years. She's never really shown much attachment to me. She doesn't even nicker. My other horses had endearing ways of showing their love."

Oh my God. What am I doing? I'm responding as though I was in a conversation with my horse.

"She was taken from her mother too young," Carol said. Her cheeks rounded and some fullness returned to her lips.

How did Carol know when Emma was taken from her mother? I didn't say anything about that.

"She didn't learn how to show affection," Carol continued. "Oh, here's something interesting. She says she's known you for a very long time."

"What do you mean?" I said, startled. "Or rather what does she mean?" I felt my pulse quicken.

"She recognized you as soon as she saw you," Carol said, her lips turning up gently at the corners. "That first meeting at her barn. She was relieved. With you, she at last had a chance to be happy."

"But I never saw her before." I said, wondering where this was going. True, our first meeting had been emotionally charged. How would Carol know that?

"She remembers you from previous lives." Carol observed me with her dark blue eyes, eyes that looked wise, eyes that appreciated the intimacy of the moment. "She knows you very well."

My mouth dropped open. I couldn't respond. It was hard enough to believe that Carol could communicate this well with my horse. But now the content of the message felt as if it was coming from a distant galaxy. That a horse could communicate telepathically was already a huge stretch. The essence of this last message was wild.

"What does she remember?" I knew of psychics and advanced spiritual beings who told their clients and students about previous lives. But this is supposed to be my horse talking.

"Please speak to her directly," Carol said, her head nodding towards Emma.

"Emma, what do you remember about us being together in the past?" I said and held my breath.

"In the most recent life, her happiest memory is of you riding her bareback, galloping over grassy plains," Carol said, her eyes focused on Emma. "She's a spotted horse. You're both ecstatic. You enjoy the freedom of running at top speed and jumping over anything in your path. She wants to know if you'd take her for a gallop now."

"Emma, we can't gallop on the hillsides," I warned. "Too many people and bicycles. It could be dangerous. Maybe someday we can go to the beach and have a gallop there. But I doubt I'd give up my saddle to ride you bareback."

There I go talking to my horse as if we were two friends having a casual tete-a-tete. Yeah, but what she said. Wow, I had probably been a Native American. That made sense with my affinity for those cultures. A big dollop of more things to process was just heaved onto my plate. I wasn't sure if I could handle or process any more surprises. My mind was stretched so far that I could feel a pinprick in my head warning me that a dull ache was brewing.

"From now on I'm going to speak with Emma's voice and simply do the translating," Carol advised me. "I'll try and mimic her feelings with my tone of voice. Oh, she's talking again."

"I know you very well," Carol translated for Emma and emphasized "well." "I didn't have a mother, either."

I felt as if a knife cut into my heart. I would never have characterized my relationship with my mother that way. I wasn't an orphan. I hadn't been abandoned to foster care. But Emma was right. For all practical purposes my mother wasn't present. With her short statement Emma had released a flood of anguish from deep within me. I choked with grief. My eyes moistened with the first few tears pressing for expression. My body embraced the truth of Emma's voice.

"What does she mean?" Carol asked, handing me a tissue.

"I did some research into Emma's history." I stroked Emma's neck. "Her early life was full of trauma. Shelly Siegel, a well-known dressage rider, bought Coming Up Clover, Emma's mother, off the race track to breed to her competitive show horse, Alissando. Shelly and a young ranch hand were brutally murdered not long after Clover was in foal with Emma."

"Murdered?" Carol's mouth gaped open.

My fingers combed Emma's mane. "At some point Shelly's husband dispersed the livestock. He sold Emma when she was two weeks old, but she wasn't taken until she was weaned a short few months later. During this time the mare and foal were kept apart from other horses. Emma received no socialization with either foals of her own age or with people. All she knew was her mother."

Emma's beginnings had some similarities to my own. For the first four years of my life I lived without friends or playmates. I knew the effects of diminished contact. No play, no exploration.

"Gosh, I'm sorry to hear that," Carol interjected. Frowning, she looked over at Emma.

Emma stood quietly by the gate, nosing for the few vagrant wisps of hay left over from her breakfast.

"When Emma was around six months old, the new owner put both mother and baby into a trailer and drove them away," I said, feeling my anger stir. "As soon as they got to the owner's horse pasture, they put Emma behind a fence. They hauled her mother away. What an unfortunate way to create separation anxiety in a foal. Emma had never been away from her mother and never away from home. Her mother was her whole world."

"What an awful story," Carol said, her lips drooping at the corners.

"A metal gate separated Emma from the last place she had seen her mother," I said. "She threw herself against the gate, catching both front legs in the slats. In her struggle, she ripped off parts of both front hooves - an excruciating injury. Analogous to ripping off our fingernails. To keep her from doing more damage to herself, the new owners installed an electric wire across the gate. But then Emma tried to go through the gate despite the pain of the shocks."

"Unbelievable," Carol said, her head facing the ground.

"She was left alone in the pasture with a few older horses, while she recovered. The previous owner said Emma seemed aloof and didn't make any friends. Between two and three years old, she was taken out to be "broken" and then returned to the pasture."

"I hope that was a better experience," Carol raised her chin and looked over at me.

"I don't know anything about it." I shrugged my shoulders. "When Emma was five, she was sent to a hunter/jumper barn to be trained.

Her form over jumps was quite nice except for one critical flaw – she didn't snap up her knees. Dangling legs are dangerous. If horses misjudge the fence and hit it on their forearms they can flip over on top of the rider. Apparently her trainers punished her severely, as if that would teach her to pick up her legs. I guess Emma got unruly. She was sent back to pasture. After a few months she ended up at the barn where I first saw her."

I stood rooted to the ground. Carol had no way of knowing about Emma's loss of her mother. I placed another check mark in the "proof" column. The reservations I had about Carol's abilities were dissipating.

"There's something else I need to know," I said, turning to Carol.

"Sure, shoot," she replied.

"Emma, shortly after I got you, you misbehaved on the trail," I said, peering straight into Emma's eye. "Why?" I still felt uncomfortable talking directly to my horse.

"I had to test you to see if you were strong enough for me," Carol translated, with a bowed head, her brows narrowed in concentration. "I'd been mistreated and had automatic responses to authority. I had to have an adjustment of my mental state. I couldn't help it. I'm sorry. You did really well, though."

"This is so totally amazing," I said. "I'm getting feedback on my riding technique from my horse." Emma's response made sense and explained her behavior - the fact that she did it only that once and never a hint of it again. How incredible. I was getting inside a horse's mind.

"Emma's quite the character," Carol said. "Rather direct, I'd say."

"I can't postpone asking this any longer," I said, feeling anxiety grow. "Emma, why are you unable to work consistently? A few days out of the month you're great. The other days you're distracted or without much energy. We can't ever progress with our work that way. I'm in a relationship with horses so I can ride dressage. I need to do that."

"I know you need to ride dressage and I can do it," Carol translated in a voice full of confidence. "I'm strong enough to do the work. I just can't do it here."

Emma's response caught me off guard. I'd expended a lot energy to build her an outside space at this barn. Pine Knoll not only has a large indoor arena, but also great access to trails. I didn't want to move.

"Why?" My head jerked back. "You've got this great paddock and stall."

"Too many horses are unhappy here," Carol translated, using a somber note in her voice. "Immense amounts of negative energy come up from the earth. I feel it through my feet. I'm distracted and can't concentrate. My ability to do the work is affected by the amount of negative energy that surrounds me. That's why I'm better some days than others. I know you've worked hard to build this stall to give me a good home. I'm very grateful for everything you've done. But I can't live here."

"Why aren't the other horses affected by the negative energy?" I asked, wiggling my feet deeper into the dirt and wondering what I might feel. All I managed to do was knock open a fresh apple of manure, releasing its pungent odor.

"They are," Carol translated. "Some feel it consciously. Others unconsciously. I'm very sensitive, so it affects me more. That's why horses get sick here."

"She's right," I blurted out to Carol. "When I came here, I noticed an inordinate number of vet visits for sick or injured horses."

I let out a breath I didn't know I was holding. "I feel better. We might have a solution to our problem. Do you know of a place where you might be happy?"

"Yes," Carol translated, "it's nearby."

"Great! Where?" My curiosity was really piqued.

"I don't know, I haven't been there," Carol translated, shrugging her shoulders.

"Then how do you know it exists?" I retorted, as if I was a prosecuting attorney.

"Other horses have told me," Carol translated, making it an emphatic declaration. "They've come from there and they don't like it here either." Carol added a defensive tone.

"How will I know when I've found the right place?" I focused on Emma. I kept looking for some mouth gestures like Mr. Ed, the talking horse. But nothing. She nosed the ground for more strands of hay.

"Take me there," Carol translated. "Let me spend the night. Then I'll let you know."

"You mean, call up a barn manager. Ask if my horse can have a sleepover to see if she approves of the energy or not?"

"Yes," Carol translated, putting confidence in her voice and ignoring my sarcasm.

"I can't do that," I complained. "Maybe we can figure out another way. Exactly how will I know whether you want to live at the new place?"

"Don't worry," Carol translated. "You'll know."

I stood rooted to the earth seeking reassurance the ground was still solid. My heart soaked in what all this meant. A flood of well-being coursed through my body. Relief transformed into joy. Emma could do the work. I just had to find the right place for her. This beautiful athlete might be my dressage horse after all. Did I realize what I just thought? I swallowed it all. As the fishermen say, "Hook line and sinker."

"I don't have anything else to ask Emma right now." My eyes reluctantly left Emma so I could better address Carol. "She's explained what's been driving her peculiar behavior. This was great. I won't have to sell her." No more than a nanosecond passed between my uttering the last word and Emma letting out a huge breath, her ribs visibly collapsing. Wrinkles around her eyes faded.

"Diana, she's so relieved," Carol said, touching her hand to her head and then lowering it to the front of her sweatshirt. "She thanks you with all of her heart."

"In my wildest dreams I couldn't have imagined what happened today," I said, my shoulders slumping into a relaxed droop.

"Do you have any other questions?" Carol asked.

"Not now," I answered, knowing that there would be more after I had time to digest everything that had just happened.

"If you need any more help," Carol said, heading to her car, "just give me a call."

Carol's old Toyota coasted down the driveway, leaving behind a mist of dust entwined with streamers of sunlight. I couldn't help but shake my head. She looked and could pass for a typical, everyday person. She didn't use any strange paraphernalia. Where in the world did she get these abilities?

After the dust drifted away, I turned and leaned over the metal gate at Emma's paddock. The rattling of the plastic bag I carried got Emma's attention. She put one hoof closer, stuck out her neck and lipped the carrot from my palm, crunching down with relish. Her eyelids descended over her eyes, a languid half close. Her breath slowed and lengthened. After she had finished the last carrot, the whiskers from her muzzle brushed my hand and I felt the slightest hint of her nuzzling my hand with affection. Joy poured through my heart. A laugh, deep from within my belly burst my shells of reserve and inhibition. My mind got busy with its own laughter. Once again Nina had provided me with the means to a solution.

Driving home I had the strangest mix of emotions. On one hand, I was elated that I would keep Emma. On the other hand, I was emotionally exhausted from the weight of everything I had to think about and try to integrate into my understanding. That animals were sentient didn't surprise me. But talking to them had only existed in fiction. Now I had a way to get explanations for things I didn't understand. It would take time for me to get used to this idea.

My heart and mind debated feelings against facts. My heart ruled. I refused to acknowledge the little gremlins of doubt that came leaping out from cubbyholes dispersed throughout my mind. Somewhere in my body I knew this was real. I knew I had just done something huge, something that would change my life. I had walked through a door that could never be closed, in a direction that could not be reversed. No longer could I be dismissive of an animal. I would have to examine how I treated every animal in my care. I felt as if I had stepped through a magic portal that led to a world whose boundaries and properties I was about to explore.

Chapter 7

My eyelids sprung open to a new morning, a morning where the world was different, a world that would be perceived with a unique set of lenses. Tiredness and emotional excess from the day before had been replaced with exhilaration. I hadn't felt so refreshed in months. I popped out of bed and sprinted across the floor. I didn't know whether I was more excited about keeping Emma or landing on the foreign shores of animal communication.

"Emma can do dressage," I squealed into the bathroom mirror.

"Emma likes me," I chirped to the robin hopping across the grass of my front yard.

"I have access to the thoughts of animals," I sang out to the squirrel scurrying up the trunk of the sycamore.

All I needed to do was find Emma a new home. Elaine might know of nearby boarding stables. I wouldn't say much to her now. At a later time and over wine, I might broach what had happened with Emma and Carol. Telepathic animal communication was not the sort of thing I wanted to spring on someone over the phone. Even good friends have limits. Besides I was still pretty new to this myself.

My cup of jasmine tea rattled on the saucer when I plunked it down on the kitchen table. Letting my eyes drift out the window, I thought about everything that had happened. I felt as if I were a kid let loose in a candy store. Which glass jar full of treats would I put my hand in first? What are the flavors of animal communication? Do spiders talk? How far down the evolutionary ladder does sentience go? How complex are their emotions? What do they really think of us? I would need time to sort this out. The erratic movement of the squirrels as they flitted across the branches of the sycamore tree across the street brought me back. They had no apparent care in the world. Or did they?

Fingering the delicate handle on my cup, I felt what hit me the hardest was that for every behavior of Emma's I didn't understand, Emma seemed to have a logical explanation. That thought kept circulating in my mind. My mind replayed videotapes. How many times have I questioned an animal's behavior? This discovery inspired me to study Emma's every movement more closely. I vowed to be a detective in search of the clues that resolved puzzling actions. My focus and perception had shifted. I couldn't wait to get back out to the barn.

I scooped up the bag of carrots from the passenger seat and zipped over to Emma's paddock. She spotted me. Like clockwork, she turned and headed up the hill away from me. I let out a punctuated tee-hee.

"Emma, the gig is up." I called up to her. "You don't need to walk away anymore." I rested my arms on the top slat of the gate.

She stopped and turned her head and neck to look at me. Her eyes seemed liquid and beamed with energy. A magnetic quality forced my eyes to hers. The carrot in my hand was still slightly cool from its nest in the refrigerator. I slid through the gate, extended my hand with the carrot as a tempting bribe and inched my way up to her. My heart radiated a controlled sparkle of compassion and love.

"I know what you're feeling," I said, lowering my voice. "Come on back down. I won't blast you with so much love. We'll ease into it."

She struck out her left foot towards me. She didn't come down, but she didn't continue up the hill either. I took that as my cue to join her. With my last step, I looked deep into her eyes. Did she really understand what I had just said? Did what I say to her change her actions?

"I can never quite look at you the same way," I said, stroking her cheek. Her lips closed around the carrot. She pulled back slowly and chomped down. "Now I've heard your voice, I know you on a deeper level. Your personality is distinct and more complex than I ever imagined. You'll be a fully participating partner in this relationship."

Emma's jaws ceased their back and forth grinding. Her eyelids and the skin above her eyes raised. She let out a deep, long sigh and dropped her head to my waist.

Chills of recognition darted through my body. How could I miss the timing of her response? Could this really be true? Do animals really get everything we say?

I slipped the halter over her head and fastened the brass buckle at her cheek. I twirled on my heel and aimed for the gate. My mind whirred with all the possibilities for using Carol's abilities to talk to animals. My mind cavorted and leapt among thoughts embracing this potential.

Emma startled me when her nose thrust against my shoulder giving me a soft bump.

"Yes," I sighed. "I acknowledge the connection between us has grown. We are getting closer. We have stepped across the entrance of something wonderful. Do you feel it too?" Somehow I knew she did.

I tied Emma in the grooming stall. The mechanics of saddling and bridling didn't need my attention. My focus was on every signal she might make. Did she shift her weight from one leg to another? Did her nostrils flare? Did she cock an ear? How did she perceive the world? What did she have to say? I wanted to understand it all.

We walked to the indoor arena. I warmed her up as I usually did. I stretched her neck and back at the walk, trot and canter. With the preparation work completed, I shortened the reins for more strenuous work. The first twenty minutes were superb. The soft, drumming rhythm of her hoof beats invited me into a state of relaxation. I had no sense of myself. My consciousness zoned out. No worries. Only joy. I was pulled into each moment as if there had not been one before or one to follow. I lived only in the immediate present. Nothing else existed. It felt as if our heart beats had melded with a universal cosmic pulsation. I could stay there forever and I did for another few minutes.

Half-way down the long side of the arena Emma screeched to a halt. Her head flew up. I felt as if I had been rudely zapped back into my body. I took a deep breath. Emma's ears strained forward – all radar antennae. She braced her legs and glared straight ahead. Her muscles were hard with no pliability. I pressed my calves against her sides. I might as well have been trying to arouse a slab of concrete. No amount of coaxing could get her to move.

Dropping my seat further down onto the saddle, I realized this was a perfect opportunity to be the sleuth. Using Sherlock Holmes' magnifying glass to detect the slightest anomaly, I investigated the area. I looked straight ahead where Emma was staring. I saw nothing but the empty indoor arena. I looked at the ground. The arena footing was smooth from a recent dragging. I looked up at the ceiling. Dust and cobwebs. No feathers, the pigeons had been captured a few months before. I looked out the door at the other end of the arena. Again, nothing unusual.

I listened carefully for sounds that might startle. I only heard the song birds and the occasional car on the road. I even smelled the air. A whiff of smoke in the wind might have caught her attention. No, the air seemed fresh. I couldn't figure out what had caused her to stop.

Emma remained motionless. The longer she stood the more nervous I became. Horses often bolt when they are that tense. Even worse, they spin 180 degrees and then charge to get out of Dodge, leaving me to cling precariously to one side of the saddle, if I was lucky. I grabbed Emma's mane for security, not knowing what she was going to do. After a couple of minutes more, she let out a deep breath and relaxed her muscles. She moved forward as if she were ambling down the path to a local Sunday afternoon barbeque.

"Lord All Mighty, what was that about?" I asked, releasing her mane.

I picked up the reins and continued my ride.

"I'm getting to the bottom of your strange behavior," I said to Emma when I put her away in her stall. "I'm calling Carol. I want to know why you put on the brakes when nothing was there. This animal communication business is going to be put to good use. Or, I suppose, to be honest, to another test." Killing skepticism was hard.

As soon as I got home, I called Carol to make an appointment for another visit. The idea of talking to my horse made my pulse race. What might I learn? In my trusty chair, I popped open my diet Dr. Pepper. Life's simple pleasures calmed me.

Luckily Carol answered the phone right away.

"You know," she said, "now that I've met Emma, I don't need to go out to the barn anymore. I've a pretty good feeling what she's about. I'm familiar with her energy. Whenever we connect, I'd know it."

"Whoa," I said, stiffening in my chair. "What do you mean?"

"Well," Carol said. "That's just the way it is."

I wondered if telepathic communication was instantaneous or had a time delay like the speed of light. Scientists could have fun testing this.

"Okay. For now I'll stipulate to that," I said proud of the vocabulary acquired from the many courtroom dramas on TV. "You're familiar with Emma's energy." I pulled my hair out of the way so I could get the telephone receiver closer to my ear.

"Sure," Carol said, her voice sounding as if she was stifling a giggle. "I got to know Emma when we met. Her energy is her trademark. She has a strong, clear voice. Her sense of humor is dry, almost sarcastic.

She's very feminine and sends a lot of love with her communications. I'd know her anywhere."

"So, how would you experience another animal?" I asked, trying to sort this out in my head. My fingers slalomed through my scalp.

"A cat I spoke to recently was grouchy," Carol said, her Texas accent tickling my ear. "To get him to say anything was difficult, pulling teeth. Emma is very chatty."

I lived in a world filled with intangibles so this made some sense to me. I often spoke about someone's energy when describing one person to another. "All right," I said, deciding to move on. "How do you connect?"

"Have you ever had the feeling someone was watching you?" Carol said. I pressed the phone harder against my ear. I didn't want to miss a word. "The feeling is so strong you turn to see what's going on, only to discover someone's staring at you?"

"Yes, at times I've felt as if someone's eyes were boring a hole in my back and discovered them looking at me.

"When I feel the animal join me," Carol said, "it's a similar feeling, but not uncomfortable. I can feel them without seeing them. Each animal has a distinctive feel, their own signature."

"How do you get connected to Emma?" I asked, looking at a picture of Emma I kept on my side table.

"All you have to do is think of Emma," Carol said, as if it were no big deal.

"Just think about her?" I asked, staring harder at the photograph of Emma's face and neck.

"Picture her in your mind," Carol said. "By thinking of her, you summon her presence. You and I are connected right now. I can connect to her through you. Then we can talk telepathically. Since Emma and I don't have a relationship, I can't summon her. That may change over time."

"But how will she hear me?" I said, picturing Emma hanging out at the barn. "She's six miles on the other side of Walnut Creek. You're a few miles the other way in Lafayette."

"The distance is irrelevant," Carol said. "She'll hear you just fine."

"Should I think the question or say it?" I washed down a big gulp of soda.

"It's better to say it out loud." Carol increased the volume of her speech. "Giving voice to the thought amplifies it. Makes it stronger. She would understand your thoughts, but it's best if you put more energy into the communication."

"Okay," I replied. "I'll try to reach her."

"Concentrate on Emma," Carol reassured me. "I promise you it's that easy. Think of her. Visualize her. Imagine her face."

I concentrated on the blank wall. The large white star on Emma's forehead appeared in my mind. I kept her image, shutting everything else out. If I wasn't determined to go along with the program, the strangeness I was feeling would have dominated my mood.

"She's joined us." Carol's voice broke the silence. "She talks loudly and is easy to understand. She says, 'Hi.'"

"Hi," I replied to thin air. A shudder ran up my back. I felt ridiculous.

"Emma, Diana wants to know why you stopped in the arena when she was riding you." Carol spoke as if Emma was on an extension phone.

Carol paused for what must have been a full minute. Then I heard her whisper, "Wow."

"What is she saying?" I demanded, my curiosity overriding my skepticism.

"Emma sees visions of horses running and screaming," Carol said, the pitch in her voice rising. "They're falling to their death. How awful. When they appear, the experience unsettles her. She stops to control her fear. It's a gripping spectacle."

"Is she having a hallucination?" I asked, my stress level maxing out over the thought of a psychotic horse.

"No, no. This isn't a hallucination." Carol said in a reassuring voice. "Emma is seeing things we can't. She sees other realms."

I sat dumb. What other realms? Could we slow this down a bit? I just got on board with talking to animals. And with plain old ordinary English. I still needed to digest talking to them when they weren't even around. Now I was supposed to believe my horse could see beings in other spheres. Overload. I was a practical kind of person. Why couldn't I just ride my horse in peace?

"I'm trying to calm myself down," I said, running out of breath and realizing I hadn't been breathing. "What other realms?"

"I don't know," Carol said. "Emma sees more than just one reality."

"I'll think about this later," I mumbled, dropping my head to my chest.

"Emma is unusual," Carol said, putting the emphasis on "is." "I've talked to several horses now and none of them are anything like Emma."

"And I'm so lucky because?" I was feeling a little annoyed. I just wanted a riding horse, not a psychic horse.

"Diana, you're a bit unusual too," Carol said.

"I suppose, but I'm not used to admitting it." I'd heard that before, from as far back as I could remember. "That may be, but I kind of stay in only one reality." I'd had some unusual experiences. But I didn't share them. How did Carol know that anyway? Did Emma tell her? How did Emma know? Who's on first?

"Emma, many riders use the indoor arena," I said to the air, still feeling a little strange speaking to a horse tucked in her stall miles away. My voice felt hollow, echoing off the bedroom wall. "I don't see other horses stopping in their tracks."

"Only a few of the horses see the destruction," Carol translated for Emma. The stress in her voice worried me. "That's why horses startle at things people don't see. Most just feel the energy unconsciously. Because I'm very sensitive, my emotions are affected more. I'm open to other worlds."

"That's interesting," I said stretching my neck to the side. This wasn't a relaxing conversation. "I've noticed the horses at this barn are especially jumpy."

"There's always a reason," Carol said, emphasizing each word with "always" getting the heaviest beat.

"Emma, I know about being too sensitive," I said thinking back to my childhood. "I've been accused of seeing and feeling things others don't. But I haven't seen other worlds."

"Not yet," Carol said, laughing.

"Stop right there," I said. Psychic abilities were for the palmists and card readers, not me. Sure I was a bit different. Ever since I was a child, my friends sought me for advice, especially when they were stuck in a thorny situation. I always knew what to say. Often they didn't immediately embrace what I said, but they always admitted it was the truth and thanked me for my help. That was an innate ability, not some spooky other realm stuff.

"Carol, I've heard of a lot of unusual stories from the other boarders," I said, thinking about previous conversations I'd had at the barn. "A really abusive trainer used to keep his horses there. One horse was thought to be so miserable, he committed suicide. The barn owners have endured suits and other legal entanglements. One boarder said she did energy work on the land around the barn, because she felt such strong negativity. I didn't think much about it, because I didn't have any direct experience."

"Emma is reassuring you no horses will be screaming at the new place," Carol said. "She doesn't want you to be worried."

"How sweet is that?" I replied. I fingered the notepad covered with phone numbers of local boarding stables. "I'm already looking. I know how it feels to be sensitive in a harsh environment. I'm doing my best to move her as quickly as possible."

"She's relieved," Carol said.

I hung up the phone and sat lost in my thoughts. The existence of other realities never entered into my thoughts. I could only wonder what else was out there.

Finding a barn to meet Emma's needs was difficult. I checked out all of the barns I'd ever run across. These barns didn't have either trail access or an adjoining paddock to the stall or didn't feed grass hay.

I had promised Emma a paddock in her next move. I couldn't count on another Tom, someone who especially loved Emma to make sure she got out every day for several hours. Discouraged, but determined, I drove around the neighborhood each weekend looking for a place that was less well known.

Three weeks into my wanderings I spotted a small placard with the hand-written word, "Opening." It dangled, slightly askew, attached with duct tape to the bottom of the entry sign for Clear Creek Equestrian Center. Maybe not so spiffy, but worth checking out. I turned into the driveway. The road recently had been leveled with a deep stratum of gravel and paralleled a turnout pasture on one side and undeveloped land on the other.

A cottage-like two-story house and a barn with peeling white paint were set farther back on the gentle slope of the hillside. The barn's high pitched roof sheltered a row of stalls on either side of the central aisle-way. The east/west orientation caught the westerly breeze and promised to give relief during hot summers. The paddock attached to each stall provided the horses freedom to wander outside. Although a little dilapidated, the place offered up a welcome feeling.

I parked my car next to the side of the hay barn. Above the buildings and spanning about two thirds of the width of the property was an expansive outdoor arena, one of the biggest I'd seen. The few halogen lights strategically placed along the fence line would probably provide adequate illumination for riding in the dark after my work day.

A woman came out of the house and approached me. She had lustrous brown hair that gleamed in the sunlight, sparkling brown eyes and a very pretty face. Her lean body fit nicely into what must have been size two jeans. I wondered what kind of diet she was on. She came up to me smiling.

"Hello," she said taking out and lighting a cigarette. "My name is Sally. I'm the barn manager here. Can I help you?"

I looked Sally over trying to assess what kind of manager she might be. For living around horses her clothing was neat and surprisingly free of dust and dirt. Her gaze was steady and her energy felt calm. I'd wait and see what she'd do with the cigarette. Horse barns and an ignition source didn't mix.

"I'm looking for a stall with a paddock," I said, taking the hand she offered. "I was wondering if you might have any available."

"We have a couple available in the main barn," she said, tucking a wisp of hair behind one ear. "Follow me."

With a long, even stride she led me past the hay barn. The bales of alfalfa and more importantly, oat hay, were stacked neatly in a basketweave pattern. On the way to the main barn entrance she stooped down to snatch up a couple of candy wrappers that looked as if they'd been blown out of the trash bin. She crushed the cigarette under her heel and placed the butt back in the pack she was holding before entering the barn.

"We clean six days a week," she said, pointing to the floor of the first stall on the right. "Bedding is pine shavings and we feed twice a day. Everyone uses the common tack room where you can put your grain can. The arena is watered when the dust gets bad and I drag the arena when the footing needs it."

My eyes adjusted to the dim light inside the barn. Sally stopped in front of two empty stalls next to each other. The stalls were solidly built of thick oak planks and an automatic waterer was placed in an opposite corner to the hay manger. So far what I saw felt good.

Tightness in my stomach glommed onto the apple that had served as my lunch. What I was about to ask was unusual, if not downright peculiar. I felt as if I was about to walk up to someone on a standing room only commuter train and ask them if they wouldn't mind giving me their seat for the sole reason that I wanted it.

"May I bring my horse over so I can see how she responds to the place?" My voice cracked. Embarrassment kept me from looking her in the eye. Still, I didn't hear her laugh.

"Sure," she said in a matter-of-fact tone. "No problem."

I sighed. If that request didn't give her pause, Emma and I might fit in here. This was a really good start.

On the way back to the parking lot, a handful of chickens darted across our path.

"I keep them for a source of fresh eggs," Sally said, waving good bye.

The next weekend I drove Emma to Clear Creek. How was she going to signal whether the place was acceptable or not? Emma had been certain I would understand her. Easy for her to say. I was the one who had to figure it out. Oh well, I'd try to not stress over it. I stressed way too easy. Worst case I'd call Carol to find out what Emma thought.

Emma backed down the ramp and out of the trailer and looked around. She had that same look of eagles, as when she was first unloaded at Pine Knoll. I was grateful Sally didn't come out to greet us. All my attention needed to focus on Emma. For the signal.

The area surrounding the barn and the outdoor pipe corrals was our first target. At the end of the pipe corrals, I turned my head to observe Emma. I waited to see a sign, some unusual behavior that clearly said, "Yes, the energy here is acceptable." She passed by my side and swiped a mouthful of grass. Hmmm. That was pretty normal behavior. Next we traversed the paths taking in as much of the perimeter as possible. I kept waiting to feel something. The only thing

I felt was the soft, warming heat of the early spring sun on my back and the blister on my toe that was forming under a tight spot on my right boot.

As a last stop, I led Emma into the barn. I chose the empty stall next to a short pony. We stepped through the stall into the adjacent paddock so I could see the view out the back. A few chickens pecked through the vegetation on the other side of the pipe fence. The pasture of the neighbor's adjoining property was large with rolling fields and a couple of mature oaks. I noticed the angle of the sun. The ground near the entrance to the stall wouldn't get much light in winter and would probably get boggy. The back half of the paddock would provide a place to soak up the rays and get warm on cold days. This felt workable.

I loosened my hold on the lead, letting it stretch out to its full length. Emma walked around the paddock. She lowered her head, sniffing the ground. When I thought she had enough exploratory time, I turned to lead her back out through the stall. She wouldn't move. She transferred her weight into her heels. I pulled on her halter encouraging her to move on. She just sank further into her feet. For goodness sakes, what was she seeing now? More ghosts? She stood still staring at me. Irritated with the situation, I pulled on her halter again. She planted her hooves into the ground. I didn't know what to do except wait it out like I did when she saw the dying horses.

"Emma, what's going on?" I said holding firm to the lead rope. "What are you seeing?" What other realm? What was stopping her now? I trembled. I'd have to call Carol again.

Emma raised her head and looked at me with what appeared to be a grin on her face. I laughed.

"Duh, I get it," I said, feeling a little stupid. "That's your signal. You aren't tense or on high alert."

With that utterance, Emma sashayed out of the paddock, seeming to give me a side glance saying "You're a bit slow." I thought I felt her laughter.

Great. Emma approved of this place. At last I could get her out of a bad situation. Mission accomplished. But was it?

I still had a lot of questions in my mind. Would Emma make good on her word? Would she start working more consistently and with better energy? Was the judge of a dressage show ever going to see our "At A, enter working trot sitting, at X, halt and salute?"

Chapter 8

O
n my first day as a boarder at Clear Creek Equestrian Center, I drove down the driveway and parked my rig in the gravel area on the high side of the main barn. Emma stood quietly in the trailer. The double-wide open door of the main barn seemed to welcome me so I hurried over to it. The two-story-high roof gave a spacious feeling to the interior and kept the baking sun at bay, maintaining a welcome coolness, compared to the outside heat.

I walked down the aisle to greet the other twelve or so horses. Quarter horses, Arabs, appaloosas, and grade horses looked happy with radiant eyes and perky ears, extending their heads in curiosity when I passed by their stalls. Emma's empty stall lay in wait with fresh pine shavings covering the ground. My nose welcomed the pungent smell of the pine.

I unloaded Emma and led her to her stall. She sniffed around the floor and hay manger eventually putting her head over the side wall. Her neighbor, a cute, dun-colored eleven-hand pony stretched his neck up in greeting. They touched noses. Perhaps a friend. An auspicious beginning.

Emma may have made a friend, but I was sad to say good-bye to Elaine and Tom. Relocating often ended friendships. Elaine was fun and lived life with gusto. We made a pact to stay in touch. That would be easy since we had had already been seeing each other socially.

Tom had been kind to Emma, even after I moved her to the outside paddock and no longer needed his turnout services. I would miss his warm smile and gentle humor. Maybe we could find a reason to get together. Losing the daily companionship of friends was a sacrifice I'd make, if this move paid off. Dressage was that important to me.

The next morning Emma's head hung out over her stall door when I arrived. Her eyes looked bright and full of energy. Change was in the air and it promised to be a better day. My excitement was as contagious as a young foal's frolic. I felt as if I was about to soar out of my boots when I tacked Emma up and headed for the arena.

"Emma, I hope this new barn does the trick." I climbed up the mounting block, settled my weight in the saddle and breathed in the fresh air and a new day.

Emma warmed up with no resistance, stretching her head and neck out and down. With energy to spare, she bounced off the ground with each stride. Her impulsion felt great. Each moment of suspension in the air provided an escape from gravity. Delicious. I didn't want to get too excited, just yet.

Picking up the reins, I asked her to collect. She responded, bringing her hind legs farther underneath herself. Her front-end lightened. Easing my calves against her sides, I felt her stride lengthen. She didn't rush, keeping her frame. Shivers went down my back.

I wanted to see how she would perform the lateral movements. I put my outside leg behind the girth, tensed a calf muscle and applied such little pressure that I wasn't sure she could feel it through my boot. Nearly an instant response. She changed her bend from poll to tail, as if she were made of rubber. Haunches-in then shoulder-in and back again. Perfect.

Time to school the half-pass. Her hind leg reached under her belly, propelling her sideways. We floated across the arena with long, even strides, maintaining her balance and rhythm. When we came out of the second corner on the short side, I closed both of my calves gently against her sides to ask for more impulsion. She floated forward lightening her front end. Both of her hind legs reached farther underneath thrusting off the ground with more energy. Excellent. Everything I'd ever taught her was there. The transitions were smoother, easier to accomplish. I was ecstatic.

"That ride was phenomenal," I said stroking Emma's neck. I released the reins to let her cool out. "If you can perform at this level every day, there's no stopping us."

My elation increased with each ride. Emma had focus and energy. Could she be the same horse from two weeks earlier? She progressed as if she was studying texts on dressage in her evening hours. I had suspected she was extremely intelligent, but now I knew it. Learning new exercises posed no difficulty for her. The concentration needed in dressage seemed to come easy for her. Some horses were quick to lose focus and be distracted or once in a movement wanted to continue doing the same thing, perseverating. Not Emma. She responded to the subtlest of cues. I made adjustments every stride. More impulsion, slower rhythm, less bend, deeper flexion, longer stride, collect more. She was right there with me. At the end of the third week, I was sure I was in heaven.

Joy and elation rampaged through my body with so much energy I felt I was going to burst. I paused to share the moment with Emma when I put her away. I leaned against the front wall of her stall. Crunching on her grain, Emma half closed her eyes, nose buried deep in her bucket. I loved the smell of a horse's breath – clean and earthy.

"I'm glad this part of my life is going well," I said, stroking Emma's neck. "This really means a lot to me. I'm not sure I did the right thing when I left my job in San Francisco to come out here and shorten my commute. This new boss has an advanced degree in abuse."

Just as I was about to launch into my list of grievances a flutter caught my eye. A red hen came bobbing down the aisle. She zig-zagged from stall to stall, as if she were checking in with each of the horses. I recognized her. She belonged to the flock of about a dozen chickens that Sally, the barn manager, had said she kept for their eggs. This red hen, whose white speckles made her look as if she was coming to town in a crocheted bodice, often left her chicken companions to meander through the barn. The chickens roosted together in the chicken coop at night, except for this red hen. At sunset, she flew into the stall of one of the horses to spend the night.

"Hello, red hen," I said as she passed by, trying out this animal communication business.

She ignored me. No surprise. Why would I expect a chicken to understand me?

The following evening, after I put Emma away, the red hen paraded into the barn and marched right up to Emma's stall. She made a sharp right turn and with a whiff of disdain passed by me. She strutted along the perimeter of Emma's stall and then pecked at the shavings.

"Hey, Emma, this is great," I said, pouring the grain into her bucket. "You have another friend."

The next morning, when I walked into Emma's stall, I checked her water tub as I did each day to make sure she hadn't inadvertently dropped some of her manure in it.

"Yuck, what is that disgusting looking thing?" I said, peering down with a distasteful reluctance. A coil that seemed to be some form of water eel or snake was wrapped around the inside of the bottom of her tub. I recoiled, shrieking.

"If I didn't love you horse...I'd back out of here." I forced myself to bend down lower to get a better view through the reflection of the water's surface, half expecting whatever was at the bottom to slither or squirm or worse erupt from the water with teeth bared like something from the movie *Alien*.

"Oh, no." Recognition provided relief to my fears but increased the revulsion. A six-inch-high pyramid of water-logged grayish ropes of poop rested at the bottom. I gagged. Good thing I didn't eat any breakfast.

Sally must have been doing her after breakfast rounds in the barn and heard me cry out. She whisked up behind me and eyed the tub.

"The red hen spent the night in Emma's stall perched on the rim," she said, backing up from the tub.

"That's one whole heck of a lot of poop for one little chicken." I wrinkled my nose.

"That's what they do," Sally said in a matter of fact tone. "You should see the bottom of the chicken coop."

"She's fouling Emma's water," I protested. I dug my feet into the shavings to drag the full tub outside.

"You have the automatic waterer." Sally leaned over to help me.

"Yeah, but the automatic waterer doesn't hold much," I said, pointing to the small bowl in the corner. "I think it's important to let horses drink as much as they want at one time." I dumped the eight gallons of polluted water next to the back fence of Emma's paddock and watched the contents tumble out and into a drainage ditch. People actually pay for this stuff to feed their plants. Let it fertilize something down stream.

"I'll go get some Clorox." Sally said, spinning on her heels.

For the next four days, the red hen left her calling card. I was annoyed. After a long day at work, I didn't want to come to the barn and have to drag and then scrub out a water tub. I caught myself saying unpleasant things to the red hen. I felt ashamed. A human being calling a chicken names wasn't improving the harmony of the world.

What was I going to do? Emma needed her water. I didn't want to spend twenty minutes every day sanitizing her tub. Then someone turned on the dimmer switch to the light bulb. Slowly it got brighter.

Wait a minute. Why can't Carol talk to this hen? Let's put animal communication to good use.

At home, I grabbed an apple and plopped down on my comfy chair. I picked up the phone and dialed Carol's number. Fortunately, I caught her when she had a free moment.

"So how's your job going?" Carol asked. "You mentioned that you were fed up with the management."

"I don't want to insult the worm kingdom, but these people are lower life forms," I said, thinking of the benign earthworm. "Their sexual harassment training class was focused on how to keep the bank from being sued," I lamented, "rather than the benefits of respecting and treating the genders equally. It's amazing how different these classes can be in theme among institutions in the same industry."

"Didn't you say that your bank is kind of sexist?" Carol asked.

"I went to a sensitivity training course for upper management," I said. "In the room of thirty there was only one other woman. When she asked a question about the apparent glass ceiling, she was ignored. The only purpose for the professional women seems to be as a ready source of mistresses for the men in power."

"Alrighty then, can't help with that one. What did you have in mind?" Carol asked.

"There's a red hen at the new stable that's polluting Emma's water every night. Do you think we could ask Emma to talk to the red hen for us?" I leaned against the back cushion, phone receiver in hand. I wondered how the world felt to a chicken. What was important to them?

"Sure, why not," she said with good cheer. "I've never used one animal to contact another one before. Let's try."

"Before you do, would you ask Emma the name of the red hen?" I wanted a polite entry to the conversation. I believed in being respectful, especially when I was asking for cooperation. Whatever it took to get clean water. After all, I was negotiating with a chicken.

"Animals have names for each other that work in their telepathic language," Carol said. "But we can't produce these animal names into human sounds. They don't translate. If I had to try to put it into a sound…hmm…Why don't we just call her Gussey?"

"Gussey, it is." I said and ran my fingers along the edges of the bronze-colored feather I had collected from Emma's stall. "Oh, does that mean Emma has her own animal name?"

"Yes, she does," Carol replied. The soft background music I heard on the phone was replaced with the squawking of advertisements. Carol must have her radio on. "Emma says the name you've chosen for her is a fine, feminine name. It's all right with her, if you choose to use it."

"Well, thank you, Emma," I said, thinking I'd never had to get the pet's permission on a name before.

"Do I have an animal name as well?" I asked. After all I was an animal too. I was curious to know what that sound might be.

"Yes," Carol translated with an intonation to imply the answer was obvious.

"What is it?" I refused to be bothered by Carol's cheeky tone.

"Emma said, 'Love,'" Carol said. "That's your animal name, but it isn't the name she uses when she speaks to me. It's unusual for animals to call humans by their name, but Emma always refers to you by your name, Diana. They usually refer to my person or the old man or the little child. Emma is different than other animals I've talked to. I keep discovering how different she is."

I got that. How many times had I been called "different?" After I had graduated with my MBA, a career counselor advised me that in terms of social position I was a drummer boy. Not the drummer boy leading the way for others, but the drummer boy for the drummer boys. I thought he chose a pleasant way to describe my being "way out there."

"Emma, please tell Gussey, we're honored she has chosen to spend her evenings with you," I said, putting the half eaten apple on my side table. "I was wondering, if she might roost in another place. Her poo drops into your water tub, making the water undrinkable." I figured a soft approach might work best.

"But I enjoy having Gussey in my stall," Carol translated, making the statement an objection. "She's good company. I can manage the water."

"I always thought horses preferred to drink as much as they wanted at one time." I pictured horses patiently standing by their automatic waterer waiting for it to fill.

"Yeah," Carol translated, as if it were a very reluctant admission.

"Well, maybe Gussey can move to a different spot in your stall." I said, remembering my familiarity with the Clorox bottle and scrub brush.

"Emma isn't hearing anything back from Gussey," Carol said.

"Perhaps, Gussey isn't a very talkative hen.

"Oh, no," Carol said, laughing. "The opposite."

"What do you mean?" I asked.

"Gussey is very talkative," Carol translated for Emma. "She's my friend. I want to know what's going on. Gussey has the freedom to run around the place. She sees everything and gets to visit with whomever she wishes. She then tells me what's going on. I don't want to be the gossip, but I really appreciate having one as a friend."

"Emma, aren't you the clever one," I said, feeling pride in my horse. "It's a good way to get data. I'm kind of like that myself." I seldom ventured out of my building at work, so I enjoyed visitors who told me about the latest rumor or political moves by the executives.

"Gussey also doesn't believe people can hear animals," Carol translated.

"Oh, really?" I said, chuckling. "I must confess it's easy to empathize with Gussey. I know what I would've said just a few short months ago. Why can't you convince her, Emma?"

"I keep telling Gussey that I know a human who can talk to animals," Carol translated, "but she said it isn't possible."

The picture of Emma chatting away with Gussey trying to broaden her belief system about humans was too much to hold. I giggled and Carol followed.

"I guess, I might as well resign myself to cleaning out Emma's tub each time I go out to the barn," I said, sighing. "Yuck. Maybe the hen will move to another stall soon."

"Sorry I can't help," Carol said.

After hanging up, I thought at last I'd found a limitation to animal communication. We couldn't change the behavior of a chicken. Life was feeling a little more normal.

For the next two weeks, Emma's training went well. Then one day her pattern changed. Right at the beginning of our ride when I got on her, she wouldn't move. She stood completely still. Not a muscle twitched. She wasn't tense and didn't seem anxious. I pulled her head around to look at her expression. Her eyes had a distant look about them, as if she weren't focusing on anything. I pressed my calves into her sides, signaling her to move forward. Her body showed no reaction at all. I urged her with my heels. No one seemed home. In her stall, her eye had looked okay. She wasn't lame. I didn't know what to do. She normally was sensitive and very responsive to the slightest pressure. Why was fate keeping me from riding dressage? Why was there always something? I wanted to throw a tantrum.

Out of frustration, I tapped Emma with the whip. No movement in response, not even a contraction in the tiniest muscle. That was odd. Emma always reacted to the whip. I hardly ever had to touch her with it. To see what her reaction would be I tapped harder. The sound of the whip making contact with her hide made me cringe. Again, absolutely nothing. Any horse would have responded to a whip being used with that much force. Her lack of reaction was beyond unusual, it was bizarre. Something had to give. I sat quietly, cleared my mind and asked for guidance. In a split second and with no reason why, it was if my body had taken over control, I shut my eyelids, raised my arm over my head and grimaced. The whip sliced through the air and slammed down on her flank. Bam, she took off with a bold, energetic trot. Out of nowhere she seemed to have been jolted alive. The rest of the ride was great and I didn't have to use the whip again. Try and explain that to a seasoned horseperson who held the belief that thoroughbred mares were among the most sensitive horses on earth.

A few days later, the same thing happened. Nothing got Emma moving until I used all of my strength to hit her with the whip. I didn't like doing it and felt trapped with no other option available. Emma didn't show any resentment and thank goodness no welts were raised to make me feel really awful. Once she woke up and trotted, she was fine. This behavior was peculiar. She wasn't sluggish. She wasn't on high alert, watching something. I had no idea what was causing the sudden change in behavior. What in the world could it be this time? On the third occurrence, I decided to call Carol.

I dialed the phone.

"Carol, listen to what she's doing now," I blurted out.

"Emma is very different from any other animal I've experienced," Carol said. "I want to come out to the barn."

"Huh? Why? Seems like a lot of trouble for you to drive all the way over."

"I get more information when I talk directly and not over the airwaves," Carol said. "Think about talking to someone face to face versus on the telephone. Same thing. Body language, emotional energy and other cues are a big help. I want to look her in the eye. It's really important that I can stare straight into her eyes when I talk to her. She's a real puzzle. Let's do it next Saturday."

Emma seemed to be waiting for me, when I got to the barn. She didn't nicker. She never nickered. But she did bob her head up and down when she saw me. That felt good.

"Hello, Emma," I said, buckling the halter behind her ears. "I get so excited, whenever we chat with Carol. I've been let into this whole world I didn't know existed. I never know what I'm going to learn next. Your world seems full of surprises."

I brushed every square inch of Emma's coat to remove imbedded dirt. The hair fluffed after several passes. She welcomed the grooming, leaning into each stroke of the brush. Raising the natural oils in her coat would make her sparkle for her visitor. Brushing her also removed some of my nervous energy.

A car clickety-clacked up the driveway. I cocked my head out a stall door that faced the frontage road. Spotting Carol's Toyota made my pulse quicken.

I led Emma to the downhill entrance of the main barn. She could nibble on the tufts of green grass near the wash rack while we chatted. I waved to Carol and she came directly to us. She stopped a couple of yards away from Emma and looked her over.

"Hello, Emma. I'm happy to see you again," Carol said, keeping her distance. "You look beautiful."

"Thank you, I know I'm beautiful," Carol translated for Emma.

Gussey, the rest of the chickens, the ranch dog, a Canada goose and assorted wild songbirds gathered around us. The songbirds lit on the beams crisscrossing the horses' stalls. They flitted back and forth like caged birds exploring their perches. A concerto of chirps punctuated the quiet of the barn. The goose hung back near the entrance to the barn and kept watch in our direction. Sandy's little dog, who usually preferred his own company, seemed content to lie down in the aisle. The horses in the neighboring stalls stopped looking for strands of hay left over from breakfast, pressed their chests against their stall doors and stretched their necks out to observe us better. This end of the barn aisle was teeming with an unusual congregation of life. We were the performers for a theater in the round.

Carol and I swiveled our heads to check out all of the animals. She cocked her head over at me. I blew air out of my lips and shrugged. I'd never seen anything like that before.

"Emma, are you settling in here?" Carol said, turning to look at my horse.

"She says she feels fine and is starting to make friends," Carol said and walked down the aisle and inspected the stall next to Emma. "She's particularly fond of her pony friend next door. I guess this is him. She says he has a go-with-the-flow attitude and nothing upsets him. He calms her down."

"That little pony is Spunky," I said. "The name seems to fit him. He is quite the personality."

Carol walked back to join us. She stood still for a moment and then burst out with a high-pitched giggle. Her smile grew to fill her face.

"What!" I demanded. "What!"

"Emma is telling the animals around us, 'See, I told you so. This human can talk to animals.' She said Gussey had to come see for herself. Gussey is dumbstruck – just didn't think it was possible." Carol giggled.

"Check out Emma's face," I said laughing. "I wish I had a camera. How could I ever describe that look?"

"Yeah, Emma is apparently feeling quite smug about my capabilities – the capabilities of her HUMAN friend." The energy of Carol's laughter joined the birds' cheerful twitters.

Most of the animals continued to hang around. They seemed to be taking their time to soak up this marvel. We were clearly a curiosity. Then I had a disturbing thought. With all of these eavesdroppers,

I would have no privacy. I wasn't the paranoid type, but I preferred keeping to myself. Kept life simpler.

"Emma, it's a bit of a concern with all of these ears around." I turned to look at her. "When we talk with Carol telepathically, do the other animals listen in? How open are the airwaves?"

"Only those I want to hear are invited to listen," Carol translated for Emma.

"That's a relief." I gestured a swipe across my forehead. "I pictured my life entering the realm of broadcast media."

"The airwaves are full," Carol said, opening her arms into a wide semicircle. "That's why I have to feel the animals' energy to identify them. I have to distinguish their communication from someone else's."

"This animal communication business," I said, brushing some of Emma's hairs off of my sweatshirt, "makes the world more complicated. Although I must admit a more interesting place." I couldn't help but notice how quickly I had accommodated to believing that Emma was not only sentient, but understood and participated in conversations. Now I thought of her as just one of the girls. Not that long ago I would have scoffed at the idea as preposterous. And here I was doing it as though it were an everyday interaction.

"Animals are pretty awesome." Carol beamed.

"Speaking of awesome animals," I said, running my hand along Emma's neck. "Why is this awesome animal stuck in neutral, when I get on her?"

"Emma, why are you having such a hard time getting started when Diana rides you?" Carol stepped a little closer to Emma, but still out of reach. She focused on Emma's face as if her eyes would hold all of the answers.

"I'm spaced out," Carol translated. Her brows narrowed. "When Diana hits me with the whip, it jerks me back in."

"What do you mean spaced out?" I asked, stepping closer to Emma and fixing my stare on her face.

"I go somewhere else," Carol translated. "I can't help it. I got into the habit."

"When did you start spacing out?" I asked, tracing my fingers over her powerful shoulder muscles. "It sounds similar to day-dreaming."

"After my mother was taken away from me, I was miserable and lonely." Carol's jaw tightened as soon as she started translating. "My feet were badly injured. I cried and no one consoled me. I didn't want to feel anything. It makes my life easier."

I felt her misery. I knew how that felt too well. If my mother or father weren't yelling at me then it was my sister pinning me down, socking me and spitting in my face. No relatives, no neighborhood friends, no where to turn and no advocate to plead my case.

My palm pressed against her shoulder. I wanted her to feel the warmth of my love through my hand. She pressed back.

"I think I know what's going on," I said, addressing Carol. "It sounds a lot like dissociation – the psychological defense to too much pain. It's a way to disengage from your feelings. It's a survival mechanism. Emma suffered from a lot of trauma before I got her."

"You told me about her early years, being taken from her mother and left alone," Carol said.

"Yes, it takes a lot of pain to develop that habit," I said, staring at the floor and thinking of my own history.

Looking back I realized that before I started kindergarten, I had already developed the habit of spacing out whenever I was uncomfortable. The world was a battleground to me. My parent's rages and punishments coupled with having no venue to express my feelings trapped me in a vise of unhappiness. If I cried I usually was hit harder. If I laughed, I was challenged to describe what I found so funny. If I said what I liked I gave my sister ammunition to take something away from me. Similarly if I didn't like something I gave her a vehicle to torment me. I learned to keep all sentiments to myself. To disclose what pleased or annoyed me gave power away.

Emma's tail in pursuit of a fly brushed my arm. I leaped back to the present and tried to shake off the dread I felt whenever I relived my childhood.

"Emma," I said, massaging her withers. "I don't want to use the whip and give you more pain. It feels too much like I'm being abusive. Is there another way I can reach you? Besides, I don't like the way people look at me."

"Since when did you care what people think about you?" Carol translated, throwing the words out with force.

That bullet hit with the speed of truth. As long as I didn't hurt anyone and my intuition gave me a clear go ahead, I generally did my own thing, ignoring the reactions of others. My feelings, though, were not immune to their verbal slings.

"Instead of the whip, how about I take you behind the barn and beat you with a two by four?" I said, thinking that I'd make a joke.

"No, no wood, thank you." Carol translated, laughing. She turned to look at me. "Emma's laughing, too. That was her joke."

"A comic for a horse," I said and offered Emma a horse cookie. Emma loved her treats, especially sweet and crunchy. Juicy, sweet and crunchy ruled, giving Fuji apples the highest marks.

"I don't mind the whip at all," Carol translated. "That's how you get my attention. It's perfectly fine. It works."

"Are you sure?" I asked. The sound the whip made when I hit her flank made my skin crawl. "It must hurt."

"O, pshaw," Carol translated.

At first my feelings lightened when I heard Emma's response. Then my emotions turned serious.

"You know, at some point, Emma, you have to do your recovery work." I gave her another cookie. "If you're still spacing out, you're still avoiding life. Sometime you're going to have to face your hurtful memories and heal your psychological wounds. You're missing out on all of the good things. It's not healthy."

"Not now," Carol translated, using a very firm voice. "I'm happy. I can't help when the memories pop up."

"All right," I said, running my fingers over the crown of Emma's head. Scratching behind her ears was quite pleasurable for her. She tilted her head and moved closer to my fingers.

The next evening as I was untacking Emma in front of her stall, I saw Gussey strut down the barn aisle and pivot straight into Emma's stall. With a flap of her wings, she jumped onto the rim of Emma's water tub. She settled herself down for the night with her butt hanging over the water. She looked over her shoulder at me with a dismissive flair.

Wowser, that chicken had an attitude. My mother protector genes activated. I was going to address this head on by talking directly to Gussey, without the benefit of Carol's presence to translate any response. I assembled all the respect that I could.

"Gussey," I bowed to the chicken. "When you sit that way on Emma's bucket, your poo falls into the water. This water is what Emma needs to drink during the day. Your poo makes the water unfit to drink. Would you please consider moving to another roosting spot?"

As soon as I finished my question, Gussey simply turned an about face, fluttered and settled down again. Her rear end now hung over the bedding in Emma's stall. I froze, staring at the chicken. Could I believe what I saw? Could the timing have been any better? I had a hard time comprehending that there was a relationship to what I said and Gussey's change in position. I turned to Emma.

"My God," I said, my mouth hanging open, "did you see that? This very minute a chicken made a direct response to a spoken request.

Not in some ancient tongue or alchemist's chant. In simple, modern English. A chicken. Unbelievable. What else can animals do?"

From that night forward Gussey never pooed in Emma's water tub and I had a new regard for chickens – not such lowly animals after all.

So that I wouldn't get too smug, during a later conversation Gussey thought it imperative to clarify that she changed her position on the water tub not because I, a human, asked, but because Emma was her friend and she didn't want to do anything to harm Emma.

Among the characters residing at Clear Creek was a Canada goose whose presence commanded attention. The full-bodied bird sported a pure white breast and grey-brown back and tail feathers. Round dark brown eyes sparkled with life from either side of the jet black head. A pure white chin strap interrupted the long, thin black neck and head. The white stripe arched over the cheeks giving the bird an elegant look, as if it were wearing a starched shirt with a raised collar. A migratory, wild bird living among domesticated barnyard animals was as incongruous as the family chihuahua sitting down to share a meal with a lioness.

The goose often grazed alongside the horses pastured in the front field, meandering from hay pile to hay pile, dining on bits of the green alfalfa leaves from each horse's hay allotment. Although the horses squabbled among themselves as to who got control of the bigger pile and guarded their own jealously, they didn't seem to mind that the goose munched at will. This interspecies relationship intrigued me.

Sally walked up to me as I stood, leaning on the fence contemplating the goose in the front pasture.

"Early last spring, a small flock of geese landed here in this pasture." Sally took out a cigarette. "They hung around for a couple of hours and left. This goose came back for visits several times a week. A couple of months later we found a nest with eggs up in the hay barn. After that this goose took up permanent residence."

"Did they hatch?" I asked, picturing goslings padding around the barn.

"Sadly, none hatched." Sally turned her back to the breeze and lit her cigarette. "In the fall when the geese migrated, this goose stayed behind. She seemed to be perfectly healthy, capable of flight. Sometimes disappearing for hours at a time and then always coming back here to eat and sleep."

"Look how tiny she is next to the horses," I said, nodding my head towards the goose. "Her head comes up level to their knees. I'm surprised she isn't afraid of them."

"I've lived here several years," Sally said, taking a long draw on her cigarette. "This goose is something new."

The next evening on my way to Emma's stall, I stopped at the uphill entrance to the barn. Gussey poked among the weeds and her fellow flock mates dashed in and out of crevices in the rocks a few feet away, heads down intent on scrounging for their meal. Too bad eating wasn't that simple for humans. I had skipped dinner to come straight to the barn. Even the goose was munching, happily parked under the elevated manger in one of the two-horse paddocks. Every time the resident horse grabbed a mouthful of hay out of the manger, stray bits of alfalfa leaves drifted to the ground. The goose dined right next to the horse's front legs, scarfing up the vibrant green litter.

With no advance notice, the horse jerked up his hoof and stomped it on the ground to dislodge a biting fly. The crashing hoof caught the edge of the goose's webbed toe. The goose squawked. The horse quickly retrieved his foot, but that wasn't the end of it. The goose honked, fluffed and fluttered in disapproval at the horse.

Catching a shod horse hoof on your foot must really hurt. I wondered why the goose stayed so close to the horses with the inherent danger created by such size disparity. A few weeks later I got my answer.

A Rottweiler came running full speed down the driveway. Clumps of gravel flew behind the dog as he clawed the ground for more traction. The goose, who had been strolling across the barnyard, spun, ran and dived towards the nearest horse, a stout, sorrel quarter horse gelding. In her rush to scoot under the fence rail she sacrificed a few feathers which dangled from slivers in the wood.

The goose braked to a stop below the horse's belly. All four paws of the dog dug into the dirt, sliding to a stop a couple of feet away. With ferocious barking and spitting drool, the dog eyed the goose and the horse. He must have thought better of his attack, or worse, was figuring out how to continue it. My heart pounded and my muscles spasmed into immobility, catatonic in my fear, the intense emotion thrusting me back into a child's emotional state and my old patterns of survival. I didn't hear the footsteps racing towards me. Sally lunged forward and grabbed the dog's collar.

"That was scary," I managed to squeak.

"This is my neighbor's dog," Sally said, catching her breath. "He won't hurt people." She ran twine from a hay bale through the dog's collar and wrapped it several times around her hand. The dog looked as if he weighed as much as Sally. "She has a pair of Rotties. When they get loose, they head over here. They've gotten a couple of my hens on different occasions."

"The poor goose," I said, "must be nervous with so few places to be safe." I kept my distance from the dog, who strained against Sally's hold pulling the twine tight forcing it to gouge it into her hand.

"There's a pond on the adjoining property farther up the hill," Sally said, pointing in the direction of the outdoor arena. "The goose spends time up there eating the vegetation growing in the water. The dogs don't go into the pond after her."

"I usually see geese in a flock," I said. "Does she have any friends?"

"Rarely," Sally said. "Once in a while her goose friends fly over. They join her either up in the pond or down here in the front pasture. I think she has a boyfriend. I've seen the pair cavort in the outdoor arena late in the evening, when things are quieter. Their antics are entertaining."

"I'm glad you were here," I said, feeling gratitude for the rescue.

"Yeah, I know this dog. I'll bring him back," Sally said, heading down the driveway.

So here was another Canada goose capable of odd behavior. What was it about me and these geese? Ten years earlier, when I lived in Danville, a goose landed in the middle of the road in front of my ranch house a week after I'd moved in. I wondered what that was about. I didn't see geese hang out in front of anyone else's driveway. The neighbors across the street told me that the goose landings were a new phenomenon. After honking and waddling for a minute, the goose would take root on the asphalt and stare at me. I thought it odd, but endearing. Over time I looked forward to the noisy greetings when I got home from work.

Two golf courses, not far from my house, provided ponds for the migrating water fowl. Sometimes I would see the Canada geese in their "V" formation wing over my house. One summer evening I had a chance to witness the fly-by. A goose left the flock formation and dropped down to a few feet overhead, honking when she got close to my roof. After she passed my house, she gained altitude and rejoined the flock. What she did looked purposeful and gave me chills. For the seven years I lived in Danville, I enjoyed the company of the goose, either from the visits on the street or the fly bys. When I decided to move to Walnut Creek to be closer to my job and the Sufism Reoriented Center, I knew I would be sad to miss the regular social calls.

A week after I moved into the new house in Walnut Creek, a Canada goose landed right outside my kitchen window in the middle of the street. Canada geese look the same to me, so I wondered if this was the same goose. It felt different, but still like an old friend. The fly-bys resumed, although not as frequent as in Danville. The goose appearances helped me feel at home in the new city.

Now with a goose living at the barn, I had an opportunity to resume my connection to these beautiful birds and observe their habits. First order of business was to name her. Talking to Emma had given me a better appreciation for animals. This goose deserved to have her individuality honored. I loved her fat body and exaggerated waddle that made her resemble a character right out of a fairy tale, perhaps Mother Goose. I decided to call her Mathilda.

Mathilda showed a lot of curiosity for a wild bird. She often left the pasture to walk around the buildings on the ranch, checking out the people when they came to visit their horses. Although she showed an interest in people, as with most wild animals, she was aloof, not letting anyone get too close. As inquisitive as Gussey seemed to be, I never saw her give Mathilda a second look. Apparently the hen's agenda didn't seem to include making friends with a wild bird. Except for the uncommon stop over from another wild goose, Mathilda was alone.

Late one night, when no one else was around, I decided to enjoy a private moment with Emma. I had gotten in the habit of talking to her about my day and felt freer to share any topic when in private. She was a good friend and listened patiently to all of my ramblings. I leaned against the low wall in front of her hay manger.

"Emma, I started spacing out again when my boss verbally assaulted me," I said, stroking her ears from base to tip. "I don't think I've done that in years. It's important that I stay present. Nina recommended that I get help from a practitioner in Berkeley who helps his clients deal with difficult work situations. I saw him yesterday. That's why I didn't come out to the barn. He showed me what postures to use to protect myself. He said instead of facing her I should aim my shoulder to her and sit sideways, shielding my core that way. I should also face the exit door to remind myself that there was always a way out. I hope it works. Knowing my boss it won't be very long before I'll have the opportunity to try it out."

Emma looked at me and I felt as if she had sent me a wave of support. I touched her cheek to say "thank you." She dropped her head and continued eating. The rhythm of her chewing and the night-time symphony of crickets and frogs down at the creek relaxed me. The fresh perfume of the hay and the scent of apple left on Emma's breath permeated the air.

The cool night air brushed against my face. I was about to slip off into a soothing meditation, when I noticed a movement at the far end of the barn aisle. At first, I resented having this delicious moment interrupted. Then anxiety arose when I remembered I was the only one out at the barn this late in the evening.

I shivered. What could it be?

The overhead lights provided a dim glow, so I had to struggle to see what had caught my eye. I saw a shadow move. My adrenaline pumped. I had no weapon. Sally, snug in her home, was farther up the hill and out of earshot. I was closer to the road and to the miscreants who sometimes wandered down this remote area looking for opportunities to do mischief.

Mathilda stepped forward into the faint glow of the overhead light. She commanded the entrance to the barn and stared at me. What a relief. I had imagined a very different intruder.

Wow, coming into an enclosure must be risky for a large bird, especially one who needs a lot of room to take wing. She must feel safe enough to enter the barn. I hadn't ever seen her do that before.

"Hello Mathilda," I said, in my friendliest voice. "How are you?" Although Gussey had taught me that animals really do understand what I say, I had a hard time getting with the program. A lifetime of believing that animals didn't understand our spoken words was a hard habit to break. It would take time to feel perfectly natural speaking to them. I had gotten comfortable talking to Emma, but my discomfort made its appearance when I tried to address another animal.

Mathilda took a step closer. She hesitated and then turned around to make a quick exit into the dark of the evening.

The next night Mathilda appeared again. She came a few steps farther down the barn aisle, staying a good seventy feet away before she left. This routine continued in the evenings when no one was around. Each visit she came a little closer. Her bravery was remarkable. Half way down the barn aisle she'd be trapped. She couldn't get air borne until she got outside. Goose waddles, even at their fastest, wouldn't get her out of the barn with any speed. I felt honored by what appeared to be an increasing display of trust. She was risking her life.

One night as I prepared Emma's grain and supplement mixture, Mathilda padded all the way down the barn aisle next to Emma's stall. She parked, raised her head and her dark eyes fixed on my face with an expression of expectation. She looked as if she was one of the girls who had just popped over for a cozy chat and I should be putting on the tea kettle. Where were the scones? The full bucket I was holding pulled on my shoulder. Grain.

I took a handful of dry COB (a mixture of corn, oats, and barley without molasses), stooped down and stretched out my arm. Mathilda eyed me and then my hand. She stepped forward and tilted her head to inspect the offering. Once she made up her mind, she made short work of the corn. Her pecks were precise and gentle. The barley and oats were left behind.

I watched Emma as Mathilda enjoyed the grain. Emma didn't seem to even notice the goose. I wondered why she had no interest, especially given how much she had warmed up to Gussey.

I guess Mathilda must have fancied my party. She showed up every evening for her treat of corn. She stood very close while she ate. Her behavior seemed relaxed and not that twitchy kind of energy that squirrels and most birds have.

Her breast feathers looked so soft. One evening I thought, "Dare I?" The back of my free hand slowly lowered and grazed her crop and breast as she gobbled up the grain. She didn't move away. My fingertips brushed against her back feathers. Her feathers were even softer than they looked. I sank deeper onto my haunches. A sweet friendship was developing.

To show my appreciation and affection for her, I wanted to find out what might be an extra special treat. I got the idea to ask Emma to help. Why not use Emma to talk to Mathilda as we tried to do with Gussey?

The next time I called Carol, I would ask Emma to help me identify what kind of food might be a delicacy for Mathilda. When that evening came, I settled into my chair and wondered what amazing things I might learn. How extraordinary to be let into their world. The conversations provided an intimacy that was immediate and lasting.

I couldn't understand why I wasn't able to sustain this kind of intimacy with more friends. The only other time I felt as intensely close was during my trip to India. The strength and openness of my experiences with people on the trip reached places previously untouched. Vulnerable, loving places. Speaking to Emma moved me in similar ways. With both I felt the verbal and non-verbal communications were immediate, open, honest and most importantly, real. I wondered if I could establish the same kind of rapport with Mathilda.

I phoned Carol and told her what I wanted to try.

"Emma," I said, putting my feet up on my ottoman, "would you talk to Mathilda for me?"

"Yes," Carol translated with a cheery voice, "I would be happy to help."

"Emma, what kind of seeds or greens would Mathilda want – perhaps sunflower seeds?" I said, imagining Mathilda and her goofy waddle. I got goose bumps waiting for the response.

"Emma will try and talk to Mathilda," Carol said, putting doubt into her tone. "But she doesn't have the vocabulary to distinguish different kind of seeds. She can't ask about sunflower seeds."

"I guess," I said, shaking my head, "horses don't have much use for sunflower seeds."

"Oh, good," Carol exclaimed, "Emma talked to Mathilda for us. All Emma is able to say is that Mathilda likes seeds."

"Emma," I asked, wanting to learn more, "do you have the vocabulary to distinguish different kinds of grasses?"

"Duh," Carol translated, laughing.

"Emma," I said, thinking she must share my love for this remarkable bird. "What do you think of Mathilda?"

"I don't like geese," Carol translated in a matter-of-fact voice.

"That's a surprise," I said. "Emma seems to like everyone. I've never seen her pin her ears back."

"It's as if Emma considers them a lower life form." Carol went on to say.

"That's unusual." I sat puzzled. "She invited Gussey, a chicken, into her stall as a welcomed friend and guest. She seems to take an interest in most living things. One time I saw Emma checking out a tarantula that was charging down the aisle way. She seemed totally absorbed in it. And that's a spider. A buggy thing."

"Emma has her own preferences," Carol said.

"So, Emma," I asked, "why don't you like geese?"

"Something about them pecking her, being annoying," Carol translated.

"Emma," I said, feeling defensive for Mathilda, "this is a very special goose. She hasn't pecked you or chased you. She's left her flock and chosen to live among horses. She can't be an ordinary goose."

"I'm still getting," Carol said, "she thinks it's not worthy of consideration."

"Emma," I said, taking the role of a parent guiding her wayward kid. "When you were young and had no friends wouldn't you have wanted someone to take you under wing - to be there for you?"

"Yes," Carol translated, lowering her voice to represent a reluctant whisper.

"Don't you feel that this goose, who is very special in her appreciation for horses, might deserve some kindness?" I thought I was clever with that one.

"The other horses don't think much of it either," Carol translated. "They don't like it. They tolerate it."

I noticed that Emma referred to Mathilda as an "it." Carol reminded me that when talking about another species, animals don't distinguish gender. Sexual orientation simply had no relevance for them.

"But, Emma," I pleaded, "you aren't similar to other horses. You're very intelligent and generous and kind. And I am sure you can find a place in your heart to give something to this goose. Remember, she has feelings, too."

"Emma, stop beating yourself up! Stop it!" Carol exclaimed. "Diana, she just got it and feels really bad about her prejudice. She'll try to be friends with this goose. Boy is she hard on herself."

Even I could feel Emma's emotions. The guilt and shame were overpowering. I waited for a few minutes for her to settle down. Emma and I were so much alike it was scary.

"Emma, you're the one who taught me to do a better job of respecting animals. I'm doing better. Mathilda is another personality in our world."

"I know," Carol translated in a whisper. "I'll do my best."

Chapter 9

The work day was over and at last I was out at the barn with my horse. Gussey and the chickens had settled in for the night. Even when the halogen lamps along the fence line got up to full power they provided just enough illumination for night riding. The pale beams reflected a dull yellow color from the sand and cast long, spooky, web-like shadows from the latticed wings of the wooden stadium jumps scattered throughout the arena. The black shroud engulfing the night relented only to pinholes of distant, faint stars. Even the white wood fence that defined the perimeter turned grey and faded into the dark.

The cool air flowing down from Mt. Diablo penetrated my shirt. I felt as if I had been dropped in the middle of a wilderness. The low foothills surrounding the barn blocked the sounds and lights of civilization. Only the muffled sounds of Emma's hooves on the dirt challenged the silence. I felt an eerie sense of isolation. I shivered when I mounted Emma and was grateful for her companionship and the warmth of her body. Riding after dark always creeped me out a little bit.

I heard a scuffle behind me. My head jerked toward the sound. A movement startled me. I could almost make out the details of a murky shadow. Mathilda's head and neck jutted over the bottom rail of the fence. The rest of her body disappeared in the dark.

A disembodied goose face with a comical tilt to her head was a sharp contrast to the surroundings. I laughed.

Mathilda had never come up to the outdoor arena before when I was working Emma. Having an audience would be fun. Perhaps she felt welcome now that Emma had changed her regard for the goose.

Mathilda didn't seem to be interested in spectator sports. She ducked under the gate and marched up right beside us. I turned Emma to walk along the rail. Mathilda followed keeping to the inside. Watching the goose waddle next to us, as if she were a pet dog on a leash, made me giggle.

Mathilda was no dummy. After the first long side, she kept abreast by cutting the corners of the arena. Whenever I changed direction, Mathilda lagged behind and then showed up on the inside again. I felt touched and honored that Mathilda joined us in this way. How strange for a wild animal to do this.

Our moving in tandem worked well for ten minutes of walking. What would Mathilda do when Emma trotted? Our slow warm-up was over. I closed my calves, my signal for Emma to switch to a higher gear.

By the time we trotted to the middle of the long side of the arena, Mathilda's little legs were thrusting in quick time. No way could she keep up. She cut across the arena to meet us on the other side. When we came around the second corner of the short side, she was waiting for us. She turned in the direction we were headed, paddled with everything she had, stretched her wings and flapped furiously.

Struggling to get airborne, she cruised a few feet off the ground barely clearing the fence on the other short side. She disappeared into the matte black curtain of night surrounding the arena. When Emma and I were half-way down the other long side, a swooshing sound interrupted the dead quiet of the night. The rhythmic whirring seemed otherworldly. Mathilda reappeared out of the shadows behind us passing within inches of my head. My face felt the currents of air stirred by each beat of her wings. I felt as if I had been transported to another realm. I kept getting images of the Headless Horseman leaving his grave to pursue an unsuspecting night rider. A tremor ran up my back.

Mathilda flew by us only to disappear into the dark where she could get more space to turn and come back. An impressive sight with five feet of wingspan, Mathilda cast an even larger shadow. Why Emma didn't spook when this night-flying apparition glided back into the dim light was a puzzle. Horses are programmed to flee when startled. The foreboding of the night left me. I stopped Emma and faced the goose when she landed in the middle of the ring.

"Mathilda, no one will ever believe what you're doing," I said, wishing I had a witness. For a wild goose to come out from her roosting spot and join us in play and offer her companionship was extraordinary. A warm flush breezed across my face when my mind grasped the depth that our friendship had attained. To be loved by a goose felt magical, rare and a divine gift.

"As lovely as this is, I want to continue working Emma," I said.

Mathilda took off after us when we trotted off. Dogs sometimes chased horses in fun. But they didn't patiently trot around an arena following their person. Maybe one lap or two, but no more. Mathilda worked hard to keep up with us. Lap, after lap. No small feat. She had to be determined to put out that much effort.

That was my new friend Mathilda, the goose.

The next night Mathilda joined us again. With practice, she became more adept at negotiating small spaces, staying in the arena the entire time we rode. By initiating her take off on the short side, she got airborne about a third of the way down the long side of the arena, flying a foot or two off the ground. I could almost see her lips pursed with concentration to keep up with us.

When Mathilda approached the narrow end of the arena after her short flight, she crashed into the ground, flopping on her face.

Her body took abuse every time she landed. Not bothered at all, she got right up, reversed her direction and ran to catch up. The pattern was the same. Manic waddling, flapping wings, short flight, crash. Repeat. Mathilda was a natural comic. She had slapstick nailed.

I didn't want to hurt her feelings, but I couldn't contain my laughter. How cute - a fat-bodied, short-legged goose picking up her skirts and scrambling as fast as she could to keep abreast of my long-legged born-to-run thoroughbred horse.

Who would ever accept this as true? How would I ever describe this to anyone? No one else saw Mathilda in action. She only joined us when we were alone.

I wanted to share this extraordinary and intimate moment with a friend. None of my friends' understanding stretched this far. Elaine didn't believe in animal communication and was spooked by it. Carol would get it, but I wanted a friend to share how blessed I felt. Nina was off on a trip to Europe for a few months. A couple of other friends would have understood, but cancer took one and a riding accident, the other. I felt a deep pit of loneliness for the loss of my friends.

I wanted to shout to the world how extraordinary animals were. I wanted to share my joy of connection to this goose. I felt as if my family was expanding. How frustrating to keep my silence.

The next weekend, I decided to call Carol. Perhaps we could use Emma to connect us directly to Mathilda instead of using Emma to tell us what Mathilda said. I wanted to get a sense of the goose's voice, especially with the growing intimacy of each evening's rendezvous. I took off my boots, put my feet up and dialed the phone.

"I can hear Mathilda's voice clearly," Carol said. "Thank you, Emma, for making this happen."

"I don't want you to think that I'm clumsy," Carol translated for Mathilda, "even though I sputter and tumble when I try to keep up with you in the arena. I know I look awkward. I want you to visit me when I'm in the pond. Then you'll see me in my element – a competent and graceful swimmer."

"Mathilda," I said, feeling touched by her concern, "I know you're elegant. You fly beautifully. I will try to get to the pond when you're there."

"Thank you, I land so much better on water," Carol translated for Mathilda.

"The other night it seemed as if you wanted me to go on a walk with you." My curiosity was bursting with anticipation. "Is that right?"

"Yes, you understood me," Carol translated. "I wanted you all to myself. I didn't want to share you."

I pumped my fist. Yes, I was right. How could I not be charmed by Mathilda's answer? I was flattered that she chose to spend time with me. Animals could make me feel special, wanted.

"Your company was a pleasure and the outing was very enjoyable," I said, remembering our stroll. I also remembered making a joke out of my "wild goose chase" as I wandered with Mathilda around the barn grounds.

Then out of nowhere a thought zapped into my head. The force was so strong I couldn't ignore it. I had no control. Before I knew what happened, my lips opened.

"Are you Noodles?" I blurted out.

The question blew out of mouth with no time to filter what I was saying. The urgency of my voice and the meaning of what I had said took me by surprise. I wondered where the impulse came from. Not from my mind. There was no logic.

"Yes," Carol translated for Mathilda. The reply came without hesitation.

I sat immobile, unable to breathe. This was entirely too incredible.

"What was…," Carol demanded, "noodles?"

I ignored her request. My emotions blotted out any thought of responding. Love and joy poured through my body and flooded my mind. My feelings were so strong I sat captured by the experience.

How could this be possible? This was too farfetched to comprehend. How could I believe this goose was a reincarnation of a childhood pet? My mind whirred, while my heart filled with love.

I grabbed the arm of my chair searching for something solid, something known, something earthbound. My lungs demanded air and a deep inhalation satisfied their craving while I regrouped. I pushed the ottoman to the side and placed my feet firmly on the floor.

"Noodles was the family pet parakeet when I was a young girl," I explained with tears streaming down my face. "I loved that bird with all of my heart. He had a dignity about him that taught me to respect his individuality."

"Mathilda says you learned your lesson well," Carol said. "She is very proud of you."

I grinned through my tears. An urge I couldn't resist whipped through me.

"Gimme kiss, gimme kiss, gimme, gimme kiss," I sung out in joy. A blast of love enveloped me. The tears streamed faster.

"What was that?" Carol asked.

"Our cue," I said, wiping my cheeks with a tissue. "I used to say that to Noodles to elicit an affectionate peck on the mouth."

Another blast of love enveloped me as though I was cushioned in a soft, warm down comforter. I turned into putty and reached for another tissue.

"Diana, Noodles is gone," Carol admonished. "This is Mathilda now."

"I know," I said, feeling my heart pounding. "I couldn't help it."

And then bam. Out of nowhere. Another thought bombarded my brain.

"Mathilda, were you the goose visitor to my house in Danville and then again in Walnut Creek?" I asked, my heart racing again.

"Yes, but I was in other goose bodies," Carol translated. "What a pleasure to see you and to be near you again. I came to this ranch because I knew you would eventually come here."

What? I sat stunned. I already had a lot of information to process. Mathilda was Noodles. Noodles, the bright spot in my tween years and throughout high school.

"How did you know Emma and I would show up?" I whispered, short of breath.

"I just did," Carol translated. "There are some things I just know. That's why I left my flock and took up residence here. I've been waiting for you."

Waiting for me? How could I believe that? I felt as if I was pushed to a place of unbalance. I was enveloped by the queasy feeling I got when a roller coaster had just crowned the apex and was plunging down, near zero gravity.

"How did you know we would change barns?" The pitch in my voice rose. My fingernails clutched at cushioning on the chair arm. "How did you recognize me? How did you get from being my parakeet to being a goose many years later?"

"It just is," Carol translated. "There's no more to say."

Thoughts fueled by the frantic dance of the skeptic careened inside my skull like ping pong balls ricocheting off hardwood. I pressed for more answers.

"You know," Carol said, "I'm just not hearing anything. You need to accept what is."

"Arrrgh," I spat out in frustration.

After Carol said goodbye, I sat immobile, trying to absorb everything Mathilda had said. Everything I had felt. The love that Mathilda sent me, that enveloped me was powerful and had made me light-headed. Emotions swirled throughout my body. I needed to slow down. Process. Love for Noodles. Appreciation for his friendship. Love of Mathilda. Her showing up at the barn.

As soon as I felt grounded, I managed to sway over to my bookshelf. My mind was back in control, my body, barely. I had a hard time believing a wild goose could possibly have been my parakeet in another life. My hands searched for a text on Eastern spirituality, Meher

Baba's *God Speaks*. This book described the evolution of consciousness. I didn't search long. In black letters on a white page. Water fowl are the last of the bird forms. I let out a pathetic croak. According to this belief system, my belief system, a bird would be a parakeet before a Canada goose. Evidence was conspiring against my mind. My heart had already responded to its own truth.

I knew what I felt when I spoke to Mathilda, but this experience was asking my mind to believe things I had little preparation to understand. Certainly I had studied spiritual evolution and involution, but that was an intellectual exercise. Mathilda was face to face with me in the world I knew as reality. My mind said this was impossible.

Nevertheless, my heart believed everything Mathilda had told me. Given time, I knew my mind would follow. Deliberations and debates, the exercises of the mind would fade against what my heart knew. Mathilda had been Noodles.

My pets - horse, dog, parakeet, hamster or fish - had always been important to me. But if the animal wasn't in my immediate sphere, in my care, I didn't give it much thought. Mathilda had just taught me how connected we all are. That somehow through time and space we meet up again.

The time Mathilda and I spent together drew us closer and closer. Mathilda's friendship pushed me farther down the path of appreciating all life. Animals were no longer ancillary creatures inhabiting my world. Whether or not they were my pet, they were becoming personalities with stature equal to my human friends.

Our talk seemed to draw Mathilda closer to me as well. As soon as I called her or she saw my car coming down the driveway, she came running - honking and flapping her wings, blasting me with a shower of love and affection. The power of her love was so strong I was wrapped and cushioned in a joy that was irrepressible. All of that from a wild goose.

Chapter 10

Next weekend as I was riding Emma around the outdoor arena, I spotted Nina, walking towards us from the parking lot. Here was the woman, who had sparked my discovery of Emma. She hadn't seen us since we left Pine Knoll, our previous barn. My hand, liberated from holding the rein, gave her a quick wave. Emma had warmed up at her best and I didn't want to interrupt our rhythm.

In telephone conversations we'd had over the last several months, Nina couldn't get over her incredulity. She refused to believe that Emma's competency in dressage had improved as much as I claimed. After the umpteenth debate, we decided the only way to settle the dispute would be for Nina to come out to Clear Creek and see Emma for herself.

"Hey, Diana, who are you riding?" Nina's arm stopped its wave mid-arc and dropped to her side. The wrinkles in her cheeks hinted at the squint hidden behind her sunglasses.

How could she not recognize my horse? Bay thoroughbred mare, duh.

"It's Emma. Isn't she doing great?" I said and closed my calves to ask for more impulsion, energy, thrust. Emma responded with exuberance.

"No, really, who is it?" Nina shouted, leaning over the fence. "This horse is moving great, an upper level dressage horse. Look at the bend in those hocks."

Yup, Emma's quite something I chuckled to myself. I guess it was hard for Nina to admit she was wrong. Nina knew that I sometimes schooled other people's horses for them, but how could she mistake Emma for another horse?

"Isn't her energy and suspension wonderful?" I called out over my shoulder. "I never thought I could afford an athletic horse with this kind of movement." I trotted Emma down the long side of the arena. Showing off felt good.

"This horse is Emma?" Nina leaned farther over the fence.

I rode over to where Nina stood. How ridiculous. She was going to make me prove this was my horse.

"Here's the white star right in the middle of her forehead." I turned Emma's head in Nina's direction. Yup, where it's always been. "No lie. This is the new and improved Emma." I did my best not to gloat.

"This much change can't occur in such a short time." Nina raised her sunglasses and looked up at me. Her eyes squinted nearly shut, she stared at me as if the truth were written on my forehead and she could divine the form of chicanery I used to fool her.

"Don't forget what Emma said." I dismounted and walked up to Nina near the exit gate. "She promised she could do the work if she lived in a place with better energy." I turned toward the barn.

"Emma said this, Emma said that," Nina taunted me and followed us down to the main barn. "Remember, I don't quite buy into this animal communication business as much as you do."

Yeah, sure, you've communicated with your dead aunt and had other psychic experiences, but don't believe animals talk. How does that work? Then again, I shouldn't be surprised. A feng shui master I recently met didn't believe me either. She heard what buildings had to say about prior owners and events, yet found it beyond comprehension that animals had voices. Go figure. Emma was right. Human beings were really complicated.

"I forget how it is for other people," I said, rubbing Emma's neck. "I'm like a little kid in Disneyland for the first time. Knowing that animals have a voice is a thrill for me. It's a privilege to be let into their lives in such an immediate and intimate way." I tied Emma outside her stall in the barn aisle.

"By the way, how's your job going," Nina asked, having heard enough of my horror stories of work.

"Same ole, same ole from the boss," I said, sneering. "I'm coping better, though. I've had some turnover in staff and the folks I've hired are awesome. They make a big difference."

"You're looking like you've picked up weight," Nina said, checking out the fit of my blouse.

"Maybe a couple of pounds," I said, tucking my blouse back into my breeches. "Since I stopped commuting, my energy has improved. I have no trouble putting on weight when I'm well. So far I've been able to duck a really big illness."

When I unbuckled Emma's girth, she bent her neck around and her nose touched my hand with a measured gentleness. My back shivered with delight whenever she did that and she always did that when I dismounted. I unsaddled Emma and motioned Nina to come closer.

"Here's something that has me puzzled." I pointed to Emma's shoulder.

A hairless circle six inches wide was home to eight or more bumps. A couple had burst out pus and now oozed fluid. Others were threatening to expulse their foul contents.

"What in the world is that?" Nina asked, coming close to inspect Emma.

"Abscesses. They used to appear on my butt as a young child so I know how uncomfortable they can feel," I said. "In my case they were the result of malnutrition, but Emma is eating well and gets supplements." I cringed remembering my past. My mother's treatment of my boils was to humiliate me by making me lay naked in front of the family on the living room sofa while she applied a slice of very hot onion on it.

"I've never seen an abscess on a horse's shoulder never mind this many so close together," Nina said, leaning her head down to get a better view. "Wow, you seem to be harvesting them."

"No signs of injury." I outlined the area with my fingers taking care not to touch the sensitive part. "No sign of bug bites. No change in diet. John, my vet, came out to take a look, but he had no idea what caused them. Rinse with Betadine was all he could offer. When I thought they were about to heal, another set formed behind them. They're playing tag team. Pretty gross."

"Have you thought of using any alternative treatments?" Nina sat down on a small stool in the aisle way.

"Yes, I put in a call to Ashley, a boarder over at Pine Knoll," I said, putting Emma away. "She's an M.D. type doctor who practices homeopathy on people and helps horses on the side."

"What's homeopathy?" Nina leaned back against the wall. "I was thinking acupuncture."

I flipped Emma's bucket over and sat down next to Nina. "Get this. Practitioners treat patients with a heavily diluted substance. If it were administered full strength to a healthy person, it would create symptoms similar to the illness being treated. Emma would be prescribed something that would tend to cause abscesses in a healthy person, but would be given only the very dilute version."

"You're right. It's a stretch to believe." Nina said, putting her sunglasses away in her purse.

"The more dilute, the more potent. Kind of the opposite from our western medicine. I'm a believer since several of my friends have been helped with it."

"Just in case Henry needs help with any strange ailments," Nina opened her purse and retrieved an address book, "let me have Ashley's number."

Two days after Ashley called me back, she showed up at the barn. I greeted her and led her to Emma's stall. A pony tail of light brown hair was tied at the base of her head. Large green eyes smiled even when her other features looked serious. She didn't need to take much time with her evaluation. She was familiar with Emma's history from when she had treated Emma at Pine Knoll for her inconsistent energy levels. Turning to face me, she raised her eyebrows and shook her head.

"This coincidence is remarkable," Ashley said, taking another good look at Emma's shoulder. "Last week I read an article in a medical journal that described a case of a woman with abscesses on her shoulder. The condition is very rare. The diagnosis was unresolved, deep-seated grief. For Emma to dissociate from her body, she may have issues of suppressed grief. Especially given what you told me about her early life. I'm prescribing the same remedy used on the woman. Anthracinum."

"Emma must have guardian angels," I said, feeling a slight tingly sensation over my body as I released the halter.

"This remedy can be extremely effective," Ashley said. "Don't be surprised if it releases repressed emotions in Emma." Ashley wrote the name of the medicine on a notepad. "Remember, the remedies are energetically sensitive so don't put them in her feed. Administer the dose directly into her mouth every day for five days,"

"But Emma is fussy about her mouth." I pictured my last battle trying to insert the syringe of worm medicine between Emma's lips. I especially remembered the last time Ashley prescribed a remedy and that was only one dose. I lucked out and tapped the tube of pellets into Emma's mouth before she knew what happened. Immediately she threw her head up, knocked my hand and flung the remaining pellets all over the place. With having to do it five days in a row she would know what was going to happen the second day.

"This wouldn't work for anyone else," Ashley said. "With everything you shared about yourself and Emma, you two are energetically identical. Go ahead and use your fingers to ease them into the side of her mouth. You won't alter the efficacy for her."

With homeopathic remedy in hand I walked into Emma's stall. I tapped a few pellets onto the palm of my hand. I slipped my finger into Emma's mouth to moisten it with her saliva. With pellets adhering to my wet forefinger I slid my finger between her teeth and her cheek. It worked. She didn't seem to be bothered at all.

The day after I gave Emma her first dose of medicine, her head didn't bob over the stall door to greet me when I entered the barn. She skulked at the back of her stall. Her wrinkled brow accentuated the worry in her eyes. Her head slumped. Wow, Emma had an immediate and strong response to the remedy. Ashley had warned me this might happen.

Gussey hopscotched down the barn aisle. Emma didn't even look at her. Wow, that's not my horse to pass up an opportunity to talk to the resident gossip.

I debated what to do. Using my muscles often lifted my state of mind and might do the same for Emma. Horses needed to move for their physical health.

I tacked Emma up. No schooling today. Maybe some sunshine and play would be good for both of us. We could canter around the arena on a loose rein and maybe pop over some of the lower jumps for fun.

In the outdoor arena, the best Emma could do was offer a half-hearted trot. She stumbled over her feet when I asked for the canter. We plodded around for ten minutes before I took her back to her stall. Her apathy hadn't improved.

"I'm so sorry you're feeling punk." I squatted down to kiss her nose before I left. On the way to my car Gussey zoomed passed me to snatch a slow moving beetle plodding across the gravel. Mathilda was in the front pasture, head down, nibbling at the bits of alfalfa left over from the horses' last meal.

The next day Emma was no better. I couldn't tell for sure, but I suspected she was a bit worse. The worried look on her face saddened me.

By the end of the week, I had no doubt Emma was sinking deeper. Her energy plummeted to a subterranean level. I had a hard time getting her to walk outside to graze, never mind carry a rider's weight at the trot or canter. Her listlessness dragged into depression. She seemed submerged in profound grief.

The month seemed interminable. Emma was losing her conditioning. Her well developed muscles atrophied. Worse, I sometimes found her manger filled with an uneaten mound of hay, a small hollow in the center where she had nosed it around. Her weight dropped. I knew that horses lost weight easily. This process was tough on her.

I stroked her neck and shoulders. At least hair had grown out where the abscesses had been. That was a good sign. I massaged her back with a tennis ball. The physical comfort didn't seem to penetrate the cocoon of misery that enveloped her. One of Emma's chiropractor's had introduced me to a Linda Tellington-Jones video. It taught me how to use light touch to soothe and heal a horse from a variety of problems. Each day, I used several techniques to bring her relief. I tapped her hooves to help ground her. My fingers made small circles along her back to relieve anxiety.

Her looks haunted me. The whites of her eyes showed whenever she focused on something and abandoned the dull, lifeless stare. A permanent film settled over her eyes and wrinkles deepened over her face. She had no interest in the treats I brought her. Slightly chilled quarter pieces of Fuji apples browned in the bag. My inability to ease her suffering was agony. In desperation, I called Ashley.

"Emma is losing weight," I explained, my heart aching. "She's not doing well."

"Can you tell what she's feeling?" Ashley asked.

What was Emma feeling? Communicating telepathically with Emma through Carol had made me more attune to Emma's feelings. Before I had met Carol I would guess at Emma's feelings based on body language and behavior. Sometimes I thought I could feel them, but I didn't have much confidence. Emma said that I had always heard and felt what she sent me, even before Carol. I didn't trust myself and felt more comfortable calling Carol when I needed to know something. Both Carol and Emma kept telling me to stop calling and to have faith in what I was feeling and hearing. Not only that I could do it, but that I had been doing it all along. Carol had validated what I felt enough times that I began to believe that they were right. Now I could be across town and get glimmers of what Emma was feeling.

"For weeks, I have sensed what seemed to be waves of misery pour over and through her," I said. "She struggles to stay grounded. I have a hard time watching her face. Her eyes go vacant and it seems as if she's been pulled deep into an abyss."

"What have you tried?" Ashley asked.

"I'm using Linda Tellington Jones' TTouch program," I said. "Especially those massages designed to relax and ground the horse. It may have helped a little."

"Sounds good. You're doing everything you can," Ashley said. "What you've described is the way homeopathy works. Emma's unconscious memories have been released. This is all good. The process needs to finish on its own."

I missed riding Emma and the intimacy of our physical connection. Listening to the beat of her hooves was a meditation. The centering that riding gave me was part of the structure of my life. As an alternative to riding and to keep the closeness of the association, I called Carol regularly to talk to Emma and to encourage her through her processing.

We must have spoken a couple of times a week at least an hour at a time. What I found extraordinary was that after each conversation with Emma and Carol, after Carol hung up, I could continue talking to Emma, hearing her perfectly well. The phone conversations seemed to increase my ability to tap into the telepathic animal communication airwaves. My confidence grew or the increased number of conversations opened a channel in me – one that Emma said had always been there.

Emma was reluctant to give specifics of the memories she was processing. She didn't want to dwell on that. She did, however, share her feelings of deep despair and how lonely and lost she had felt during her early life. What she described is exactly what Ashley had predicted would happen.

Meanwhile, I struggled to get through each work week. My annual performance review was about as much fun as Chinese water torture. My boss said that I was not meeting her standards and should look for another job. She had no data to substantiate her remarks. The measurements that are typically used for a marketing manager were all good. The accounts we added from our campaigns performed well. Our market share had increased. We were above target for results and our expenditures were below our budget. My staff worked hard. I had developed a good relationship with my peers. My therapist agreed that she would have a hard time firing me and I should continue doing a good job.

And with my increased sensitivity to Emma's emotions my life grew more complicated. My emotional reality had grown larger than my own skin. What had once been just a hint or glimpse of Emma's feelings had evolved into my experiencing their full force as if they were my own. The boundaries between us had disappeared. If I felt a strong emotion, I had to ask if it was Emma's or mine.

What a peculiar exercise to go through. Whose misery is this? I had to sort it out. In this case of intense grief, the emotions originated with Emma. But our intimacy made her misery, my misery. I had had enough of my own and sure didn't want any more. Anything that might help Emma helped me.

Emma and I were fortunate to have found each other. That she really understood me was her gift to me. The work that I had done for my recovery could now be used to help guide her through hers. My gift to her. The empathy I felt for her re-energized memories I had long thought had been processed and completed. I felt re-traumatized. Both for her sake and my own I hoped her current state would soon resolve.

Nine weeks went by since Emma's dark days had begun. For the last couple of weeks I had given up calling Carol since Emma hadn't wanted to talk. I needed reassurance that she wasn't stuck somewhere in a horrible void. I needed to hear her voice. So I settled in my chair in the den, picked up the phone and dialed the familiar Lafayette number.

"That medicine you gave me was very powerful," Carol translated for Emma, putting stress into her voice. "It went through my whole body unleashing stored memories and feelings. I couldn't suppress them anymore. The memories keep coming up. As soon as I think I'm done, I remember more."

"What a testimony to how homeopathy works," I said to Carol. I fingered the vial of remedy pellets I had stored on my side table. "Too bad her experience won't make it into the scientific journals."

"I never want to endure this again," Carol translated. "I've never experienced anything so black and bleak in my life. I feel that there is no return and no end, utter hopelessness."

"That was how you felt as a foal," I said, trying to give Emma a spark of hope. "At some point, the process will end and you'll have chucked a lot of baggage. I know how hard it is and I'm proud of you."

"I understand you're trying to help me," Carol translated, "but I'm lost in grief. Losing my mother was unbearably hard. The other horses ignored me. I had no friends. I was terribly lonely. The alfalfa hay made me sick. Boys used to throw rocks at me and call me names. They laughed at me. No one cared."

Each memory on Emma's list of traumas crushed my heart as if I had received the blow directly. I groaned.

"Animals are very much in the present," Carol said.

"I understand the process quite well," I said. "Although the pain is from her past, she's feeling it as though it were happening right now. There's urgency to it. It's very real to her. It's almost as if she has become that unhappy young horse and lost her adult perspective. She'll have a different view when she isn't in the middle of it."

"It is really hard for her," Carol said.

"Emma, at least it's a small consolation your abscesses cleared up as soon as you took the medicine," I said.

"Only a small help," Carol translated using the voice of a young child.

A couple of weeks later the light in Emma's eyes returned for a few moments. My shoulder muscles released when the wrinkles of pain in her face melted away for a brief hiatus. My gut relaxed as though our bodies were connected with invisible filaments of living tissue. Her relief was my relief. These moments made me realize how much stress we were under. I wondered why neither one of us had developed ulcers.

Each day her moments of respite got longer and the wrinkles across her brow grew softer. As her pain exhausted its course, a fresh vitality appeared. Her eyes were bright. She ate more of her hay. Seeing her happy again infused my heart with nourishing packets of joy. Lightness returned to my steps. I would wait to celebrate until I was sure the process was completely over.

Early one evening after work, I arrived at the barn. Emma thrust her head and neck over her stall door. Her head bobbed up and down. She looked at me and kicked her stall door with her knee. The act felt like a signal – time to ride, time to get on with our lives.

Getting on Emma, I wondered what I would feel. I pressed my calf to her side. She strode off with an energetic walk. She was fully present. I was so relieved - no need to use the whip to get her back in her body.

I dropped the reins and let her speed around the arena. Her ears perked up. Her legs stretched into a ground-covering trot. With a squeal, she shot her legs forward into a gallop. Her pleasure in the freedom to run and cavort coursed through my body. I shared her feeling. I too had been released from months in solitary confinement. The warmth from the setting sun and the delight of moving over the ground bathed me in a joy that vibrated at the level of each cell in my body. The wind whipped my face, the angle of the sun blurred my vision and the thunder of Emma's hooves resounded in my head. I disappeared into a cascade of gleaming threads of golden ecstasy. I never wanted this ride to end.

As Emma took a wide turn in the arena, I spotted Mathilda and Gussey standing to one side, spectators silently cheering.

Chapter 11

E ven though we occasionally talked by phone, two months had whizzed by since Elaine and I had last seen each other. I missed Elaine's company and the visual feast she provided with her tasteful and interesting clothing. We both missed each other and wanted to catch up. We agreed to meet at a local Mexican restaurant after our morning ride.

Few things gave me more delight than watching Elaine's fabulous appetite at work. While Elaine didn't have to fret about pounds, my struggle to keep my weight off was constant when I wasn't sick. And she was a great conversationalist, too. Elaine could source more captivating stories than Joyce Carol Oates. Elaine seemed to know everybody and everything. If I weren't so entertained, I would have been tempted to eat more.

Elaine slid into the seat across from me. As usual, right on time. She practiced the best etiquette.

Our conversation covered news about our mutual friends, whose horse was lame and what beautiful horses had moved into our respective barns. Beaming with anticipation I wanted to show her my new purchase, but waited until we were served.

"Look what's in here," I said. I reached down to pull out a shopping bag.

"A black, lacy thong?" Elaine grinned, biting down on an enchilada smothered in a creamy, cheesy tomato sauce.

I returned a beatific smile. I understood where she was coming from. Elaine's black-lace-thong query was her hope I'd start dating. She felt people were happier with partners. But with my job, my commitment to Sufism Reoriented and my horse, I didn't have time for men. Both my father and my sister's boyfriend who later became her husband were abusive. My husband couldn't accept my love of horses. At some point I must have decided that it was better to live unattached. On rare occasions I would yearn to be held, but that didn't last long. At times I wondered why I had been born a heterosexual since the kinder ways and emotional sensitivity of women seemed to make them better companions.

"I have something much more exciting to show you," I said and with a flourish pulled out a bundle neatly cushioned in wrapping paper.

"...and whatever could that possibly be?" Elaine said, her eyes focused on my hands as they peeled back the paper.

"So much better than sexy underwear. Emma's new bridle." I draped the German-made bridle over my arm. "She's going to be ready to show soon."

I fingered the soft, smooth Havana-brown cheek straps as if they were made of the finest silk. The silver-metal buckles were polished to a high sheen. A fine spun cotton cloth had brought out the reflective quality of the metal. Creases in my fingers, still blackened from the Brasso, held the bridle out to Elaine.

"I bet that set you back a paycheck or two." Elaine reached over to stroke the leather brow band. "Just imagine what you could do with that kind of money at Victoria's Secret."

I crossed my eyes, puckered my mouth, worked my lips like a duck bill and made a sucking sound. Elaine's eyes sparkled. Elaine, the fashion model, the ever so gracious and appropriately behaved hostess, suddenly blew air through her mouth and flapped her lips to resemble a motor boat taking on water, droplets of spit spraying the table. We both laughed with school girl glee. Nothing like a couple of middle aged women acting silly. We muffled our giggles when the two men across from our table shot us a glance. Elaine got control first.

"I can add the double bridle pieces to it when Emma gets to the upper levels," I said, showing Elaine the dressage equipment catalog. "All I'll need is the headstall, cheek pieces, curb bit and another set of reins. Fortune's double bridle is too big for Emma."

"The workmanship is beautiful." Elaine took a bite out of the chicken taco. "And the style suits Emma's elegance."

"Show world, here we come." I put the bridle away, taking care to nestle it back into the tissue paper.

"So do you have any new Emma stories?" Elaine asked, perhaps expecting yet another one of my wild tales.

"Get this," I said, toying with a leaf of lettuce on my fork. "Leslie, the hunter/jumper trainer from the barn called me to tell me that Emma is giving her grain away. The last thing I do before I leave the barn is give Emma her bucket of grain mixed with her joint supplements, MSM (methylsulfonylmethane), DMG (N-dimethylglycine) and chondroitin sulfates. Apparently as soon as I'm in my car, she picks up her bucket and places it outside of her stall where the horse next door could reach it."

"No horse would give up their food," Elaine said, looking up at me with a wrinkled nose.

"It's true," I protested. "It's not because her supplements, which Emma refers to as her "white powders," taste all that horrible when mixed in with her grain. It's not about her avoiding something. Emma said that the horse next to her needed the supplements I was giving her more than she did. He's an older horse and probably has some arthritis. As soon as I made an arrangement with the owner to give her horse the same supplements, Emma stopped giving her food away."

"Why do I ask?" Elaine said, laughing. "Most of what you tell me is too hard to believe."

"You ask because you are intrigued, because you know I don't lie and because at some subconscious level you do believe it," I said, playing with a radish on my plate.

Near the end of the meal, Elaine hinted at some juicy piece of news. She took pleasure in teasing me.

"What's the big secret?" I pushed my half-eaten plate of house salad to the side.

"Something you've been wanting for quite awhile." Elaine sopped up the last bit of tamale from her empty plate of the Mexican Grande combo. "I was talking to a friend of mine."

"Now, that's a surprise," I said, dipping my head and looking up at her.

"I think I know where Emma's mother is." Elaine smiled as if she had just eaten the last snickerdoodle from the cookie jar.

"What? No joking?" I leaned forward.

"I heard." Elaine gingerly liberated a compact from her purse to reapply her lipstick. "Suzanne Allen down at Kentfield Farm ended up with a brood mare from Shelly Siegel's estate. I'm pretty sure it's Emma's mother."

"How do you know?" I asked with wide eyes.

"Didn't you tell me that Emma's mother was named Coming up Clover? Well, the name of the mare that Suzanne got was Clover." Elaine dabbed her lips with the edge of the paper napkin, folding it back into a neat rectangle with the smudged side hidden. "I bet it's the same horse. Call and find out."

"What a gift that would be." I relaxed my back against the slats of the wooden chair. "Emma won't have to mourn the loss of her mother anymore. I'm hauling her down there ASAP."

"You'll do anything for that horse." Elaine put her lipstick back in her purse.

I grabbed a soda and headed straight to my den as soon as I got home. On the occasional table next to my chair, I found a show prize list from Kentfield Farm. That was a stroke of luck. Saved me from finding the California Dressage Society's membership hand book piled amidst the jumble of papers, magazines and mail overflowing my desk. The rest of the house was clean and orderly unlike my desk where I let it all hang out. I ignored the mess and dialed the number.

"Yes, I have Coming Up Clover," Suzanne replied to my question. "She's been a good brood mare and great mom."

"I have Clover's first foal, a daughter. Her name is Emma and it would be great if I could bring her down to see her mom, if that works for you."

"You can bring Emma down here anytime," Suzanne replied. "Are you coming to the dressage show this Saturday?"

"No, Emma isn't quite show-ready yet. But the timing is perfect." I glanced at the array of dusty trophies piled in a corner of my room. "Emma needs to experience a show atmosphere before I enter her. I'm not sure what she'd do with all of the hub bub."

"Clover is in the last stall on the right of the little barn," Suzanne said. "Can't miss her."

"I'm curious," I said, looking at Emma's registration papers, "how you ended up with Clover?"

"She was a giveaway," Suzanne said. "Had a nasty shoulder injury and they needed a home for her. We nursed her back to health. I needed a brood mare to breed to my stallion. She's a good looking mare and has thrown beautiful babies. You can see two of her off-spring, colts, in the main barn. A two-year-old and a three-year-old."

I hung up the phone and sat still. Emma had two brothers. What a lucky girl.

I was determined to give Emma a happier family life than I had. Besides, I would feel her joy as if it were my own. I couldn't wait to tell Emma and called Carol.

"I hear your excitement," Carol said, her voice sounding tired. "Spit it out."

"I want you to tell me Emma's reaction to something." I fiddled with the phone cord.

"For goodness sakes, I just got off of a long shift and you want me to do more work." Despite her exhaustion, Carol laughed. "If your horse wasn't so fascinating…"

"I know, I know. She's different."

"Give me a minute to sit down," Carol said. Her breathing slowed and the rhythm steadied. "Okay, Emma's on line."

"Hey, Emma, I've got great news." I couldn't imagine a better gift than to be reunited with a loved one. "I've located your mother."

Feeling pleased, I sat back in my chair. Emma must be excited to hear the news. I pressed the phone receiver closer to my ear.

"Emma was caught by surprise," Carol said. "She's getting used to the idea. She never expected to see her mother again."

"I'm thrilled to make this happen," I said, squirming in my chair. "After all her suffering, I can't wait."

"My mother?" Carol translated for Emma, using a tone expressing incredulity.

"Your very own mother," I said and sent Emma wafts of my love.

"When are we going?" Carol translated with urgency in her voice.

"This weekend," I shouted, half expecting my energy to send me hovering above my chair. "You're going to visit your mother this weekend."

"Can you feel Emma's joy?" Carol said. "She's trembling. I'm not sure that she can quite believe it. Her euphoria is bordering on rapture."

"I'm not sure," I said, trying to calm down. I looked at Emma's picture. "I can't tell whether the happiness and anticipation I'm feeling are mine or hers."

I imagined giving Emma the gift of her mother's love, giving her what I probably wasn't ever going to get. I sighed. Through this act I felt as if I were healing myself. I sighed even deeper. I felt powerful.

I could do something to ease another being's pain. What could be more awesome?

At least twenty horse trailers were parked in Kentfield Farm's overflow parking by the time I got there mid-morning Saturday. Rusted out quarter-horse sized Mileys were parked next to shiny, fifth wheel Logans with a tack room in the nose and space for the biggest warmbloods. The sport of dressage made the rich, poor and the poor, indigent. My Circle J with paint intact was a step up from the bottom rung.

After unloading Emma, I led her past the main barn to the warm-up arena. Horses braided up snazzy, riders with tight lips, grooms giving boots a last minute polish, mega-phones blasting the riding order for the show ring, readers practicing the dressage tests. The commotion resembled a transfer station during commute rush. There was a lot to absorb.

Emma sidestepped and stopped to gawk at a groom with a towel flapping from her back pocket. She settled down quickly after a few minutes of cruising the grounds. She handled the buzz so well she proved she was ready for her first show. Stroking her neck, I radiated pride and told her she was a good horse.

I tied Emma to the trailer. An even bigger experience was about to happen. I headed to the back of the property. Would Emma's mother have a sixth sense that her daughter was near?

I negotiated my way through the labyrinth of horses and riders scurrying back and forth between riding rings and trailers. I couldn't help stopping for a minute. Watching the dressage horses gave me a thrill. Their pride in their capabilities gleamed out of their eyes. Their gaits were animated and expressive. When they were amped for a show, they exuded a "look at me" posture.

Oops. Almost stepped into a pile of manure. That pulled my mind back. What a stroke of luck to find Clover. Emma hadn't seen Clover since she was a baby. That was eight years ago. I wondered if Emma had the feelings of an adopted kid who was about to have her first meeting with her biological parent. My stomach did a flip flop.

The little six-stall barn nestled under a spreading oak tree was tucked away from the activity of the show. Emma's reunion with her mother would have some privacy.

At the entrance, I screeched to a stop. Just ahead a bay horse hung her head over the wood stall door. My breath caught. For a moment I was confused, thinking this horse must be Emma. I rushed outside. In the distance, I could see Emma - still tied to the trailer. I walked back into the barn to take a closer look. No white star, otherwise this horse was an exact replica of Emma.

Clover had the large, intelligent, deep-brown eye of Emma. I felt a shiver. I stepped back and studied her from head to tail. Oh, my God. The color of her coat, her black markings were identical to Emma's. The same sloped rear end, straight legs, long shoulder and elegance of frame. Emma's doppelganger. But the expression was different – distant. No light on, no one home. I walked into her stall. She didn't greet me. She didn't nuzzle me for treats.

On the way back to Emma, I swung by the main barn. Standing outside in the end paddock was a young horse. A bay, darker than Emma, had the same incredible eye and regal pose. Again the resemblance was striking. Emma's mom put her stamp on her babies. The second brother was just as easy to spot - another bay with large brown eyes and a commanding presence. How exciting – a family reunion.

I wasn't in communication with either of my sisters. I supposed life without them was better. But Emma's brothers had the look of kind horses. Their expressions exuded calmness and intelligence. We hit the jackpot. Not only Emma's mother, but also two half-brothers. Emma would be pleased.

I untied Emma and led her towards the little barn. She pranced the whole way, her excitement mounting with each step. She arched her neck, looked straight ahead and didn't even give an occasional glance to a passing horse or rider. This was different from her first walk-about where she checked everything out. She must be focused on meeting her mother. We reached the barn.

"Emma, how awesome is this?" My fingers stroked her neck. "Fate was on our side."

Emma usually paused before entering a new space. Especially when she went from the bright sunlight outside to a dark, small interior. Not this time. She didn't even slow down. She marched down the aisle of the little barn. Eyes open wide, staring at her mother. Her feet skimmed the ground. She was almost levitating.

We reached Clover's stall. Ears strained forward, Emma stretched out her head with an innocent eagerness. With no time for us to react, Clover, her ears pinned flat back and teeth bared, lunged at Emma. Her gnashing incisors narrowly missed Emma's neck. Emma and I jumped back at the same time. Emma threw her head up, falling back on her hindquarters.

The speed and viciousness of the attack surprised me. I looked at Emma's face. Her eyes bugged out showing the whites. The wrinkles around her eyes revealed distress. The muscles of her neck and shoulders stiffened.

"Emma," I cried. The horror of the rejection whipped through my body.

Clover's action wasn't the typical territorial response warning us not to get too close. I felt malevolence from Clover. I pulled Emma's head around. As soon as she faced the open door of the barn, she rushed past, pulling me behind her. I caught up with her and ran along her side to the trailer. I kept one eye on where I was going and one on Emma. She didn't seem to see or react to anything. She just kept staring straight ahead with a look of confusion.

Misery flooded my being. My heart pounded, and my stomach cramped. I felt as if I had tunnel vision. All I could do was concentrate on getting Emma away from there, fast. I fumbled with the trailer door, releasing the bolts with trembling fingers. As soon as

Emma faced the ramp she leapt in and stood shivering. I locked the doors behind her and scrambled to the cab. The truck started right up and I headed down the road.

I remembered Carol's advice. Even at a distance, Emma would hear everything I said if I directed my comments to her. I looked in the rearview mirror and spotted her face through the trailer window.

"Emma, it's different now." I softened my voice. "You have me. I'll take good care of you. You're stronger. You have friends. Mathilda, Gussey and Spunky, your pony friend, will help you heal. We have our own family now."

Later that evening I called Carol. The cushion on my easy chair felt cold. The phone felt hard and unyielding against my ear.

"You got me in the middle of cooking dinner," Carol said when she picked up the phone. "Let me turn down the heat so I can talk. Only a few minutes, though."

"Let me guess, you're steaming vegetables." I couldn't imagine Carol eating animal flesh.

"Yup, broccoli and asparagus." A lid banged. "Tell me how fabulous your visit was."

"Emma's mother rejected her," I said, feeling an empty pit in my stomach.

"That's lousy," Carol said, dropping her voice.

"How's Emma doing with it?" I asked, with a dry mouth.

"Give me a minute, would ya?" I heard her put down the phone and then pick-up an extension in another room. I heard deep breathing. "What in the world happened? She's very sad."

"Clover tried to bite Emma. Not a playful nip, but a full frontal assault," I said, feeling guilt spread in a hot flash across my face. "Emma, I'm so sorry I took you there."

"No, no. I'm glad you took me," Carol translated. "I realize I can't ever be friends with my mother. She sees me as a competitor now.

Not as a baby needing protection. Finding her was important. Since we were separated, I have yearned for her love. I won't long for her anymore. I have closure now."

Closure with her mother. Emma was ahead of me on that score. Conflict ruled my emotions. On one hand I envisioned that my mother and I could learn to be friends. I clung to hope as many abused children did. On the other hand I prayed for closure, so I could get on with my life and build other satisfying relationships.

The next day when I arrived at the stable, Emma's expression surprised me. It appeared bright and upbeat. I paused in front of her stall. Outside the sun broke through the cloud cover and dispelled the hint of humidity in the air. The barn aisle captured a gentle breeze.

Although I didn't sense any residual discord in Emma's emotions, I did feel a subtle shift in her energy. She seemed better grounded. Her legs shot straight down to the earth with a strength I hadn't seen before. I used to think that Emma walked slightly above the earth and not on it. Much the way a ballerina moves. Today, her weight seemed to settle down through her entire foot and not on her toes. I'd know more when I rode. My body often validated and expanded on what my intuition sensed.

Emma warmed up with easy fluid strides. I didn't need to whip her to get her started. Her spacing out had stopped after she processed the homeopathic remedy. Today her concentration was as focused as ever – no wandering mind, no apparent pangs from memories of the visit to her mother. If anything, her movement had more energy, more brilliance. The lightness in her feet hadn't changed. What had changed was the vibrancy I felt when she pushed off the earth. For that split second I felt a strength that was solid. Wow. How cool was that?

To engage her hind end, I cued Emma for a shoulder-in followed by a haunches-in. When I had asked her to do that in the past, she would hesitate while she figured out how to respond. Probably something no one would ever notice. Today I felt her glide from one bend seamlessly to the other. She moved with more confidence. Good for her.

Something had been resolved. If she lost some baggage, then the trip to visit her mother was a gift. And good for me, too. Emma's dressage work was improved. Who would have guessed that visiting her mother would help our dressage career? Why not write a letter to the United States Dressage Federation or the American Horse Show Association with that helpful hint? "Does your horse have abandonment issues? Are your dressage scores too low? Take your horse to visit her mother." I laughed.

Emma had given up hope of attaining her mother's love with an alacrity I admired. But then, Emma had experienced a loving mother for the first few months of her life. She had happy memories, something to fall back on. She knew what it meant to have the benefit of a mother's protection. As a newborn I hadn't seen the adoring face of a mother. I was born into a climate of rage, frustration and terror.

Emma reassured me that her grieving for her mother was over. Mine wasn't. My therapist had warned me that when my parents died I would have a hard time. As long as they were alive, I had the hope of working out some kind of satisfactory relationship. When they were gone, I'd have to admit the void would never be filled. Wasn't that a cheery something to look forward to?

The next week when I walked down the aisle of the barn to greet Emma, I saw her bobbing head. That greeting tickled the joy spot in my belly and spread warmth across my body like immersing in a warm pool of water. The velocity and depth of her head bob told me how happy she was to see me. Emma's physical affection had slowly grown over the last couple of years. The bobbing head was a powerful reminder of how far we had come from the days she had walked up the hill and away from me. I stood and watched and was grateful for this display of her love.

Today though, along with the nodding head, I heard something. I'd never heard a horse make that sound. A croak. Frogs croak, not horses. Was she well?

Dread took birth as I marched up to Emma's stall door. She nuzzled the plastic bag in my hand rooting out a quarter-slice of slightly chilled Fuji apple. Her eyes looked clear. She didn't act sick. I took no chances and reached into my tack box to retrieve a thin plastic container. I took out the thermometer and spit on it before inserting it into her rectum. For safety, I tied the string that was attached to the end of the thermometer to Emma's tail. I had no interest in calling out the vet to retrieve it from a place I wasn't qualified to search. Or hunting for the glass shards in the shavings. Three minutes later the mercury read 99.8 degrees. Normal. No infection. Whew.

If Emma wasn't sick, maybe the croak was her attempt to imitate me. My sinus and upper respiratory infections were doing a job on my breathing. Sometimes the coughing wouldn't stop. I had a hard time getting rid of the illnesses. At my previous job I'd missed a lot of work. It was a good thing that horses don't catch human germs. Real or imagined, I didn't want Emma to develop a sympathetic reaction. The expression "healthy as a horse" was a crock.

"I'm checking up to see how the new guy is cleaning the stalls." Sally said as she walked up to Emma's stall and inspected the shavings. She eyed the thermometer in my hand. "Is Emma sick?"

"I don't think so." I closed the stall door behind me.

"People don't realize how delicate horses can be." Sally leaned against the half-wall in front of Emma's stall.

"To the average person horses seem incredibly strong," I said, turning to face her. "All they see are the huge muscles. I have a hard time getting my non-horse friends to understand how easily I could lose Emma."

"Isn't it amazing that their intestinal tract seems to be one of their real weak points." Sally pulled out a stick of nicotine gum.

"Horse-care scares me." I sat down on Emma's upturned bucket. "So many things can go wrong too quickly. Why were they made this way?"

"It seems nuts that they can't throw up." Sally sat down on a bale of hay in the aisle.

"Yup, moldy hay causing fermentation to go wild in the gut – colic. Bam. Dead horse." My own stomach felt a knot of indigestion. I was on a roll. "Got into the grain bin, drank water and burst a stomach. Bam. Dead horse."

Sally nodded in agreement. She put the wrapper from the gum into her jeans pocket. She motioned to a stall at the other end of the barn.

"The chestnut who used to be in that stall rolled the wrong way to scratch his back and twisted his intestines. Dead the next day." Sally bent over and re-tied the shoelace of her hunt boot. "A horse in the outside paddock up at the house had an enterolith that blocked his intestines. Miserable death."

I shivered from the conversation. We had conspired to let our thoughts roam to the dark side. Knowledge was supposed to be power, but it increased my levels of stress and anxiety. When I first started out with horses, I was more relaxed, more naïve. Sally looked at me and shook her head.

"How many tragedies have you experienced?" I asked, half not wanting to know.

"All of what we've talked about and that's not the half of it." She stood up and headed up the aisle, checking out each stall and picking up strays bits of litter as she went.

I leaned over and smelled Emma's breath. Sweet. I pressed my ear against her flank. The gurgling sounds of gut movement. I sighed. All good indicators of a healthy horse.

I wouldn't give Emma's croak another thought. Maybe it was some kind of weird tracheal spasm. I had enough vet bills. Until I had something of substance, I wasn't calling the vet out again. John had invited phone calls at home to discuss my health worries about Emma at no charge. He had been extraordinarily sensitive. But John was no longer my vet. He had at last succumbed, withered and died of AIDS. I had been deeply saddened to lose John, both my vet and my friend. The horse community was deeply distressed as well. He was popular, accessible and a master of common sense. He could handle horses and people. I'm not sure that anyone would measure up to what John offered all of us. I couldn't call on Ashley. She had moved out of town.

Not surprising then, that I found the new vet wasn't so helpful. I could imagine the phone call. Emma made a strange sound. Say what?

A little more than a week passed by. On my usual walk down the barn aisle, I pulled up short when I was two stalls away from Emma. In between one of her bobbing arcs, she made a peculiar sound. This time it wasn't a croak. The sound had a guttural and hoarse quality. My heart raced. I didn't need to be spooked.

I went into her stall and scrutinized her. All her vitals looked fine. She had cleaned up her breakfast. The level in her water tub had dropped. Ate and drank. Good signs. I told myself to calm down. I was determined to keep my imagination from slipping into a hysterical rampage of ills. Maybe this was just a strange coincidence. I believed in the law of three's. If it happened a third time I'd call Carol.

This time a week didn't go by. The next day Emma choked out a sound as if she was trying to cough up phlegm. I lost control over my imagination. What if she had a tumor growing on a bronchial tube? What if she was coming down with a case of strangles, that hideous infection of the mucus membranes which sometimes led to the rupture of lymph nodes and the expulsion of thick, gooey pus from the nose? Or could it be pigeon fever manifesting in a rare location and about to burst forth with cup loads of pus to suffocate her? My only chance for a good night's sleep was to call Carol when I got home. Emma might tell me it was a mild allergic reaction and not to worry.

Yeah, right. Not with my luck.

Once in my den, I headed for my favorite chair. I stared at the phone. I could have used a bag of Cheetos. I needed to know what was going on with Emma. A part of me worried that it couldn't be fixed. Things were going too well. I had a habit of getting nervous when things went well. Life had taught me that's when stuff happened.

My hands trembled as I dialed Carol's number. She picked up on the second ring.

"Calm down, calm down," Carol insisted. "What are you trying to say? You're talking way too fast."

"Emma is making noises," I said. "I've never heard her vocalize in her stall before. She has coughed or sneezed a few times. I think she's sick." There I'd said it. Now I'd have to wait to hear the truth.

That the University of California at Davis vet school was only a little over an hour away gave me some comfort. I kept my truck and trailer ready for a mad dash as an ambulance. But I had always pictured that desperate ride would be for a friend's horse, not mine.

"So," Carol said, "you want me to ask Emma how she's feeling." Carol told one of her dogs to be quiet.

"Yes, yes." I stammered. "I can take it. My truck is filled with gas."

"Your truck is farting?" Carol's laughter filled my ear.

I didn't want to laugh, but I had to. Carol had a way of defusing my hysteria. Good thing. My adrenaline crept back to more normal levels.

"Okay, hang on." Carol's breathing got deeper. "It's going to take me a minute. I've got a lot of work stuff on my mind."

I bounced up and down on my chair. I flipped the stainless steel band of my watch so I could see the face. I always wore watches with a second hand so I could measure my horse's respiratory rate or heart beat.

"Tell me what's going on with you and your job while I'm getting settled," Carol said.

"Great news," I said. "The rumor I heard has turned out to be true. Those of us with staff positions are going to lose our jobs, including my boss. The timing hasn't been released yet. It may be as long as six months from now. That means I get a severance package and unemployment compensation. I can't wait to get out. I'm not even trying to find a job within the company. I want a well deserved long rest."

"Your health needs to improve," Carol sighed. "Aha, Emma's joined us. Emma, what's going on? Diana thinks you're sick."

The big second hand crawled from tick mark to tick mark around the face of my watch. I held my breath. My eyelids stopped blinking.

"She says she's fine." Carol breathed into the phone. "There's nothing wrong with her. She wants to know how YOU ARE." Carol's laughter escalated into raucous guffaws.

"That's not funny." My muscles relaxed a notch. "I was worried."

"Emma is worried that you're worried." Carol was having too much fun at my expense. "You two are a circus team."

"I'm glad we amuse you." I flopped back and rested my head against my chair.

"I needed comic relief after my day," Carol said and then reminded her dog Bailey to be quiet. "Too many doctors' egos needed stroking."

"Tell me why Emma is making strange sounds." I twisted the curly phone wire around my fingers.

"She's been practicing," Carol teased.

"You win, I bite, practicing for what?" I felt impatience stir.

"She knows how your heart feels when you hear a nicker." A cabinet door shut. "What you've been hearing are her attempts."

"Oh, Emma," I said, emitting my own version of a small croak.

All my other horses had nickered whenever they saw me. Maybe a horse's nicker substituted for never hearing a mother's cooing. Maybe some deep, primal need was being satisfied with that sound. All I knew was how much I loved hearing it. The place that was touched by that sound was aching for nourishment.

Pans clanked. "Carol, what are you doing?"

"I'm putting the dishes away."

"I'm glad you can multi-task; tell me what Emma is saying."

"Emma says that her pony friend Spunky in the stall next door has been helping her," Carol said. "She's been practicing at night when there aren't any people around. The other horses have been making fun of her, but she's determined to do it."

"I've been puzzled why you didn't nicker like other horses. I thought horses were born knowing how to vocalize."

"My mother didn't teach me." Carol translated, making her statement a lamentation. "It takes two years to learn to be a proper horse. I didn't have anyone to help me with social behaviors. Baby horses are taken away from their mothers too early. It's humanity's crime against horse."

"I'm so sorry," I said. I wondered if the Native Americans knew better and kept babies with their mothers.

"Spunky just popped in." Carol interrupted my thoughts. "He says he thinks Emma sounds stupid."

"What? Shut up, you little pip squeak." The mother protector in me reared up in full force. "She's showing a lot of courage. I appreciate that you're helping her, but keep the criticism to yourself."

"He heard that loud and clear." Carol's breaths became even. She must have stopped her chores. "He's gonna think twice before he insults Emma again."

"Emma, you touched me." My right hand involuntarily lighted over my heart.

"That's what I wanted," Carol translated.

I felt Emma's love. I felt loved and with that love, I felt worthy. We deserved each other's love.

Chapter 12

A small local dressage show at Heather Farm Park provided Emma the opportunity to do her job at a specified time and place. We could look fabulous in the arena at Clear Creek under known conditions and yet our performance could fall apart in a show ring a few miles down the road. I had trailered Emma to a variety of venues so she could get accustomed to trips away from home. Putting it all together at a show was different.

Despite her show nerves, Emma put in solid tests in both of our classes. I wasn't much help. Bronchitis had settled in my chest causing a hacking cough that sapped my energy. Emma was the better partner. I was the one not in top form. Under normal circumstances, I would have been elated over Emma's first outing, but I was too tired to feel much.

I knew my luck. My riding was progressing well. Too well. Emma was my hope to school a horse to the FEI, Federation Equestre Internationale, levels. Emma might have a healthy body, but I didn't. I prayed that the trajectory that my health seemed to be traveling would reverse and we'd have more test results to file. All I had to do was keep well another two months - until the middle of June – my layoff date. Then I would sleep and recover from the stress I had been under.

The bronchitis was almost healed when I contracted a cold. And then on its heels another cold. Each episode of upper respiratory infection diminished my health. Exhaustion dogged me for weeks after my immune system vanquished the infective agent.

A sore throat, more of a nuisance than a plague, sickened several of my associates at work. At most they were inconvenienced with popping throat lozenges. When the illness got to me, the affect was totally different. My body was not unlike Florida after Andrew. The virus stormed through my body and left in its wake a decimated immune system like the ruined houses after the hurricane subsided. Why, now that I was on such a promising path to realize my dream of upper level dressage, did my lack of health need to raise its ugly head?

Getting dressed in the morning was difficult and took longer than the normal amount of time. Just putting on a single piece of clothing taxed my energy. I had to sit on my bed to recover from the effort and to gather the strength I'd need to put on the next piece. These episodes of debilitation started ten years earlier and I knew the pattern well. I lived in constant fear of the particular viral infection that would set me into a tail spin. My sword of Damocles was a microbe.

The day I heard Emma croak I thought the other shoe had dropped. I thought there was going to be something wrong with Emma, not me. I had hoped my bouts of illness wouldn't recur. After all, I had been in pretty good shape for the last three years, for as long as I had Emma. When I quit my job in San Francisco four years earlier and stopped the long commute, my health seemed to improve.

If I had been a sloth instead of having abundant physical energy when I was well, the adjustment might have been easier. When ill, I needed to sleep ten hours a day which crimped my style. I preferred to live in denial, to forget how sick I could get. As soon as an attack was over, my will power got me back to a full scale of activities, pronto.

But this time I wasn't rebounding very well. I fought it for as long as I could. Too often I had to beg off invitations with friends to go to a movie or out to dinner. I think I disappointed my friends and eventually they called less often.

My lack of energy was on a luge track to the South Pole. I knew I needed to face my situation with more realism. I hired a gardener and house cleaning service. A caterer cooked dinners because I was too tired by the time I got home to prepare healthy meals. I struggled to exercise Emma.

One Saturday morning when I finished riding Emma, I nearly blacked out. Dismounting, I fell backwards splaying out on the ground with a thud.

"Are you all right, are you hurt, what happened?" Sally asked as she raced over to me.

I looked up at her from the floor of the sand arena, shielding my eyes from the sun. I felt as if I had just gotten off a spinning joy ride at Great America. Sally reached down and helped me sit up and then stand.

"Emma didn't do anything." I brushed the dirt off my clothes. "I lost my balance when I was getting off. I'm really tired."

"Do you think you should be riding?" Sally said, holding my arm to steady me.

"Would you put Emma away for me?" I handed her Emma's reins when she nodded.

Too tired to think, I drove home and crawled straight to bed sleeping through until the next day. Pulling myself out of bed midmorning, I knew I needed some sound advice. After breakfast I called Elaine and told her what happened.

"Read the tea leaves, dear," Elaine's tone of voice scared me. "It's about time that you put more energy into taking better care of yourself."

"That's something that I'm not very good at." I felt my stomach sink. I didn't look forward to these kinds of talks.

"Fortune and your other horses managed to survive through your illnesses and I'm sure that Emma will manage as well. They didn't last all that long." This wasn't the cheery Elaine that I was used to. "You need to spend more time resting and less time at the barn."

"Okay, okay." My back stiffened with resistance whenever anyone suggested I see less of Emma. "I admit I do feel worse this time."

"Do I have your promise?" Elaine was playing hard ball.

"Yes, yes." I hated to admit she was right. Where was my kind, gentle friend?

My family practice doctor shook his head and said that it looked as if I had Chronic Fatigue Syndrome. I had many of the symptoms to support that theory. My sinus infections were too mild to account for the severity of my exhaustion. There was no definitive test to support his hypothesis but he had seen enough cases to be pretty sure that was what I had.

In order to protect me, he suggested that he continue to log in my chart a series of chronic sinus infections. He was concerned about my ability to get health insurance in the future. There was no sense putting a label on what I might have when there was no certainty about the diagnosis and there was no treatment. He put down his pen and apologized that there wasn't anything he could do. Not that much was known about the syndrome other than it tended to affect women who were abused in their early life and/or who were under a lot of stress.

I'd already tried homeopathy. I asked my friends for help and was referred to a variety of alternative health care providers. I'd try anything.

The nutritionist I consulted surprised me by confessing she didn't know how I could work in my condition. She said people as sick as I was were unable to hold down their jobs. My body was unable to digest food and get any nutrition. I had to agree. Shoving in calories didn't seem to do anything. My clothes hung loose. The requirements of maintaining a home mortgage and a horse ensured that I had to keep working until June. I had no choice.

Next I tried an acupuncturist. I drove all the way to Emeryville to see her. When she read my pulses, she frowned.

"You're one of the weakest patients I've ever seen." She pulled up a stool next to the table I was lying on. "I'm not sure you would get any benefit from my treatment."

"What do you mean?" I'd never heard that from a practitioner. "Many of my friends have been helped with acupuncture."

"I need energy to move energy," her fingers pressed into my wrist. "You are so weak I'm afraid that if I treat you, I might pull out the few props that keep you upright."

Her voice penetrated my skull with the same precision that her needles would target the acupuncture trigger points.

If my health continued to decline, I wouldn't be able to keep my job. I wanted that severance package. I needed that to support me through a few months of rest and a job search. Others with chronic fatigue became bed bound. Researchers had suggested that the illness sometimes morphed into multiple sclerosis (MS). My sister had MS, a familial disease. If I was going to get through the next day, I couldn't give these thoughts another moment of life in my brain. I was a survivor. I knew how to keep pushing on.

I left the acupuncturist's office feeling depressed and exhausted. On the drive home I forced my eyes wide open. I wanted to sleep, to rest. Keeping my car pointed in the right direction challenged me.

This melancholy was a rare low. I pulled my convertible Mustang over to the slow lane of a six-lane highway and slipped into bitterness. Memories of unpleasant prognostications added bile to my despondency. Everywhere I had turned, I was forced to face miserable predictions. A palmist in India gulped hard when he looked at my hand. His grin and nodding head that had greeted my traveling companions faded into a downcast visage when he saw me. He avoided looking at me. The best he could say was that I was a self made woman. He got rid of me as soon as he could. Everyone else had been told about wonderful experiences that awaited them. I remembered feeling demolished.

Here I was half-way around the world only to be told what my astrologers had been telling me for years. They had warned me I had signed up for a tough life, full of challenges and a lot of growth. Nothing would be given to me. I was paddling my canoe upstream – no, up river – no, up Niagara Falls. At least a psychic had been kinder. With concern written all over her face, she suggested that I had wonderful opportunities to learn a lot this life. A whole lot. They weren't kidding. Thump, thump, thump interrupted my ruminations. My tires had drifted across the broken white lines punctuated with raised circles. Thank you Bott's dots. I steered back into my lane. Maybe I needed to concentrate on one thing at a time.

Through will power and teeth-gritting force of determination, I made it through to the big June lay-offs and received my severance package.

I may have skipped out of the building clicking my heels on my last day of work, but the jubilation didn't last. Although I was no longer subjected to the stresses of my job, my health didn't improve the way I'd hoped. A couple of months of rest was followed by a plummet into the worst attack I'd ever had. My energy was so low that I had to plan a bathroom break in advance to accumulate the physical strength to crawl to the toilet. At first I wasn't concerned because I had budgeted to be off nearly six months. With the extra caregiving I required, my funds spewed out of my checking account as if I were supporting four horses and not just one.

On one of my good days and only three months after I had been laid off, I managed to get out a cover letter and my resume to a classified ad in the *Wall Street Journal* for heading up the home loan marketing and product development department of a Fortune 500 company. The low odds of being contacted through want ads assured me that I wouldn't be called. When I was, I took the last appointment they offered so I would have all morning and afternoon to dress.

My corporate uniform, wool suit with silk blouse, helped me look the part. I used all of my will power to look lively when I arrived for my 4:30 p.m. interview. The hiring manager interviewed me and as luck would have it my mind was sharp. My experience matched their requirements and they appreciated my mathematics background. At the end I drove home and staggered into bed.

More interviews were scheduled with other executives in the bank. I spaced them out as best as I could to give me some time to recover between them. Fortunately I interview well and I needed those skills to impress the evaluators. I can project high energy, intelligence and cordiality. One person in particular liked that I was both right and left brain competent and said that he would hire me if his peer didn't select me from among the other candidates.

To my amazement, the hiring manager called me and offered a signing bonus, a salary larger than I requested and an appointment as an officer of the corporation. How I would deliver a creditable performance was my next challenge. I managed to function by sleeping at a friend's house on my lunch hour and collapsing as soon as I got home. Sheer will power got me through the day. My nutritionist and acupuncturist didn't think I would be able to do it.

Because Carol enjoyed talking to Emma and found some of her responses fascinating, she occasionally made herself available in the evenings. She may also have felt a little sorry for me. I was pretty miserable. My only connection to a social life was through the telephone. No wonder these visits with my horse took on importance. I soon discovered that Emma had far more interesting things to say than many people. And unlike some of my friends and more like a faithful dog, Emma didn't put any demands on me.

For several hours a week Carol, Emma and I explored a variety of subjects. Carol was in her home in Lafayette, I, in my bed in Walnut

Creek and Emma, in her stall at the barn. It was open season for any topic esoteric or banal. I learned more about how Emma thought and her answers to my questions were often captivating. With each visit I was drawn even closer to her. Carol seemed to need to keep reminding me that Emma was an extraordinary horse – that she was so evolved that this was probably her last life as a horse. In the years since Carol first met Emma she had the opportunity to talk to many other horses. Emma was more sensitive, aware and simply did things that other horses didn't.

When Emma wasn't distracted with her own business, she was connected to me, observing what I was doing. Psychologically she was spending a lot of time in the human world. It used to annoy Emma whenever Carol suggested that she was probably going to reincarnate as a human. Emma resisted the idea saying that humans were far too complicated. She was fond of being a horse and would continue to reincarnate as a horse as long as I needed a horse in my life.

Because Emma spent most of her day attending to what I was doing, I could ask her what other people with whom I interacted were thinking, what kind of energy they were putting out. She advised me of situations that had totally escaped my awareness. One time I was confused by the attention of a woman at work. What she was saying and what I was feeling weren't aligned. After a particularly baffling conversation, I asked Emma what was going on. She explained that the woman wanted to partner at a sexual level. That energy had never made it into my consciousness. After Emma said it and I replayed the puzzling behavior, it all became clear.

I could be wise for others, but when it was about me I could be quite naive. Emma could help me understand the origin of some of the difficulties I experienced with other people. She explained how relationships in previous lives affected our current exchanges.

During one of these telephone gatherings, Emma was particularly talkative. She had been telling us that she had no concept of money other than it was something important to me. She was appalled that someone would give up their horse for money. She found it unfathomable that someone would sell their horse, their partner who had devoted themselves and given their heart so completely. After I explained what might be the human viewpoint, Emma changed the subject.

"When you are better, would you take me back to Pt. Reyes?" Carol translated.

"My pleasure," I said. "I love the seashore." I cradled the receiver on my pillow so I could keep my hands under the covers.

"I'm getting that she had a fabulous time," Carol said. Bailey and Janie, Carol's dogs, barked in choral disharmony in the background. "What did you and Emma do?"

"We took a loop between the trailhead and the beach." Remembering that day brought back images of spectacular views. "The change in ecology in such a short distance was amazing. The trip began in dense forest dripping with mosses, ferns and delicate wildflowers only to emerge at the shore where sea gulls flew over jagged sea cliffs covered in salt grasses. Definitely my kind of day."

"Sounds beautiful," Carol said. "Oops, wait. I'm not getting that's what had Emma's interest." A bag rattled and then canine crunching. Probably the destruction of Milk Bones.

"Maybe it was the fallow deer." I pictured the meadow where we had stopped. "At dusk we came upon a herd of about fifteen miniature, grayish-white deer with magnificent racks. The diminutive herd seemed gentle and timid. They wandered around us as if we were invisible to them. I'd never heard about these small, pale animals before. Walking among them was a rare and special privilege. I was enchanted and felt as if I had been dropped into a fairyland."

"No, that's not it either." More barking. More crunching.

"You got me." I searched my brain for anything else unusual about the trip.

"Emma wants to go back in February." Carol said. "Isn't that typical of your horse to specify the conditions of a request? It goes along with her preferring her Fuji apples slightly chilled. She has Rolls Royce tastes."

"But remember. She always has a reason. You taught me that."

Carol laughed. And then a series of coughs. She was having some health issues. Minor health issues. A common cold. A cold that would go away in a few days.

"I'd be happy to take you back when I'm better," I said, "but why in February when it's chilly?"

I turned the heating pad up one notch. Since getting sick, I couldn't drive the chill out of my body. No matter how many layers of thermal wear I put on under my business suits, I couldn't get warm.

"I want to talk to the whales," Carol translated. She took in a deep breath.

"What whales?" I hadn't seen any whales at Point Reyes.

"I spoke to them when we were there," Carol translated. "Their voices were weak because they were so far away. They said that when they migrated in February they would be closer to Pt. Reyes and there would be more of them to talk to. The ones I spoke to were focused on catching up with the others in their pod. Stragglers."

"Why do you want to talk to whales?" I asked. Emma continued to surprise me. Maybe that was why my few free wake hours were spent on the phone with her.

"They're interesting," Carol translated. "Remember tarantulas got Emma's attention."

"What makes the whales interesting?" I sat up in bed. I focused on what she would say next.

"I'll show you," Carol translated.

Before Carol even finished the sentence, my bedroom became blurry. I blinked. When I opened my eyes, the white Techline dressers blended into the walls. My heart pounded. Was I having a stroke? Was it MS? My sister's MS started with visual problems. Emma blasted me with warm love. I was blanketed, surrounded with her energy. This vision must be coming from her and not be a burp in my brain.

Then my bedroom's warm-white walls dissolved into a wash of blue. My furniture and bed transformed into muted grey shapes moving against a background of a rich shade of vibrant, shimmering marine blue. Schools of herring-sized fish darted back and forth, reflecting prisms of light when their shiny sides caught the sun. Wherever they darted, they left a trail of sparkling bubbles of silver. But they weren't fish. They were muted flashes of light streaming through a beautiful blue expanse. If the flashes of lights were notes of music, I witnessed an uplifting symphony of shapes blending and weaving into complicated rhythms that merged, separated, but stayed in some indefinite relationship to each other. Ah, Bach, you would know what I meant.

The twinkling lights gripped my eyes. I was absorbed in the visual display when I felt something brush against my face. What felt like a gentle stream of air rushed past me. Only softer and fuller. I raised my hand. The air left tendrils in the wake of my fingers as if I were giving flight to filaments of the finest silk. The viscosity of air increased until I felt weightless, but supported. I moved in three dimensions. Somehow I left the bounds of my human form. I was transported to another world. For a few minutes I knew what it was to be a whale. I sat in my bed breathless.

"What's happening?" Carol broke the silence, whispering in a barely audible tone.

"Something...uh…" I rubbed my eyes, blinked and squinted at the off-white walls staring back at me from across the room. What an experience. To glide through water effortlessly. To be another animal. To see as a whale sees. To know what it feels like to be a whale. I had a hard time grasping what I had just experienced.

"Emma says she sent you whale energy." Carol spoke the words as if they were a prayer.

"It was awesome." I flopped back against my down pillows. "I don't think I can put it into words."

"Emma is pleased that she was able to share her experience of the whales." Carol said.

When I had landed fully back in my body, I sat still, trying to hold on to the place I had been invited. But I was human and my science mind returned.

"I remember when we were heading back home on the trail," I said, pulling the covers up over my shoulders. "Emma turned around a couple of times and stared out to sea. One time she got bug eyed. I wonder if that's when she connected to the whales."

"Yes," Carol translated, lowering the pitch of her voice.

"Emma, I will never forget what you just shared with me." My mind whirred with the images I had just seen and the sensations I'd felt. "Carol, did you feel it, did you see it?"

"No, she didn't send the experience to me." Carol cleared her throat. "The gift was for you."

"Emma, I thank you with all of my heart for this offering," I whispered.

"Oh, Pshaw," Carol translated.

"My friends think I'm nuts for talking to my horse for hours each week. If they only knew."

"Maybe someday they will," Carol said, with optimism in her voice.

As the home loan marketing and product development head of a Fortune 500 company, I had to inspire others. That meant I faked abundant vigor. For the first two months I only made it to the barn on Saturday or Sunday. In the third month of my new job I recovered some energy and managed to get out to the barn once or occasionally twice during the week days.

But then my energy took another dive. One weekend I couldn't make it out at all. I knew I needed more help. Fortunately there was a hunter/jumper trainer at the barn, who provided caregiving services. She met Emma's needs for exercise and nutritional supplements whenever I couldn't make it out.

The focus of my life became keeping my job. Without a job, I'd be living under a freeway overpass and there would be no Emma in my life. To preserve energy I became a recluse. Besides, whenever I had been sick, I didn't want anyone around. Everything went but my job and the horse. Priorities.

It became clear that I needed to jump start my recovery if I was going to be able to keep this job. In my last conversation with Elaine she focused on my health and responded with a generous offer. She believed her land in the foothills of the Sierras had healing qualities so she invited me to join her for three days in mid-December.

In talks with Carol, Emma said she wanted to go as well. She thought if we spent more time together she could share her energy with me and help me recover. The additional work needed to take her would be worth it if I had a bigger payoff. Emma and I would have our first sleep over together. Besides nothing substitutes for invigorating mountain air and I would have Elaine, my horse and nature to nurture me. If Emma could transport her energy to me, even better.

I had enjoyed trips to Elaine's vacation home for summer retreats. Her cabin, although residing in the middle of nowhere, was cozy and felt homey. Her forty acres of unfenced forest yielded to panoramic views of mountains dotted with the cool, blue-green of pine trees and the warm, red-brown of manzanita bark.

My lack of energy wouldn't stop me from doing what I needed to get rejuvenated. Disability was not in my vocabulary. If I could force myself through a day of a demanding job, I could certainly make myself get out in the mountain air. During the day I would ride Emma while Elaine hiked alongside of us through the hills on one of the many logging roads that crisscrossed the area. Trail riding, unlike dressage, would let me slump like a Raggedy Ann doll in the saddle with Emma doing all of the work. At day's end, Emma would be bedded down outside my window and supplied with a mound of hay to keep her busy. Whenever we talked about the trip, Emma expressed her excitement about the "sleep over." She thought spending three straight days near each other was an extraordinary opportunity. She was confident that she could help me. I welcomed the idea of the intimate contact. At night Emma's gentle sighs and snorts as she chewed her hay outside my window would lull me to sleep.

Emma and I were giddy planning the trip as if we were a couple of Girl Scouts preparing for a wilderness adventure. It mitigated my disappointment of not being able to ride much and certainly no dressage training. I was practical enough to know that I had to keep my job. I vowed to Emma that as soon as I was better we would resume our career. Emma was my dressage horse after all. And one way or another I was going to return to my sport. I was tired of the well-worn, dog-eared copies of my dressage magazines. I didn't make a good spectator.

On the Saturday three weeks before the trip, I was too tired to get on Emma and plunk around the arena so I turned her loose. She kicked up her heels and cavorted with bursts of speed and sudden, sliding stops. Her energy, exuberance and joy of life sent a ping of delight through my body. I felt as if she was transferring some of her delight and energy to me. Maybe she had a point about the sleep over. I couldn't help but feel better when I was around her. Running at nearly full speed, she came barreling down to the end of the arena where I was standing. Within a few strides of the gate, she checked her speed. Her head bobbed up and down as she trotted by. She favored her left front leg. Drat! Not now. She must have taken a misstep in a depression in the sand. My only utterance, the equestrienne's lament, "A lame horse!" spurted out of my mouth and splattered on the ground with a thud. I inspected every inch of her left leg and hoof. No immediate swelling or hot spots. I hosed her leg for twenty minutes, put her away and headed home with a sinking heart.

At last snug in my bed and warm enough to feel my hands, I reached for the phone. Emma appreciated being consulted about her medical needs and wanted to fully participate in any decision making. She felt it was her body. I called Carol to get Emma's input on the injury.

"Is the new diet giving you any energy?" Carol asked before I could speak.

"Not that I notice," I said. "My friends call bieler soup, green slime. Pureed zucchini, string beans and parsley aren't doing it for me."

"Keep up with it," Carol said. "You are seriously ill and it'll take time."

"I have one bit of good news," I reassured Carol. "Even though Emma is injured, I'm not hysterical."

I felt proud of myself. With my own health challenges, Emma's lameness was put in perspective. The injury was far from her heart. Eventually she would be all right.

"Hey, give me a minute to get organized," Carol said. The TV chatter went silent. "Emma is sending me clear pictures of the part of her leg that's injured. I'm not familiar with horse anatomy. It's the thingamajig that is connected behind the knee, but isn't the big tendon. No bone involvement."

"I think I know. She may have pulled a suspensory ligament," I said, propping a pillow behind my back. "Is that right?" I pictured that part of her leg.

"Yes, that's the place," Carol translated, coughing. A light one, not a hacking one like the week before.

"If I'm right, it's not a disastrous diagnosis." I sighed with relief. "I need to have the vet out. Do you agree, Emma?"

"Yes, I want it fixed so we can go on our trip," Carol translated giving the word "fixed" extra emphasis. "Gee, Diana. Bad timing. You've been looking forward to this trip."

"I don't know if we'll get to go," I said, picturing Emma's legs swaddled in cotton quilts and standing wraps. "Soft tissue injuries can take time."

Three weeks wasn't very long to heal a ligament. At least it wasn't her tendon. That could take months to heal.

The following Monday, my new vet, Dr. Andrews, arrived at the barn and joined me in front of Emma's stall with his black satchel in hand. Elaine had recommended him. I had used John Taylor's young associate a couple of times, but his bedside manner wasn't to my liking.

Taking in the smell of the sawdust and hay, I relaxed my shoulders. I was happy to take a half day off of work.

"Emma says she pulled her suspensory ligament," I blurted out. Oops. I saw his face change. I had mistaken his kindness over the phone for acceptance.

His eyes stretched open and his nostrils flared as if he had brushed against some stinkweed. He looked at me as if I'd been consorting with aliens. In his world, animals didn't talk. His jaw muscles bulged as he marched by me and into Emma's stall to examine her leg.

I wondered what John would have thought of telepathic animal communication if he were still alive. He would probably have been okay with it. Or at the very least tolerated my belief.

Dr. Andrews came out of Emma's stall and seemed reluctant to admit that the injury was "consistent with" a pulled suspensory ligament. His discomfort was palpable. I made a mental note to myself – find ways to relate what Emma says without giving her attribution.

Emma's leg needed icing and wrapping daily. She was to be confined to stall rest with thirty minutes of hand walking – no jumping around. The vet guessed that it would take about three weeks from the day of the injury to heal if all went well and was hopeful that we could still make the trip.

Wow, exactly three weeks. I hadn't thought it would heal in time. Now, for once, luck was on our side.

The trainer I had hired to help care for Emma during the work week took care of the bandages and the icing. On the days the trainer wasn't available Sally volunteered to hand-walk Emma.

Friday, the day before I was to leave for our outing and nearly three weeks from the date of the injury, I met the vet out at the barn. I removed the flannel wrap and quilted standing bandage to uncover a tight leg devoid of any swelling or heat. The vet ran his fingers up and down Emma's tendon and on either side of the back of her knee. He stood up, smiled and pronounced her good-to-go. The mini-vacation was on.

At home, I collapsed into bed and called Carol to go over last minute details with Emma. I reasoned that if I talked everything through there would be fewer mistakes. Energy deficiency taught me to be clever about planning ahead.

"I'm glad Emma is better," Carol said. "You didn't think her injury would heal in time."

"The trip will take about three hours," I said pulling the down comforter over my shoulders. "That's a long time for Emma to stand in a horse trailer."

"And a long time for you to be behind the wheel," Carol said, taking a parental tone. "Are you really sure this trip is a good idea? I was thinking that Emma's injury might cause you to postpone it."

"I want to do something to try and get better," I said. "Forcing myself to work everyday is the hardest thing I've ever done."

"You're an adult," Carol said, laughing, "sometimes."

"Your point has been received," I said with irritation. Carol was echoing my friends' warnings. "Now I want to chat with Emma."

"Well, enjoy yourself," Carol said. "You deserve some relief."

"Thanks," I said. "Remember, Emma, Elaine has no fencing." I used a stern tone. "You will be on your honor to stay close and not wander off the way most horses would be tempted to do."

"No problem," Carol translated for Emma. "I'm not like other horses."

I smiled. Yup, Emma was not like other horses. This holiday would provide me the opportunity to get to know Emma on even deeper levels. What else might I discover about her? Did she snore?

Chapter 13

The buzz of the alarm clock invaded the haze in my mind. 10:00 a.m. Twelve hours of sleep wasn't enough. I used to need only six or seven hours with a brief nap on the BART train during my morning commute into the city. Then it hit me. Today is Saturday and I'm going to Elaine's. I forced my legs out over the edge of the bed. Panting, I pushed into a sitting position. This was so hard. If it weren't for my excitement, my rising time would have been closer to noon. The thought of going to the mountains helped make my muscles come to life, but the response was slow and paltry.

The weight of my arm pulled on the cord of the blinds to unveil a grey sky blanketed with a high, thick fog. For the last several days a hard rain had pelted the area and more of the same meant the trip would be cancelled. I rested my forehead against the window for a better look, but also to hold up my head. No threatening rain clouds loomed on the horizon. I turned on the radio. The forecasters predicted no precipitation for the next few days. I felt a tiny twinge of energy. After all of this anticipation, the trip would happen.

My energy level was usually at its lowest on Saturday mornings. Weekends were used to recover from the work week, so I would have to be clever with my preparations. I went through a checklist in my mind. Being well organized would save me precious steps. One trip each to the bathroom, kitchen and truck.

In order to get dressed and packed, I had to take long rest breaks. At last my things were loaded in the bed of the truck. Check. I left the house at noon. Elaine was taking care of the food, and all other arrangements so I could concentrate on my and Emma's needs. Although a three-hour drive pulling a horse trailer was daunting, my mind was stoked. I could do this. At least that is what I kept telling myself.

On the way to the barn, I went through my mental checklist again. Get the trailer. Gather the hay, grain, tack, buckets. Load Emma. Hit the road.

The rains had thoroughly soaked the ground. Water-logged adobe soil turned into gloppy, sticky glue. Rain had a way of converting what was perfectly sound footing in the summer into mire in the winter. I would have to be careful and inspect the ground near the trailer before I hitched up.

I drove down the driveway to the barn and was relieved to see the trailer resting on a mound of gravel next to the road. Sally must have moved it nearer the parking lot when the rains started. That was like Sally to be kind and thoughtful. Hitching up the trailer was easy. Getting the things Emma would need was harder. My all-purpose saddle was heavy. Thankfully, the bridle and saddle pads were lighter. I collected brushes, water buckets and all the accoutrements needed for horse care out of my tack locker. Stumbling only once, I managed to load all of it into the compartment in the nose of the trailer with three trips. Traveling with a dog would be so much easier - kibble and a bowl.

Food was next. I filled a feed bucket with rolled oats from my plastic bin in the grain room. My shoulders sagged while I hauled it out to the trailer. A half bale of oat hay from the hay barn was next. I took a few flakes at a time to the trailer. A horse eats about fifteen pounds a day. Better to have too much. Four trips later I was done. Everything Emma would need was now stowed away. Check. I sat down for a minute to get my breath.

All I needed to do was put Emma's padded shipping boots on her legs and she'd be ready to load. She was already heavily blanketed since the winter weather had been quite cold. In order to save myself some steps I intended to park on the gravel driveway near Emma's stall. I would load her from there. Then we would be under way and I could relax and recoup in the truck.

I pulled the trailer off its perch and eased down the gravel road. About halfway to my destination I saw something large moving slowly down the frontage road. A semi truck turned into the driveway and headed towards me. What was it doing here? The truck and trailer were one of those behemoths you see on the freeways with gazillion axles and a load stacked a couple stories high. Then under the flapping tarp I saw hay bales. The hay order wasn't delivered on weekends. The rain must have delayed it. What crummy timing.

The rig crawled towards me. I heard the grinding of gears. The motor strained when it encountered the slope. It gained momentum. I wasn't about to play chicken. I didn't know what to do. In order to make a passageway on the narrow road I had to move way over to the side. I couldn't see the ground to the right of the truck from the driver's side so I had a hard time judging how far the strewn gravel extended over the road base. I inched over. The hay truck was so huge it blotted out the sky. The driver motioned me to move over more and waved in gratitude. I crept a couple of inches more to the right. Too late I realized I was sinking in the mud.

With a quick flip of the gear shift, I put the truck into low and tried to edge to better ground. Getting back on the road failed. I spun to the right onto the driveway at the back door of the barn hoping to find a firmer base on what appeared to be hard packed gravel. The farther I went the deeper I sank. The tires lost traction. The truck halted with a jerk. I put it in reverse. The tires spun. I put it in low. The tires spun again. The sound of dirt splattering against the mudguards, so vehement I thought it was the work of pellet guns, alerted me I was sinking lower. I turned off the engine and stared out the windshield. Foul words spewed from my mouth.

I slid out of the truck landing in the mud with a squish. Halfway to the road, my mucker boot stuck, my foot pulled out and I lost my balance. To keep from falling I had to put my free foot down. Now I had one wet, cold, gooey sock. I reached down and ripped my shoe out of the mud. The attached gunk added another pound. I grimaced and put my foot, coated with mother earth, back into it.

Dressed in her down jacket, Sally came out to greet the hay truck. She looked down the driveway in my direction. Motioning to the driver where to unload the hay, Sally continued to ramble down the road. She looked at my half-brown white crew sock and laughed. Then her eyes shifted to my truck and trailer. She stopped laughing. We picked our way over to the rig. Mud climbed half-way up the hubcaps of the sunken tires.

"That's nasty." Sally let out a whistle.

"Can I use your phone?" I whimpered. My shoulders slumped as I pointed to her house.

"Sure, I need to go supervise the hay delivery." Sally turned and followed me up the driveway. "Do you have road insurance?"

"Thank goodness, yes," I blurted. "AAA road service." I reached into my purse for my insurance card.

Thirty minutes later when the truck arrived, I was relieved to see AAA had responded to my request and sent a big one and not one of those mini-trucks dispatched to fix flat tires and dead batteries. The operator got out of his vehicle, pulled on calf-high mud boots and tramped over to my truck. He stared at the wheels wallowing in mud and plodded over to the trailer, shaking his head.

"I'm sorry." The driver looked at me with sympathy. "There's nothing that I can do. The situation is really hopeless."

"But I need my rig." I stammered.

"You're too far off the road." He raised his hand motioning in the truck's direction. "Your truck is at a bad angle. Beside your AAA insurance doesn't cover the trailer."

I went on to explain about my trip to the Sierra's, how sick I'd been, how much I needed to get away and asked if he wouldn't just try. The pleading and desperation in my voice emerged much stronger than I had intended. I felt embarrassed. Whining was not a behavior I admired. I stared down at the brown gooey, soppy mess clutching my shoes like a starfish to rocks during ebb tide. No amount of stomping released the tentacles.

After a couple of minutes of silence, I looked up. I saw what must have been a thought flash through the driver's mind. A trace of a smile swept across his lips. The flicker was so tiny it might have been subliminal. I will never know what changed his mind, but I felt that the part of us which makes humans divine was touched.

Without a word, he detached the horse trailer from the hitch. He grabbed the hook and steel rope from his winch, yanked it across the mud and attached it to the front bumper of my truck. He pushed a lever to extend the boom as high as it would go. His body moved with efficiency and purpose. This kind of confidence must mean he had a plan.

"I'm concerned about the orientation of your truck," he took off his baseball cap and wiped his brow with a red cotton cloth he had stashed in the hip pocket of his overalls. "I wish it faced us. When I start pulling it, I think the wheels will just dig deeper into the mud. The boom isn't high enough to lighten the front end of the truck and lift it so it will swing towards us."

His head turned to the right. He slogged through the mud over to the side of the barn where some plywood panels were stacked – a leftover from a stall renovation. He took one of the panels and tried to work it under the truck's front tire so that the wheel stood a small chance of sliding onto and across it rather than deeper into the goo.

"Now is the time for prayer," he said, flipping the switch of the winch.

The metal rope tightened. The winch groaned and his truck creaked. My truck leaned towards us. The mud held fast to the tires and clawed higher up the hubcaps. I held my breath. Then I heard a small pop. A sucking sound told us the mud had lost the struggle. The wheels slid onto the plywood and the truck's front end swung around. As soon as the truck faced the road, the driver let out a soft whistle. At this angle, the winch had no trouble pulling the truck clear of the mud. Once the back wheels were on the gravel shoulder I released the tension around my chest one notch.

Next the driver turned his attention to the trailer. He tried the same maneuver of sliding the plywood under the eight inch front wheel. Positioning the plywood proved more difficult so he used a small shovel to clear away some of the glop.

When the winch rope was pulled taut, the small wheel sank deeper, faster. The driver repositioned the winch and the plywood. Three tries later, the trailer swung around and was pulled free.

The driver could have left at this point. Instead he helped me hitch my truck to the trailer. He stood to one side while I put on Emma's shipping boots and loaded her. As soon as she was safely in the trailer, he approached me.

"AAA does not allow for this kind of rescue," he dragged his muddy hands across a grimy towel he had retrieved from behind the driver's seat of his truck. "You need to be more careful. Now, get in your truck. I'll follow you to Ygnacio Valley Road. I want to make sure you have a safe start to your trip."

If he hadn't turned and disappeared into his truck so abruptly, I would have hugged him. My verbal thanks weren't enough to show my appreciation. Getting this kind of help from a stranger didn't often come my way. I felt as if he was an angel in a workman's uniform.

I waved good-bye to him when I made the right turn onto the main road. He smiled and shook his head. He must have thought I was one crazy person. My shoulders sagged. I pressed my back into the seat cushions and breathed more freely. I knew this part of the route. Time to go on autopilot. This trip's beginning might have been rocky, but I felt as if a miracle worker had been sent our way. What a sweet man. I heard Emma whinny behind me. She agreed. The silver lining in this cloud was made of platinum.

Either Emma's ligament injury or getting the rig stuck in mud could have scuttled the trip. I offered up a multitude of thanks to my guardian angels and to all those invisible entities that came to my aid.

I settled back to enjoy the view. The green grasses of winter lined the levees in the Central Valley. Blue sky broke through puffy clouds and the sun dusted the rows of winter crops with its warming light. A few cassette tapes later the flatlands morphed into foothills. I pushed against the foam cushioning of the truck's seat to stretch and relax my muscles when we were about twenty minutes from Elaine's property. At last I could begin to enjoy myself.

The light was fading. I would just make it to Elaine's by dark, if I didn't make any mistakes. I made a left turn off the main road and headed into the thick, dark-green forest with Emma calmly standing in the horse trailer behind me. About a mile off the main road, the asphalt ended and the pot holes in the gravel road forced me to slow down. We had left behind signs of civilization – street lights, street signs, power lines and houses. No twinkling lights in the distance. Small red reflectors peeking up from eighteen-inch stakes marked forks in the road.

At the first two reflectors, I was to make left turns and then a right turn at the third. As I drove down the road, I strained to see the gleaming red lights beamed back at me. Plants had grown up and partially covered the first one. The brush would probably be cleared in spring before the onslaught of fair-weather guests.

Going slow let me take in the scenery. Snow, ensconced on the larger boughs of the pine trees, enjoyed a nap on the bed of needles. The density of the trees provided deep shade where pockets of pristine, crystalline snow clung to the ground refusing to retreat despite above freezing temperatures. The low light reflected a beautiful marine blue off of the snow. I opened the window. Pure, sweet mountain air glided past my face. I breathed deep and luxuriated in the crisp smell.

About a quarter of a mile after the third turn, the road seemed to grow increasingly narrow. The ruts got deeper bouncing the truck up and down and jerking the trailer every which way. I wasn't sure if it was the impending dark that gave me that feeling or if the roadway was really getting that tight.

"Sorry, Emma. Try and use your sea legs," I cautioned under my breath as I heard her hooves scrape against the metal sides of the trailer.

Trees closed in on either side, and low hung limbs brushed the roof of the rig. A knot growing in my stomach warned me that things weren't quite right. I must have missed my turn. I hadn't passed any turnouts where I could reverse direction so I drove on. The passageway got tighter. Tree branches whacked, slapped and scratched against the trailer. Where did this road lead? The knot in my stomach hardened.

Five minutes later the road ended at a small clearing a few yards ahead. The canopy of green forest had at last succumbed and exposed human habitation. I jerked to a stop alongside a dilapidated, single-wide trailer perched to the right on the steep hill. The backside of the trailer touched the earth and the front side, supported by a few strategically placed four-by-fours, dangled a good six feet above the ground. Rudely crafted patches to the side of the trailer suggested some form of maintenance.

I looked for signs of life and didn't see anything. No lights shared their rays through curtains. The trailer looked more like a summer rest stop than a year-round home.

I heard a door creak. A woman with disheveled brown hair came out, stared at me and then descended her front stairs. Her eyes went from my face, to my truck, to the trailer and back to me. I rolled down the passenger-side window. She leaned into the truck and asked how I managed to get the rig that far. I responded that I was looking for the home of my friend, Elaine, and asked her if she knew her.

"Yes, Elaine is one of our neighbors." She pointed her finger in the direction from which I had just come. "I think I know which turn you missed. My husband, Chuck, will be home soon. He'll know what to do."

"Great." I felt relief that help was on the way. "I wouldn't even begin to know how to turn this rig around."

"Do you know how lucky you were today?" the woman said, leaning farther into my truck.

I didn't know how to respond. Was that supposed to be a rhetorical question? I looked at her, expecting her to go on.

"Logging roads are all over this part of the country," she said, gesturing with her arms in a wide circle. "Some of them go deep into the forest without ending at anyone's home. They can go for miles, end nowhere and you'd have no way to turn around."

She looked at me and shook her head, shivering in her light sweater. She turned and disappeared back inside the trailer. I didn't expect her to invite me in. I was a stranger. Still, when the door closed, I felt entirely alone.

I decided to check up on Emma while I was waiting. Patience was as foreign to her as it was to me. I opened the door on the driver's side of the truck. Whoops. My head spun as I looked at the drop-off. I had to be careful. A narrow terrace of boulders held the downhill side of the road in place. In the gloom, I didn't know how far the drop was if I were to fall.

Without looking down, I side-stepped along the rig until I got to the side door of the trailer. I popped it open. Emma craned her neck to look at me. It'll be fine, I told her. She sank her weight into the wooden floorboards. Whew.

The sound of a car engine drowned out the rustle of the pine needles. A man, this must be Chuck, drove down the road in an older model car whose grey paint had suffered too many seasons in the weather. Dull, white, oxidized spots dotted the hood. My rig blocked his way.

He pulled his car as far off the road as he could manage. He got out and stood still, ran his eyes over to me and rubbed the stubble of his short blonde hair with his palm. His plaid flannel jacket outlined a stocky frame. He climbed up an embankment and his eyes widened when they scanned the full length of my rig. I strode up to him, held out my hand and offered an introduction.

"Hi. I'm sorry to be in your way. I'm trying to get to Elaine's place."

"Yeah, I know Elaine," he said, maneuvering to the front of my truck. "I've done work up at her house."

"Do you think you can get this rig turned around?" I looked at him, hope stirring.

"Yeah, no problem," Chuck said, his voice strong and confident. I needed confidence. "Get back in your truck and follow me."

Chuck walked ahead and waved at me to drive forward into a clearing of undulating piles of gravel, small rocks and mowed-over plants. The ground looked as if raw dirt had been moved around by a bulldozer. The space was just a few feet longer than my rig and about half as wide. I couldn't imagine turning around there.

"I want you to take a hard left and move towards the downhill side." He guided me forward through the left turn.

"You have to be joking." I yelled out the window. The truck faced a gap where the trees parted.

"Trust me, you can do this." His waved his hand faster.

I gulped. I faced a sheer drop to a gorge below. The ground didn't look committed to permanence. A couple of wispy plants whose spindly roots clung to loose rocks fought for life. That was all that separated me from a free fall. I stopped the truck. At any other time I could have admired the view. But a hundred foot drop wasn't doing it for me.

"Keep coming," Chuck yelled. "You can do this."

My foot eased ever so gently off the brake. With each advance of a few inches, Chuck's voice got more insistent. My adrenaline hit fever pitch when the cab of the truck looked out over the cliff. I saw no ground below me and felt suspended in air. From my vantage point I was heading into space. I wasn't sure the front tires were still on the ground. The few rocks scattered among the dirt were only loosely planted and didn't offer any sense of a balustrade. The water-logged dirt on the edge of the cliff might not hold the weight of the truck. I prayed that this guy knew what he was doing.

"Come on, come on," Chuck directed, his arm waves growing more animated.

I held my breath and inched forward. When I was convinced I was going over the cliff, his palm jerked up. My foot stomped on the brake pedal with all of my weight. I took a deep breath and panted. I thought I might pass out.

Chuck waved at me to back up. With joy, I threw the truck into reverse and eased away from certain death. The rig had managed a few degrees of angle. All together I had to make four passes to the edge of infinity. "Breathtaking view" had a new meaning for me. As soon as the truck and rig faced back down the road, I collapsed against the back of the seat. The hammering of my heart slowed to dull throbs. With the adrenaline surge gone, my exhaustion took over again.

Chuck and his wife took turns describing in careful detail how to identify the turn I missed and how to stay on the right road. They insisted that I repeat the directions. I obliged them although there was no way I was going to screw up now. I thanked them again and eased the truck past Chuck's car. All I wanted to do was get to Elaine's. That's all I had wanted to do for the last few weeks. That's all I'd focused on since I woke up this morning.

How many miracles was I going to need to get to my destination?

I very carefully followed Chuck's instructions and I sang out a hallelujah when the truck faced the slope that ascended to Elaine's property. I hung onto the steering wheel for support. I could barely move my arms. The trip had been so difficult that I felt as if I'd been out scaling rock walls all day. A strained ligament, a wallow in mud and a death-defying dangle over a cliff were not keeping us from our destination. Like our country's pioneers, I set my jaw, kept going and pictured the Elysian Fields ahead.

The hill was steeper than I remembered. The truck engine strained. A few yards past Elaine's entrance gate and about a quarter mile from her home, the tires spun out on the wet dirt. I backed up to negotiate the hill with more speed. I didn't get much farther. By now I was bone weary and emotionally spent. Discouraged to the core of my being, I buckled over the steering wheel. Hunger and thirst had drained the early settlers' energy. I had Chronic Fatigue Syndrome.

I felt Emma shift her weight in the trailer. Ah, ha. That's it. Let Emma out. She weighs nearly 1200 pounds and with a lighter load the rig could get up the hill. I was so tired I nearly fell to the ground when I opened the door and stepped down. A deep breath of the cool, crisp air shocked my system into moving. I unloaded Emma and led her to the front of the truck.

"Just head up this road" I said, stroking her neck. "It ends at Elaine's house. You can't get lost. I'll be right there to give you your dinner."

I led Emma a couple of steps up the hill. She turned her head and brushed my arm with her nose, her endearing gesture of understanding and connection. I loved that touch. I unbuckled her lead rope and let her loose. With slow, even steps she picked her way up the hill. Good horse. I tripped on the step up when I pulled my body into the truck and groaned when I sank back against the seat cushion. To keep Emma in view and to illuminate her way up the road, I turned on the high beams.

The moment I turned the key in the ignition, Emma threw up her head. She let out a high-pitched whinny, spun around and took off at full speed down the hill towards me. My mouth dropped open as she flashed by. At the bottom of the hill, she made a hard turn to the left and sped down a logging road, disappearing into the murky night. I flew out of the truck and ran after her, calling her name. Branches cracked and muffled hoof beats faded into dead quiet. It all happened so fast. I stood in disbelief, too tired to have much of a plan. An unwelcome, eerie silence settled around me.

With the sunset, warmth had withdrawn its influence. Cold advanced to light's retreat and an icy chill and dampness oozed around me. I climbed back into my truck and let the tears spill. Why me? Why now? With everything that it had taken to get here? I shivered, dried my eyes and put on my jacket to get some protection from the winter chill. My reserves of energy, like belly fat stored for a lean winter, had already been tapped. I needed civilization, Elaine and the support they would bring. I stepped on the gas.

The truck responded and lurched forward. The tires took me about three yards farther than my previous best effort. Rats. My truck blocked the road. I backed up to take advantage of a wider space just outside the gate. In the process, the trailer started to jack-knife. When I tried to pull forward to straighten the rig, the truck tires spun out again. I felt as if I was one of those summer hikers in the high country who encountered a freak snow storm in July. I understood the surprise and desperation of the ill-prepared.

The disappearing sun waved goodbye with the tiniest bit of light. The moon hadn't risen. With no moon, I couldn't see the road under my feet. No time for the luxury of a rest. I grabbed a flashlight from the glove compartment and lumbered my way past the gate. The flashlight batteries hadn't been touched in a couple of years. Or maybe more. Pink bunny, you better come through. I struggled to climb the hill. Altitude was no help and my breathing got more difficult. I couldn't rest long. The beam from the flashlight mimicked the sun and proceeded to bid adieu. I hustled up the hill the best I could. Hustle is what I thought, plod is what I did.

Near the crest, I saw lights beaming down at me from Elaine's house. I welcomed the break in monotony from the dark. Civilization. My breathing came easier knowing I was a few steps away.

"I'm here." I yelled with what was left of my strength. "I finally made it."

The door flew open and a trapezoid of light dazzled the ground. Beautiful, welcoming light. Elaine ran out onto her porch.

"Where in the world have you been?" Her voice sounded anxious. "I've been worried about you." She sprinted down the steps. "What took so long? Where's your truck?"

"I'm so sorry I'm late," I apologized. "It's a long story. I'm exhausted and Emma has run away." I climbed the steps.

My clenched jaw relaxed into a weak smile on seeing my friend. And with the relief, tears flowed. My body wanted to sink to the floor and rest. Elaine set me down in the kitchen on one of her wood spindle chairs. My mind was spinning with images from the last half hour. I felt hysteria racing up and down my back with agitated feet like a penned greyhound in a dog run. In a high-pitched voice I described what had happened with the truck and Emma.

"I know the road Emma took," Elaine put her hand on my shoulder. "Don't worry she can't get far. Everything will be fine."

The warmth of the kitchen revived me. I took a deep look at my friend. She was dressed in khakis with a dark brown turtle neck sweater. Her shoulders seemed broader and her posture gave a feeling of substance. She pulled a woolen cap over her luxuriant red hair and faced me. Dark blue eyes radiated compassion, concern and a deep sadness.

Elaine strode with strength and determination over to the kitchen counter and swept up her car keys. Throwing on her heavy flannel car coat, she grabbed gear from the mud room and guided me outside. We set off down the hill in her large sedan, bright beams projecting hope into the distance. We passed the truck, dead and lifeless by the side of the road with the trailer strangely angled behind it.

A quick left turn and the sedan rumbled down the old logging road where I had last seen Emma. Brush scraped the undercarriage. Elaine stopped when a couple of hardy saplings blocked our way. We left the warmth of the car and tackled the dirt road on foot. The only light to beat back the black of the night came from our flashlights. We had to bounce them up and down to watch for uneven ground below and low hanging branches above. Manzanita, pine and oak had begun to obliterate the old logging road, the only evidence that humans had ever been in this part of the country. To avoid tripping on the larger plants, we stepped on the smaller mountain misery, crushing its leaves and releasing its aromatic scent into the cold air.

"Emma, Emma, where are you?" We took turns calling.

After trudging over and around thickets of overgrowth for a few minutes, the beam of my flashlight illuminated a crumpled mound of light-colored material caught on a nude branch and draped against the dark ground. I lurched towards it. The remains of one of Emma's shipping boots. My heart pounded. I fingered the plush lining hoping to feel the warmth of her body. Silly. It was cold. Never mind. She came this way. I felt heartened.

Further down the road we found another shipping boot which was in better condition with only one Velcro strap ripped off. Emma must have raced through here at speed. I carried the boots under my arm, pressing them to my side. They comforted me, suggesting that we were on the right road and that maybe Emma was near. Elaine and I plodded on in silence another couple of minutes, expecting any minute to hear Emma's footfall or catch a beam of light on her head and neck framed by her hunter-green winter blanket.

"Can't be." Elaine's voice exploded, a sharp contrast to her usually modulated voice. A five foot metal gate secured with a thick chain blocked the road in front of us.

"What's up?" I asked, turning my flashlight on the chunky padlock.

"This is where I expected to find Emma." Elaine flashed her light on the other side of the road. "This gate is always locked and I don't know any way around it."

"Emma is very clever." Too clever. I used to appreciate that quality. "Let's look to either side of the gate and see if there's a break in the fence."

We picked our way through the brush and small trees on both sides of the road. Compact vegetation and brambles made passage impossible. We turned back.

"It's as if she disappeared into thin air." Elaine said, breaking the silence.

"Where could she have gone?" I said, my stomach twisting into knots as hard as the granite rocks under my feet.

"Don't worry, we'll find her." Elaine picked up her pace. "Let's drive to all of the neighbors in this valley. One of them will have seen her."

"When horses get loose, they usually run off to join other horses." I offered, feeling renewed hope. "Who has horses nearby?"

"I pretty much know all of my neighbors and none of them has horses," Elaine said.

"Maybe something has changed," I countered. Elaine's words had crushed my tender sprout of an easy find.

We drove in a big circle jumping off at each spoke to reach Elaine's neighbors. No one had seen Emma and they couldn't help but ask how my horse got loose. I struggled to find a response that didn't make me look like a complete idiot. My heart sunk when we left the house of the last neighbor. No one had seen a horse or knew of anyone with horses in the vicinity.

Back at her house, Elaine poured an aperitif into her water glass. I crumpled down on a kitchen chair, remembering what exhausted meant. I was so beyond that.

As the minutes ticked by, I became extremely agitated. My horse was out there all by herself - in winter, in the dark, in the cold - in the wild. With coyote, rattlesnakes, mountain lions and bears. Elaine glanced over at me and her look of concern evolved into worry.

Then it hit me. Maybe Carol could help. Elaine stretched the kitchen phone over to me and I left Carol an urgent message when she didn't pick up. Elaine renewed her drink and offered one to me. I declined. She didn't have any diet Dr. Pepper so a cup of Earl Grey would have to do.

An hour later the phone rang. I jumped. The sound of Carol's voice lowered my anxiety a notch. I used all of my self control to slow my speech down and explain what happened.

"Can you help?" I noticed the stress in my voice.

"Give me a minute," Carol said.

I heard Carol's breathing slow. I kept forgetting that she had to tune into Emma. That she had her own life. When it came to my animals, I didn't get that I could be demanding.

"Emma is okay, but scared," Carol said in a matter of fact voice.

"Emma, why did you run away?" I couldn't restrain anger from my words. "I thought we were going to have a great get-away together. You promised to stay close."

"She says when she started running, it felt really good," Carol said, defending Emma's behavior. "She was fully in her body and enjoyed the experience. She says she had been cooped up. I guess being stall-bound for three weeks and then standing in the trailer for three hours was too confining. The energy in her muscles was ready to burst."

"You need to come home now," I said, my anger subsiding to irritation. "I'm worried sick."

"She says she was having such a good time she didn't pay attention to where she was running." Carol's words halted my irritation and increased my anxiety. "She says she hasn't been to Elaine's before. Her homing instinct can't take over."

"How are we going to get her back?" I gulped.

"Talking to the lost animal usually doesn't help much," Carol said, softening her voice.

My breath caught when my brain absorbed the meaning of Carol's words. I was afraid to hear what she was going to say next. I was counting on her.

"I had a client whose dog was lost," Carol explained, her voice taking on a strength that ensured I got the message. "All the dog could say was that he was near a road and very hungry."

"What does Emma say about her location?" I asked, feeling the muscles in my back stiffen.

"She ran for a long way," Carol said. "Not a long way in human terms, but in horse terms, which is much farther. She's under some trees and near a stream."

"Far away?" I moaned. "Trees? Stream? That could be anywhere."

Carol's breathing quickened and her voice took on a pleading tone. "She promises she will never run away again."

"Never run away again." I exclaimed, ensuring my voice didn't release the scream I was feeling. "If we can't get her back, what does that matter?"

Elaine tugged at my sleeve so I related what Carol had said. We both looked at each other. An elephant could disappear in this part of the Sierra foothills with its deep gorges and jagged hills. Planes had vanished. I groaned much louder than I intended.

"I'm sorry," Carol said. "I tried to help several clients before, but it was no use."

"Did they eventually find their animals?" I asked, afraid to hear the response.

"No, sorry." Carol confessed.

My anxiety escalated even more as my mind digested what Carol told me. If she couldn't help us, how would we ever get Emma back?

"Carol, I'm going crazy." My fingers thumped the table. "You have to do something."

"Okay, okay. Wait a minute," Carol said. "Let me give it some thought."

I fidgeted in my chair. The silence on the phone puzzled me. What was Carol thinking? At last, I heard her let out a deep breath.

"I may have an idea," Carol's pensive voice trickled over the phone line.

I didn't hear the confidence I wanted. Carol was usually self-assured and right now I wanted guarantees of safety. I wanted my horse back.

"I couldn't try this with just anyone," Carol said. "You and Emma have a unique relationship. Although this may seem strange, it may help. Do you think you are up to it?"

"Of course," I said. "What is it?" I would do anything to get Emma safely back.

"Here is what you need to do," Carol assured. "Clear your mind and then imagine yourself as a lighthouse with a powerful beacon on top. Once you have that image, I want you to concentrate on projecting a beam of light in all directions just the way a lighthouse does."

"I think this is a bit out of my league," I said, impulsively rising from my chair.

"You can do it," Carol said, her voice taking on a tone of authority. "You must try."

"Why am I doing this?" I couldn't imagine the answer.

"Just trust me and do it," Carol said.

My brain didn't come up with any other options. I sat back down. The red and white stripes of the West Quoddy Head lighthouse popped into my head. I imagined the expanse of Atlantic that the lighthouse faced. I pictured the light source under the red-capped roof and did my best to project a beam. My mind had a hard time holding the image of the lighthouse; no illumination came winking out from the tower.

"Have you got the lighthouse and beam yet?" Carol prodded.

"I'm doing my best." The mental image of the light house faded in and out of view. I blotted out everything else so that I could hold onto the picture and add light. I had only seen the lighthouse during the day and wondered if that mattered.

"Emma, do you see the beam of light?" Carol's voice interrupted my thoughts.

"What did she say?" I held my breath.

"She says she doesn't see anything," Carol said.

No time for frustration. A lighthouse. A beam of light. I knew how to concentrate, to focus. That was one of my strengths. But, this exercise was entirely too weird. How was I supposed to project a beam of light that Emma could see? Real photons, real electro-magnetic waves traveling through space. What was Carol thinking, for goodness sake? My horse was lost out there somewhere and I was practicing parlor games with a mental Ouija board. What else could I do but try again?

"Does she see it now?" I asked, struggling as hard as I could to get my lighthouse to turn on its beacon.

"No, she still doesn't see it," Carol said.

Then all of a sudden my heart glowed red, emitting a soft light, the color of embers in a fire. I froze. Scared. I felt my pulse hammering in my temples. A cold sweat trickled down the middle of my back. Dropping my chin, I took a better look. I stared at the muscles of my heart beating as if there were no chest wall. Flaps of skin and chest muscle were peeled back like a banana skin. This was spooky stuff. Nothing had ever happened to me to prepare me for this experience. What was going on?

I sat rigid and watched the chambers of my heart squeeze and release. I felt as if I were watching a fluoroscope of internal organs hidden deep within my body cavity. Without warning, a thin cylinder of muted red light emerged, headed out parallel to the floor and disappeared through the wall of the kitchen into the dark outside. With each heartbeat I saw a pulsation of red light pass down the beam, across the floor and continue into space. If I didn't trust Carol I would think I was losing my mind. How freaky is this?

"Carol, I don't know what's happening." I sat staring at my chest. "My heart is on fire and light is pouring out from it. There's a beam of red light."

"Emma, do you see the light?" Carol said, as if we were doing nothing more extraordinary than discussing laundry detergents.

How could Carol be so totally unfazed? Did she understand what was happening to me?

"Yes, I can see the light, though faintly," Carol translated. "I'll be able to follow it. But not right now. I ran a really long way. I need to rest a little while before I go on. This is really hard on me. I can feel ticks crawling on my body. I'm frightened."

"Please, just hurry home," I pleaded.

How could she think of resting in the middle of nowhere? She didn't have chronic fatigue. She was a healthy horse. What happened to all of that exuberance that forced her to run away? Didn't she know how anxious I was?

"My dog, Bailey, has offered to stay up all night to amplify the beam of light." Carol's tone was reassuring. "She'll keep watch so you can get some rest, too."

Carol's dog is going to amplify the beam? What in the world does that mean? How can Bailey see it? How can the dog do it? How is all of this happening? Why can't I live in a normal world? An aching throb bounced around in my skull.

"I don't want to rest," I said, my emotions escalating towards panic. My palms moistened with sweat. "I want my horse. I want to go look for her."

"Don't worry. Bailey will keep the beam going so Emma can follow it back to you." Bailey's distinctive bark came through the phone receiver.

"This is really weird." I looked at my chest.

I looked over to Elaine. She was staring at me with an expression somewhere between anxiety and despair. Our eyes met.

"I don't know how this works either," Carol stated as if this were an everyday event. "I can't explain it. When I lost a cat, my friend suggested I leave the porch light on to guide her home. That's how I got the idea for the lighthouse."

The wooden spindles of the chair bit into my back when I sank back down. The beam of light moved with me, its angle to the wall of the house changed with my movement. I was too frightened and exhausted to worry how all of this was happening. I might be bone weary, but my anxiety was making my body have minor tremors.

"If I go look for Emma, this beam is going to move with me," I said. "How will Emma be able to follow a moving target?"

"I have a thought," Carol said. "Anchor the beam on something in the house."

Since her suggestion was no more preposterous than anything else I was doing, I stood up and looked around the open space of the cabin. I decided to anchor it, whatever that meant, to the largest chair in the living room. I stared at the chair as though it might manifest some kind of intelligence.

Elaine followed me into the living room. She clung tightly to her glass. Her face was drawn and she looked several years older.

"All right, I'm going to anchor the beam to a soft, easy chair in the living room," I said, my voice cracking mid-sentence. I was uncomfortable living in a world whose properties were unknown to me.

As soon as those words came out of my mouth, the middle of the back of the chair glowed with red embers as if a hole had been burned through the covering. I jumped back. How could I trust my eyes with what I saw? I was afraid to touch the chair.

The beam of light passed from my heart to the chair and out through the wall of the house. I circled the coffee table as a test. Wherever I moved, the light beam moved with me, continuing to pulse with every contraction of the muscles in my heart. The beam went from my heart to the chair, then out into the night.

"The anchor works," I whispered into the phone receiver. "Thank you."

"You've done everything you can do," Carol said with a calm voice.

"All I want is my horse back," I said into the phone but made it as a prayer to God. I hung up the phone and sat collecting what energy I could tease out of my body. Only my gut wrenching determination provided me the will to rise.

On the way to the mud room I put my hand on Elaine's arm. She rested her hand on mine. Moisture swelled in her eyes.

"I swear we will not lose Emma," she said, squeezing my hand gently.

Her teary eyes stared into mine. She helped me put on a heavy coat. She turned me to face her. I watched her hands as she buttoned my coat. Her actions mothered me. I ached for that kind of support.

Elaine hopped in her car and I dragged myself onto the passenger seat. The door felt leaden when I pulled it shut. We headed down the hill. Despite the chill, we rolled down the windows and yelled out Emma's name. We drove down as far as we could on each leg of the spider web of logging roads that emanated from this part of the valley. An hour later, we headed home in silence, resting our hoarse voices.

My feet barely cleared the rise of the stairs into Elaine's house. I crept to my bedroom, struggled with getting my clothes off and into sweats. The sheets of the bed were stone cold. Even when I warmed up, sleep didn't come. Every time I opened my eyes, I saw the red beam pulsing though the covers and out to the living room. My mind was blown away by everything that happened. I felt eerie, peculiar, as if I had stepped onto the set of a sci-fi movie, only to discover it wasn't a movie set. I was living in one of those episodes from the *Twilight Zone* with its twisted plot flips. Goose bumps rose over my body. Maybe when I woke up, I would emerge from this nightmare and be home in Walnut Creek.

Elaine's muffled voice managed to permeate my consciousness. A dense fog encased my brain. Sleep had not regenerated sore, spent muscles. I forced my eyelids to part. Light. Thank God, light. The gentle bath from the early morning sun made me feel better. Memories of the night before forced my eyes down to my chest. The red glow was gone. Relief. I pulled up my sweatshirt. No marks on my chest. Maybe it was all a bad dream and Emma was grazing outside my bedroom.

Elaine yelled my name from somewhere in the front of the house. Adrenaline pumped into my bloodstream. I jerked into a sitting position. Sleeping in sweats had its merits. With a quick shove of my feet into my shoes I was dressed. I jumped out of the bedroom and paused in the living room. The back of the easy chair looked intact. No burned marks anywhere. I leapt down the back steps – I gasped. There was

Emma trekking alongside Elaine up the driveway. Emma's halter was still on and her two winter blankets were intact. All of her shipping wraps were missing from her legs, but she appeared unharmed. Relief flooded my being as tears welled in my eyes.

As soon as Emma saw me, she raised her head. I sprang forward and nearly fell. Elaine handed me the cotton lead rope. I pulled Emma's head towards me so I could look her in her eye. The muscles around her face were pulled taut. She looked stressed.

"I am so glad to see you, Emma…Do you know how frightened I've been?" I stroked her neck.

My palm pressed against Emma's shoulder. She was solid. She was here. I led her to a sturdy tree. Using a triple knot, I tied her to a thick branch and gave her body the once over. Convinced she wasn't injured I parted the hairs in her tail. No ticks there but I found two in her mane. They were still flat, not having had time to bloat with blood. I easily dislodged them and crushed them against stones on the gravel road. I slid my hands over Emma's body testing for heat or swelling. She seemed unhurt.

"How did you find her?" I faced Elaine.

"I woke up and knew where to go. I met Emma coming up the driveway down by the gate," Elaine said, pointing downhill. "I concentrated all night on bringing her home. I promised you, you weren't going to lose her. I lost my dog up here and I couldn't bear to repeat that experience."

"Thank you," I said. "That means the world to me." I turned and stroked Emma's forehead with my fingertips. "I'm so glad you're back. You're very important to me."

Emma turned her neck and her nose brushed my arm. I shivered. My love for Emma had grown far deeper than I'd realized.

Satisfied that Emma was okay, Elaine and I headed back into the house. I settled at the kitchen table as Elaine prepared breakfast. With Emma back, we were able to do the catching up that we had planned all along.

The morning sun, smiling through the plate glass door, delivered a generous dose of warmth and cheer. My stomach, full of comfort food from a big breakfast, nurtured me.

I needed to relax. What a crazy beginning to my vacation. This weekend was supposed to jump start my recovery. Some recovery. I was more exhausted then when I came. And I didn't think that was possible.

I pressed back in the wooden chair to get a better view of Emma. Elaine put the last dish away from the morning meal and faced me.

"How about a real quiet, stay-at-home, hang-out and kick-back kind of recreational activity?" Elaine said as joined me at the kitchen table. "You can play computer games. I brought my laptop."

"What? You're kidding." I said, unleashing my most charming smile. "I didn't come all this way and deal with all these problems to sit inside. I want to stick to our plan. Let's hike and see the mountains. I've spent too many of my free hours housebound. I need to get out and breathe the mountain air."

I bent over and laced up my tennis shoes. Elaine sat there picking at the crumbs left on the table. She wasn't excited about my idea. Stubborn joined impatience as another of my less endearing qualities.

With free-flowing easy strides, Elaine struck off down the road to a scenic route that she'd been telling me about. She looked as if she had stepped out of a Ralph Lauren commercial with her cashmere turtle neck, hunt coat and well-polished hiking boots tapping a steady rhythm on the dirt. I rode behind her. Emma started out with a quick, jerky stride. A little too quick. I worked the bit to negotiate a slower speed, but she didn't show much response. With each step her agitation grew. She tossed her head and tried to trot. I had to concentrate to keep her quiet. On the narrow trails, she could knock Elaine down or step on her if I wasn't careful. The terrain was beautiful, but its healing qualities were diminished by my restive horse. After twenty minutes of struggle, I gave up.

"We better turn back," I said, disappointed in our outing. "Emma's not cooperating."

"Yeah, she looks a little wild," Elaine said. She pointed to a trail a few yards ahead. "I know a short-cut to take, not as pretty, but it'll work."

Emma must have known we were headed back. Her muscles turned rock hard and her head tossing grew more violent. She pulled at the reins. Elaine decided she was safer hiking behind Emma. Even with my handling skills, I had to agree.

I was happy as soon as I saw the clearing around Elaine's home. Securing Emma's lead with multiple knots to a tree and convinced she was secure, I gave her her grain.

"You're making a lousy partner this weekend, Emma," I said, thinking she deserved a bucketful of coal, not her tasty oats. "We were supposed to relax and go for an easy saunter around the hills, a dude ranch kind of trail ride."

"Well, that outing couldn't have been more fun," Elaine said, teasing me. She turned to go into the house.

"I didn't know Emma was going to jig the whole way," I called out after her. "Yeah, yeah, yeah. You were right. We should have stayed around the house."

Elaine and I visited for the rest of the day, enjoying our lunch on the patio next to the house. The rickety wooden chairs creaked and swayed whenever we moved and the old cable spool serving as our table rocked whenever we touched it. Our world seemed in constant motion as we swapped job stories and "you'll never believe this" escapades.

Even though it was mid-December, the day was mild. The sun blazed through a cloudless sky penetrating our bodies with its infrared fingers to massage our muscles with its warmth. Little birds darted among the pine trees where we sat, captivating us with their play. Maybe I didn't need to go chasing around the hillsides. Hanging around the house was starting to feel good.

Emma was tied to a tree next to the house showing little interest in her pile of hay. The mound remained untouched from where I had left it in the morning. She didn't eat her hay the night before so I thought she'd be hungry. I began to wonder if I should have brought her.

During dinner I watched Emma from the kitchen window. She must have gotten bored. She discovered the bits of grass at her feet. Her insistent pawing and straining at her lead rope to nibble the last standing blade of grass within reach made it clear she wanted to graze on the sweet and tasty grasses that bordered Elaine's house. These generous tufts of clumping greenery had survived the cold and popped up like villages on the reddish brown dirt whose barrenness resembled a moonscape.

As soon as dinner was over, I went outside. After all Emma deserved to eat well if I was. I went around the yard collecting hand-fuls of luscious, thick blades of grass and offered them to Emma who scarfed up the treats as if they were premium Belgian chocolates.

I went back inside and cleared the table. The light faded outside. Evening came early in winter. When we were ready to sit down to a game of cards, I decided to go outside to check on Emma. Despite the fact that Elaine had no fencing, I didn't want to tie Emma up for the whole night. She needed to have the freedom to lie down if she wanted. Last night she had promised she wouldn't run away. Emma's word had been good in the past and I felt secure in trusting her pledge. Carol had said on many occasions that animals don't lie. Besides, the green grass dotting the clearing around Elaine's house would keep her busy.

"Emma, remember your promise," I said as I unbuckled her lead rope.

Something made my stomach a little uneasy. I stood in the clearing next to Elaine's house watching Emma's every flick of an ear. She meandered from one clump of grass to the next. Head down, quiet munching, but keeping her eye on me the whole time. Climbing the stairs into the house, I kept her in view until I closed the front door.

After a few hands of cards were over, I got up to look outside the kitchen window to make sure Emma was still grazing where I had last seen her. She wasn't in view. My stomach did a flip flop. I told myself not to panic. She must be around the side of the house. I jogged outside and looked all around the clearing. She wasn't to be seen. I didn't know if I was more annoyed, scared or angry. I bounded back into the house.

"My stupid horse is gone again," I grumbled to Elaine. "I'm calling Carol."

"Not again," Elaine cried, sweeping the cards into a pile.

My fingers drummed the table while the phone rang. I was emotionally frayed. I didn't need any more stress. Carol answered the phone on the second ring and I told her what happened.

"How could you let her get away again?" Carol exclaimed, exasperation coating every word.

I explained my reasoning with logical precision. Especially the part about Emma promising not to run away and Carol always saying that animals never lied. This was not the time that I wanted my horse to be different.

"Carol, will you help?" I pleaded.

"Yes, of course, I'll do what I can." Carol's breathing slowed. "But Bailey thinks she's too tired to stay up another night."

"I appreciate all that Bailey has done," I said, picturing the little brown and white spaniel.

Holding the receiver close to my ear, I stood at the kitchen window looking at the spot where I last saw Emma. An edge of the setting sun silhouetted a stand of pine on a distant ridge. Farther across the valley I saw what might be the glint of a satellite tower. Worlds connected by phones, telecommunications devices and animal communicators.

"I'm not sure what's going on," Carol said, her words rushed. "I think I'd better call one of my friends in Texas who is an excellent animal communicator. Don't worry. I think Emma is okay. I'm just not sure what's happening. I need to consult with my friend. I'll call you back as soon as I know more."

Being left in limbo only increased my anxiety. Some vacation. I sat down in the living room and traced my fingers on the jacquard pattern of the fabric covering the arm chair. My foot bounced up and down making tiny circles in the air. About an hour later the phone rang.

"Are you sitting down?" Carol's voice seemed agitated.

"Yes, I'm sitting." Dead-in-a-ditch thoughts raced through my mind. "Is Emma all right?"

"What I heard from Emma didn't match the pictures she sent," Carol said, her voice having a quality of unease I hadn't ever heard before. "Emma said she was unhurt, but she sent pictures that were mixed with violence, some thrashing about and heightened emotions. My friend said it took some convincing to get Emma to communicate with her. Basically Emma told my friend to leave her alone since she was occupied. To get rid of my friend Emma finally relented, sending pictures that were very clear."

"What?" I felt the knots in my stomach harden into boulders. "What was happening?"

"My friend says Emma is currently enjoying the companionship of a stallion," Carol said, a bit breathless. "She didn't know if it was a real horse or a spirit horse. She says that it appears as if Emma is engaged in a sexual liaison."

"What? No. It can't be," I protested. "All of Elaine's neighbors say there aren't any horses around. Not within twenty five miles."

"It could be a spirit horse." Carol's voice had regained composure. "Emma sent pictures of a black, muscular horse. She said she prefers them buff."

"What is a spirit horse?" I said almost afraid to hear the answer. This was getting spooky again.

"A spirit horse doesn't have a body," Carol said. "Not a ghost. Just a horse living in another world."

Her words buffeted my ears. What was with my horse and other worlds? My mind couldn't conjure up any picture to match Carol's description. Confusion rampaged inside my brain. I was aghast at the idea of my horse associating with some kind of bodiless entity. Emma had sent pictures of the stallion to Carol's friend. Was he real?

"I don't know how it could be a real horse when there aren't any horses in the vicinity?" I said, looking over to Elaine who nodded in agreement. "Certainly no breeding stallions."

"My friend couldn't discriminate whether it was an actual horse or not," Carol said. "There was something a little other worldly about the whole thing. It had me stumped as well."

"I can't wrap my head around this right now," I said, rubbing my forehead. "I need to know why she ran away a second time. She promised she wouldn't."

"In Emma's mind she didn't run away, but ran towards," Carol explained. "She says that the first time she left it was a run away. But the second time she knew where she was going. She simply chose to make a visit. She said that the stallion had been calling her and she couldn't resist his call. That's why she's been agitated. The force of his call was so overpowering that she had to leave you and go to him."

"She didn't run away. Right," I said, rubbing my fingertips against my forehead. "My horse should be practicing in a courtroom. She has a way with words. Is she at least safe for the moment?"

"Yes, she's safe and she wants you to know that she can find her way back," Carol said. "This time she paid attention to the paths she took. She says you'll know where to look for her in the morning. Go there and you'll find her. She's very distracted and is letting me know that she's not really interested in talking right now."

I thanked Carol and hung up. Elaine had been milling around the living room with the occasional glance to check me out. Even in her everyday moves she looked as if she was walking on a runway. She eased down on the sofa across from me.

"So what is this about a spirit horse?" Elaine asked, curling her legs under her and balancing her coffee cup on the sofa arm.

"You're not going to believe this," I said, shaking my head. I told Elaine what Carol had said.

"You mean I'm going to be an aunt?" Elaine said, smiling.

"What?" I said, grimacing. "I didn't even think about that."

"A foal, a sweet foal," Elaine said, her smiled widened.

"No, no." My palm pommeled the chair arm. "I can barely pay for one horse, never mind two. I can't compete in dressage waddling through the movements with a pregnant mare and her burgeoning belly."

"Maybe Emma would want to keep the foal." Elaine sipped from her coffee mug.

"Who exactly are you supporting?" I waited for a response. When none came, I shrugged my shoulders. "My head hurts. I think I want to go to bed now."

My legs barely worked when I tried to stand up. I used my arms to push off the chair. Exhaustion was debilitating. I dragged my feet to the bedroom. I needed time alone. My brain was fried and I was out of gas. Sleep often brought a new perspective with its restorative qualities.

That night I drifted in and out between restless dozing and thrashing of the bed clothes. My mind flitted from Emma consorting with spirit horses and other bodiless entities to the monstrous creatures that this union might produce. Then images of gargoyles protruding from atop gothic churches galloped through my mind. Nightmares of what might be happening to Emma besieged my brain.

The next morning the house was quiet when I woke and headed to the bathroom. My toothbrush had made it to my back molars when I heard the crunch of footsteps on the gravel driveway. With a hopeful heart, I ran outside. Miraculously, there was Elaine leading Emma home.

"Where was she?" I said as I hurried over to Elaine.

"When I woke up this morning I knew where to look." Elaine handed me the lead rope. "She was exactly where I pictured, coming down the path behind my nearest neighbor's house. At first, she wouldn't let me catch her. There was no way I was coming back here without her. I was more afraid of facing you than hanging on to this unruly horse."

"Look at her, she can't stand still." I circled Emma around me. "I'm so sorry you had trouble getting her."

"She frightened me. She plunged, reared, spun." Elaine used her arms to act out what she did to keep hold of Emma. "She even tried to use her shoulder to shove me off the trail."

"If I was there, I would have set her back on her heels," I said, turning to take a better look at Emma.

Her expression was dazed. The whites of her eyes showed. The skin was pulled taut over her forehead. She forced each leg forward as if she was taking one more step on a trek of thousands of miles.

As I walked beside her, I looked her over. Her winter blankets were in place and there were no apparent wounds. What looked as if it might be some kind of hair gel caked her face. Saliva? Could this have been left from the kisses of the stallion? I tied her to a mature oak tree and examined her rear end. Although her tail was a little mussed, there were no tail hairs caught in the lips of her labia. Maybe it wasn't a real horse.

I had already made up my mind that if she conceived, I would have the foal aborted. I couldn't embrace the idea of another mouth to feed and another responsibility to worry about. Emma gave me more than my share of angst.

"I'm calling Carol to let her know that Emma has returned home safely," I said, dragging myself up the steps, having expended my energy on the dash outside.

The kitchen provided a good view of Emma while I dialed the phone. I blew out a sigh when Carol picked up right away.

"Emma has come home," I blurted out. "There is some evidence that points to her having fooled around with a real horse, but I'm not sure." I held my breath while I waited for Carol's reply.

"Emma is very proud of herself," Carol said, relief evident in the lower pitch of her voice. "She said that the fence surrounding the stallion was high. When she jumped into his pen, she pulled up her knees. She's grateful for all of the jumping lessons you gave her so that she could put the knowledge to good use. Her winter blankets got in the way of their lovemaking but she sheepishly admits that they managed anyway. It was a fantastic experience for her."

"Emma, what were you thinking?" The question rushed past my lips.

"He began to call me as soon as we arrived," Carol translated. "That is the reason I had to go to him. His silent call was enticing and intoxicating. I love you. But this was something different. I couldn't help myself."

Emma said she couldn't resist his song. I remembered the way the ancient sailors described the call of the Sirens. No sooner had I completed that thought, my body felt an attraction as strong as when the opposite polls of a magnet get close to each other. Wow, no wonder she had to go to him.

"Carol, Emma sent me what attracted her to the stallion," I said. "I understand why she left."

"Emma says she's deeply in love with him and wants to have his baby." Carol sounded as if she was in favor of the idea.

I suddenly had empathy for parents of unwed pregnant teens. The drama surrounding an unworkable situation. From my horse. I put the topic on hold for another time.

"Emma, why hasn't anyone ever seen this horse you visited?" My science mind originated that question.

"You may not see him," Carol translated. "He is black and lives among the shadows."

Oh brother! More spooky stuff. I thanked Carol for her time and hung up.

Elaine took a break from cooking breakfast and joined me at the kitchen table with a couple of mugs full of hot tea. I blew across the swirling steam and then explained what Emma had said taking time for the occasional sip. Despite the warmth of the liquid in our bellies, we both shivered.

"If she gets pregnant, she should have the baby." Elaine said, looking at me with her big, soft blue eyes. "I'll help." Elaine got up to finish preparing breakfast.

"I've already made up my mind." I insisted, taking a sip of tea. "If she conceives, the foal will be aborted. I can't afford it. I don't have the energy."

"Now's not the time to make that kind of decision," Elaine said.

"I think I need to go home," I said. "This trip hasn't worked out as I had hoped."

"I understand." Elaine said, nodding her head. "You came to get energy, not lose it. I'll go down the hill and see what I can do about your truck after breakfast."

The truck's engine came screaming up the hill. My mind went into hyper-drive to figure that out. How could Elaine straighten the jack-knifed trailer? How did she make it up the driveway when I couldn't? So many incomprehensible things happened this weekend, why not one more. I felt as if the world I knew had abandoned me, as if the laws of physics had been altered. Maybe Newton's laws of motion as it had been taught in my college physics classes didn't apply.

Elaine loaded my luggage in the back of the truck. A set of polo wraps stored in the trailer were going to have to suffice as a stand-in for Emma's shipping boots. Emma looked uneasy and jumpy. I opened the trailer door and stood back. She rushed the ramp and scrambled in, trembling when she stopped.

"I guess that says it all," Elaine said, her downcast eyes avoiding me.

"We both need to get back to something we know," I said, slipping the pins to lock the trailer doors shut. "Security and a world where we know the rules."

With a big hug I thanked Elaine for her support. She had offered up her home as a healing retreat and did everything she could to make me comfortable. I had to stay with my truth. I couldn't thank her for a good time, but I did thank her for an interesting experience. We both managed a weak laugh.

By the time the truck made it to the bottom of Elaine's hill, warm air replaced the cold air blowing out of the vents. Something small went whizzing by my head. Then another. Then several. I stopped the truck. Wasps. I jumped out.

"I don't believe this," I screamed to the sky. "This is winter. Where did they come from?"

Okay world. I've had it. I have so totally had it. NO MORE.

Chapter 14

Snuggled in the enveloping cushions of my living room sofa, I tucked myself in under a comfy afghan. Safe at home I could mull over the events of the weekend with Elaine at her property in the Sierra foothills.

Some of the things Emma had done were extraordinary. I'd been around horses long enough to know that when they ran away, they didn't usually come back of their own volition and breeding pairs weren't easily separated. Horses tended to respect fences and didn't go hopping from one field to another for kicks – especially a horse with Emma's background who had very little jumping experience and certainly had never been a hunter who enjoyed a cross country romp. Even seasoned hunters tended to avoid fences without the encouragement of their rider. Not much of what happened with Emma at Elaine's house would make sense to the typical horseman. The world wasn't ready to accept how different Emma was from other horses or how much the depth of our relationship influenced her behavior. She left her mate to come back to me.

After I showed my perky face to my boss Tuesday morning, I disappeared into my office and shut the door. The huge walnut desk welcomed me with stacks of paper and my computer. Brochures, story-boards, statistical reports and video scripts called out for inspection.

The blinking light on my phone would have to wait. I picked up the phone receiver to call the vet and hesitated. Constructing an explanation of how my horse might have had an unplanned breeding, by an unknown stallion, at the wrong time of year and in the middle of nowhere was a challenge. I rehearsed what I would tell him. All he would need to know were the high points, not the details. Certainly no mention of red beams of light. I dialed his number.

"You say your horse ran away and came back on her own," he said, his disbelief palpable. "No horses live nearby, but you think she got bred by a stallion you never saw?"

I couldn't blame him for having a hard time with it. The story would sound preposterous to most people. The honking horns and bustle of the streets below my office brought me back to the professional world I occupied. I sat amidst a world where high-powered executives executed transactions in millions, even billions of dollars. The products I managed accounted for hundreds of millions on the bank's balance sheet. I felt as if I were leading a double life - the corporate manager in a conservative financial institution where accounting principles ruled and my home life where there seemed to be no order, no precedents, no tenets.

"I doubt she could be pregnant," he said, his incredulity resounding on his every word. "Nevertheless, to be safe, if what you say is true, I should come out to check her for venereal disease."

"What?" I stammered. "Horses get venereal disease?" I have even more in common with the parents of sexually active teens.

"It's an easy test," he said in a matter of fact tone. "I just need to take a culture,"

"Will you check for pregnancy at the same time?" Great, my horse may be pregnant and have VD.

"I can, but the test is really expensive," he said cautioning me. "If you wait for twenty-one days, it will be easy for me to check for a fetus. You would have to wait the three weeks to do the abortion even if you knew she was pregnant early on."

"Not knowing is a limbo I don't usually go for," I said, flipping my check book open. I frowned, staring at the balance in my account. "I'll wait." House payments, care-givers for Emma and me and horse board absorbed my paycheck.

At the end of the week Carol called me in the evening at home. That was unusual. Carol wasn't the one to initiate contact. I wondered what could be wrong. Anxiety crept up my spine. I curled up on my sofa and pulled my down comforter over my legs.

"What did the vet say?" Carol asked, not wasting any time.

"The VD test came back negative." I said. Good, she's asking about Emma. Maybe something bad didn't happen. "At least the stallion was healthy. One less vet bill."

"Emma says she thinks she's pregnant given what the older mare in the barn has told her about how it feels and the rush of hormones. She really wants this baby," Carol asserted. "She's been contacting me almost every day. Whenever my mind wanders, such as when I'm driving, she pops in. She's opposed to an abortion."

Emma pregnant? Oh, no. My fears had materialized. I didn't want to face an ugly decision. This was so unfair. How many people go away for the weekend with their horse, in the middle of winter, in a virtual hinterland and come back with a foal in the making? Why me? Maybe Emma was wrong.

"I have to be practical," I said, pulling the comforter up to my shoulders.

I was tired of the whole mess. I needed to rest and get some energy to keep working. I didn't need a phone call from Carol pressuring me. But then what was Carol supposed to do if Emma was asking for her help. Emma and the Catholic Church ought to get together. Maybe I should make a Pro-Choice placard for her stall door.

"You won't have to worry about a good home," Carol said as though she had just provided the happy ending. "I contacted a friend of mine in Texas and she said she would take the foal."

Wow, someone has been busy. First, Emma with pestering Carol and then, Carol calling friends.

"That's very kind of you to broker an adoption," I said, snorting at Carol's naivety. "Remember, Emma has made it clear that mares are supposed to be with their foals for at least two years to teach them to be a proper horse. She won't consider a separation at six months or earlier which is the common practice in the horse industry. If I had my own property, that would be different. But I have to board my horses out. Never mind the vet bills and the energy needed to train a foal."

"I guess I was trying to help make it work for Emma," Carol said.

"Let's wait and see what the vet says." For once I was the voice of reason.

A couple of days later, while I was sitting at the kitchen table opening my day's mail, the phone rang. In the past I would enjoy responding to the ring, wondering what happy exchange was about to transpire. But, my week had been so bad that I cringed to think what unpleasant message might be coming. In defense I dashed to my bedroom and got deep under the covers. I felt safer in my bedroom. When I picked the extension up, I held the receiver a few inches from my ear as though that would lessen the blow of any unpleasant message.

"Is Emma pregnant?" Elaine's first words didn't ask how I was doing.

"She thinks she is," I said, "but the vet hasn't confirmed it." The knot in my stomach predicted where Elaine was going with that question.

"I'll be there for you with the foal." Elaine said, sounding hopeful. "I'll crochet a little winter blanket so the foal stays healthy in the cold."

Right, Elaine who rides other people's horses because she doesn't want the emotional or financial commitment. Will she be out there every day? In the cold and the dark. Will she be mixing up the hot bran mashes for Emma?

"That's very sweet of you," I said, picturing a tiny horse blanket crocheted in baby-pink yarn. "Are you willing to pick up the extra board and vet expenses?"

"No," Elaine said in a reluctant whisper.

I loved baby horses. Raising one would be fun. As a kid, before I understood much, I often thought I would love to give birth to a foal. Emma would probably make a beautiful baby.

I struggled to go to work, forcing myself to rise when the alarm clock went off and plowing through the day somehow convincing my fellow employees and staff that I was vivacious as ever. My mind had to be sharp. My team had to write the creative strategies for our campaigns. We had to come up with our marketing positions and a way to differentiate our products from our competitors. It was my job to balance the needs of my team, ensure that all of our projects were moving forward and would be ready by the drop dead date. After work, I flopped into bed often too tired to eat.

One night my disposition plummeted in to a particularly foul place. Since our return, Emma was more emotionally volatile than ever. Anything set her off, jumping or leaping without warning. I wasn't about to ride a jittery horse.

There would be no discussion of the baby business with Emma, Carol or Elaine. I needed to sort out how I felt about the whole thing by myself. Even though abortion was the only sensible solution, I was willing to take a step back. It was murder and it was final.

My mind knew what needed to be done but my emotions were all over the place. I felt Emma's pain as if it were my own. Almost every time my mind went on cruise control I could feel Emma pop into my consciousness. Her lovely face appeared in my mind followed by her entreaties to keep her baby. I resisted letting her in. Driving down the road, dozing off to sleep or daydreaming, Emma was there with her soft doe eye and her longing. Her persistence was unrelenting.

For goodness sakes, I had been working at banks for years. How to calculate loan payments and create budgets was my forte. Equity had built up in my home. A second mortgage or an equity line of credit could pay for the foal. With steady employment and decent raises, I could make the extra payments. Maybe I could find someone out at the barn who would help with the care giving. My dressage career had so many fits and starts. What was one more? But I didn't want that.

My heart beat a heavy rhythm as I drove out to the barn to meet Dr. Andrews. This was the day that I would be forced to make a decision.

Abortion would be final. I'd be a murderer. Letting Emma have the foal would put me at risk financially. And what about my health? What if it got worse and I couldn't do my job anymore? How would I feed and care for another mouth? I trusted that, when the moment came, my "Higher Knowing" would guide me.

Dr. Andrews showed up all business, not wasting any words on polite greetings. I could tell that he thought his visit was a waste of time. Never having had a pregnant mare, I didn't know what he was planning to do. He came into Emma's stall and asked that I take hold of her by her halter. He rolled a plastic examination glove over his arm. With no warning he turned and thrust his hand into Emma's rectum. His arm disappeared up to his elbow. Emma's eyes rolled back and she dropped her haunches. The wall kept her from springing forward. The jar of her experience resounded in my own body.

"Sonograms are much more accurate than rectal palpation," he said withdrawing his hand. "It's too early for me to feel much."

He backed out to the aisle and reached into his bag for an extension cord. He turned and handed me the plug, attaching the other end to a metal box with a small rectangular glass screen.

"Dr. Andrews," I said, wanting Emma's cooperation, not resistance. "Please explain to me what you're going to do to Emma before you do it."

He nodded in agreement and then motioned to the cord I was holding. I found an electric outlet. Dr. Andrews turned on the power and adjusted the knobs. The screen lit up.

"Why?" He looked at me with a puzzled expression.

"If I can let Emma know what to expect, she'll be easier to deal with," I said, turning to face him. "It's better not to surprise her - especially unpleasantly."

He stared at me. There it was again – that look that he was dealing with aliens. His back stiffened and he rocked back. I waited.

"You need to take her out of the stall," he said, a crispness in his voice that was barely masked. "I want her hind quarters next to the machine on this cart so I can insert the probe into her rectum. Please keep her from moving. The oscilloscope will show us what we need to know."

Once in Emma's stall, I turned to face her. The vet turned his head and stared at me with that look. I didn't care. I wasn't going to be shamed into hiding my beliefs.

"I'm going to take you out of your stall and lead you down the aisle to a sonograph machine, the big metal box." I stroked her neck. "The vet is going to insert his arm in you again. I know that will feel uncomfortable. Do your very best to stand quietly."

Emma followed me out of her stall. Once in the aisle, she increased her tempo to get ahead of me. She strode past the machine on the roller cart and stopped when her rear end was level with it. Then with a purposeful weaving motion, her haunches swayed over to the side, deliberately giving the cart a light push before standing perfectly still. With feet planted, she turned her neck to look at the vet. The intentionality of her behavior was apparent even to the vet. His face morphed from astonishment to discomfort. He coughed and regained his poise.

Things Emma was capable of doing surprised me. Horses live in horse consciousness and attend to and respond to events very differently than humans. I had learned that asking her to do something and that thing being done was separated by a chasm created by the species. Even though I could explain why she needed to pick up her knees over a fence, her muscles generally didn't do it. She didn't have that kind of volitional control. My instructor had to place jumps in such a way that taught her to snap them up and even then we weren't very successful. She could do it occasionally but not consistently. I could explain why she needed to take her nasty tasting worm medicine. Right. In that regard she was more like a two year old than my wise friend.

I didn't know when explanations would work. It did this time. She stood still when the vet's plastic clad arm disappeared into her body. Her expression changed, but she didn't move. The vet maneuvered a small probe with a thin wire attached. The screen flickered with shadows. He repositioned the probe.

"That is the wall of her uterus," he said, his left hand pointing to a shadow on the screen.

The grey and white image meant nothing to me. I turned to watch his face. I knew he thought my story was lunacy and was expecting to find an empty womb. His face froze and he sucked in his breath. His finger traced a shadow on the screen.

"That is the outline of a foal," he said, shaking his head.

"So she is pregnant." My stomach dropped. I had hoped Emma was mistaken.

"There was a foal, but it's in the process of being reabsorbed." His index finger made a circle on the screen. "Here's the outline of what remains."

"Reabsorbed?" I asked. "What does that mean?" I couldn't make out the blobs on the screen.

"Horses have all kinds of fertility issues," he said, removing the probe. "They seldom have miscarriages. Instead of expelling the fetus, their body reabsorbs it. It's fairly common. It's nature's way of eliminating mistakes."

"Emma won't need an abortion," I whispered more to myself than to the vet. My stomach relaxed and worry vanished into the atmosphere. I had no agonizing decision to make. "So this is positive proof to corroborate Emma's story."

The vet ignored my comment. No matter. Satisfaction that Emma's experience had been validated flooded my body. No one at the barn had believed what I told them either. The vet packed up and headed for his car. He came back into the barn and handed me the bill. I folded it and put it in my back pocket without looking at the amount.

I stood with Emma. The skin around her eyes wrinkled and her nostrils dilated. Her shock was reeling through my body. It was clear she understood the bad news. I was sad for her, but relieved that I didn't have to make a tough decision. Fate, not I made the foal unviable.

Emma was probably so inundated with hormones and since this was her first pregnancy, she probably didn't realize when the foal stopped growing. Her anguish broke my heart.

After a few days I could no longer bear Emma's distress. Every time my mind wandered, I saw her stressed face and felt her emotions as if they were my own. Her deep sorrow invaded my bones. Retreating to my bedroom, I crawled under the covers. Emma's pain was more than I could bear. My call to Carol found her home.

"I can't stand Emma's suffering." I looked over to my desk in an alcove of my bedroom. On top was the budget sheet I had worked up. "Does she want me to bring her back to the mountains and let her loose so that she can visit her stallion again?"

The intensity of her distress was causing a discomfort I had felt before. Not getting something I desperately wanted and yearned for with all of my being was a pain for which I was all too familiar. As a young girl, all I dreamt of was having a horse. The ache that I had felt for two decades was excruciating. I couldn't do that to another being.

"Emma doesn't want to go through that again," Carol said. "She is emotionally exhausted. Besides, the wildness of the land was too frightening."

I didn't expect that answer. Wouldn't Emma's desire for a baby overcome her concerns? How was I going to get her past her unhappiness?

"If I could find the stallion and make it safe so you didn't have to travel though the forest, would you want to go back and visit him?" I asked and held my breath.

What was I saying? Was I a total moron? I couldn't find him before, why did I think I could do it now?

"No, she just wants her life back." Carol sighed. "She wants to get back to her career, her job – dressage. She's suffered too many emotional excesses."

My body collapsed against the pillows. Emotional excess. I knew what she meant. Our sensitivities had been whipsawed. Emma had the promise of new life, hope, expectations of her own baby and then horrible disappointment. My agonizing over the decision whether to keep the foal was a miserable, ethical and moral quagmire. The last three weeks had been difficult. Emma wanted normalcy. I felt the same way. I wanted to regain my health and realize my dreams in dressage. I didn't want to worry about money. I wanted my life back too.

Chapter 15

The warming spring breezes seemed to stir improvement in my health. I felt as if the buds bursting from their long winter dormancy transferred their vibrant energy to my body. Currents of force seemed to move through my muscles and open up channels that had been clogged. The first hints of recovery were small, but perceptible. Each day I could do a little bit more, stay awake a little longer. I stopped taking lunchtime naps at my friend's house during the work week. The first time that I had enough stamina to ride Emma when I got home in the evening marked what I considered to be a major turning point in my recovery. The end of this persistent debilitation was perhaps in sight.

By early summer I was back to riding most evenings. To Emma's credit, she was ready to get back to work after her layoff. I felt like I was starting all over again. Besides getting my muscles built up I had to get Emma back in condition, at least a couple of months of going slow. The higher level movements would have to wait.

The dressage show season lasted fairly long so I pulled out the California Dressage Society's *Omnibus*. It listed the calendar of events and I targeted a couple of dressage shows in the fall that would be close to home and provide a familiar venue for our renewed attempts at putting a test together. Emma's natural gaits were beautiful and with the dressage training her suspension and expression of movement had become even more defined. It was not uncommon to have several boarders stop and watch us work.

A fellow dressage rider had proclaimed that Emma's way of going was so spectacular that I should have a successful show season. But coming in first wasn't why I rode. Placement wasn't as important as getting a high score from the judges to confirm and recognize what we had accomplished with our hard work.

By the end of summer Emma was working beautifully.

"Blast it," I blurted out. Emma had been doing exceptionally well and we were only ten days away from our first fall show. Now this. I dropped my seat in the saddle and brought Emma back to a walk, stopping our warm-up.

For the last couple of weeks I had felt at some subliminal level that Emma might be slightly off somewhere. It was one of those haunting feelings with no defined source and no visible proof. Now I could feel her weight realign. At the trot she bobbed her head ever so slightly as I surveyed the ground ahead between her ears. Emma seemed to be shifting her balance to offload weight from her right front foot. I slid off and led her over to the exit gate of Clear Creek's arena. Now I had the evidence. My eyes had seen it. More importantly, a vet would be able to see it too. The lameness would no longer be called an owner's hysterical suspicion. Leading Emma to her stall, I told her I'd call the vet when I got home. I felt she agreed.

Her lameness shouldn't have been a surprise. The footing in the arena hadn't been maintained for some time. The depth of the sand footing was uneven exposing the sandstone base in several areas. For the last two years Emma had been living there, no new sand had been added to Clear Creek's arena. Dragging the arena would only move the topping from one hard spot to another, much like trying to cover a large serving dish with a smattering of garnish.

The uneven footing caused breaks in Emma's rhythm. She would trot along just fine paying full attention to the adjustments that I communicated every stride. Then her feet would hit hardpan or a deep spot. Her cadence and concentration were interrupted as she tried to accommodate to the change in hardness and consistency of the ground. When I had spoken to Sally, the barn manager, about improving the footing of the arena, she explained that the owner of the property didn't want to expend any money on this marginal business. He had purchased the property as an investment for his retirement and would eventually sell the land for suburban development. He wasn't interested in incurring expenses for a business that would eventually be dismantled. Besides, many of the boarders were trail riders who were in no need of an arena so I was in the minority.

The vet arrived at the barn on time. He nodded at me and went straight to Emma. His hands moved up and down the tendons on both front legs. Next he grabbed his hoof testers and pinched the frog, bars and soles of Emma's right foot. She flinched each time the testers closed. The same on her left foot, only less so.

"Sore feet," the stoic vet said, letting Emma's front foot drop to the ground.

"That's what I was afraid of," I said, stroking Emma's neck.

"What kind of footing have you been working her on?" He dropped the testers into his bag.

"Sand, but a bit uneven." I dropped my eyes. I felt guilty that I hadn't acted sooner. I knew the footing wasn't the best, but the few other horses using the arena were doing fine.

"Have you thought about moving her?" He turned to face me.

"It's really hard to find a place that meets Emma's needs," I said, shaking my head.

"You really need to work her on better footing," he said, closing his bag. "The concussion isn't good for her."

After Dr. Andrews left, I nuzzled my face into Emma's neck trying to ease my sorrow. Whoever ran the boarding stable established the tone for all who lived or visited there. Sally understood horses and did what she could to make them comfortable. She observed their behavior and suggested moving stalls based on their preferences for one another. I admired the way Sally respected each horse and their individual personality. She was straight forward and would gladly brainstorm solutions to help make your horse healthier or happier. Her care ensured that whenever you walked down the barn aisle placid, contented faces reached out in cordial greeting. Not all barns had happy inhabitants.

I felt someone staring at my back. I turned to look down the barn aisle. Ah, Mathilda. How can I leave you? She stared deep into my eyes, cocking her head to one side.

"Mathilda, you are not only a good friend, but part of the family." I walked towards her and bent down to pet the soft feathers on her back.

Mathilda pecked at the cracked corn I spilled on the aisle floor. Love bathed me in a warm wash of well being. My throat closed and my eyes wetted.

"I'm going to have to move Emma to another barn," I said brushing my fingers over the downy feathers of her breast. "My heart will ache if I have to leave you. I'll call Carol so we can talk. Think about what you want to do."

Networking with my horse friends brought me to the entrance of Sweet Mountain boarding stable near the Sugarloaf open space. The small stable had been recently purchased by Joan, someone I'd met at a previous boarding stable when I still owned Fortune. I knew from the way she treated her own horse and household pets that she was committed to doing the best she could with the animals in her care. It would be reasonable to expect that her barn would be a calm and healthy place for Emma. A call to Joan gave her the opportunity to describe the renovations she'd made to the facilities. High on her priority list had been an overhaul of the arena. She wanted to do dressage with her Hanoverian mare and appreciated the need for good footing.

I parked the car, passed the barn and headed straight out to the arena. While not as large as the one at Clear Creek, Sweetwater's arena was big enough to do our work. A recently painted white, wood-plank fence enclosed the space. Laurel, oak and pine trees lined two sides and a creek ran along the eastern side. The toe of my boot wiggled back and forth digging into the footing. The sand was thick enough that I didn't scrape the base. The ring appeared to have been constructed professionally. I was about to turn to the exit gate when a door slammed and Joan approached from the backdoor of her ranch house.

"The bedrock has been graded for proper drainage and all new base material has been laid down." Joan said as she picked her way through the mounds of sand outside the arena. "The base should hold up throughout the winter protecting the footing from the adobe soil."

"The sand looks great," I said, turning to face her.

"Several truckloads have been spread over the base to create this cushy footing," she said, leaning over to pick up a handful. "I used Angel Island sand which doesn't compact and stays fluffy."

"The setting is lovely too," I said, admiring the surrounding hills.

"Thanks, the barn still needs work, though," she said, turning to face the low flat-roofed L-shaped building.

"Are there any ponds nearby?" I said, pointing to the open space.

"Ponds? No," she said, turning to face me, one eyebrow lifted. "Only the creek but it dries up in late summer. Why do you ask?"

"There's a goose I'd like to bring with me," I said and pictured Mathilda waddling through the gravel area between the barn and the arena. "She's family and I hate to leave her."

"You're certainly welcome to bring her," Joan said. "She'll be a welcome addition to the goats and other animals I plan to get for my children."

"Do the stalls all have paddocks?" I inquired, knowing Emma's need to have the freedom to go in and out at will.

"Each stall has a decent sized pipe paddock attached at the back." Joan turned and headed towards the barn.

"Do you feed any alternatives to alfalfa?" I asked, looking over to a corrugated iron structure that probably was used to store hay.

"I'll always have a supply of alfalfa and either oat hay or orchard grass." Joan detoured to the hay shed and showed me samples of her hay before continuing to the main barn. "A straight diet of alfalfa isn't healthy for horses and has been linked to the formation of enteroliths. I have some boarders here who insist on it or I wouldn't feed it at all."

The barn's low roof didn't promise a cool space the way Clear Creek did. The stalls were in fairly good repair and were bedded with a couple inches of pine shavings. The adjacent paddocks were about twice the size of the stall. Not perfect, but acceptable. Emma would have her patio.

"When can we move in?" I asked, stopping in front of an empty stall.

Nestled in my chair, I ran my fingers up and down the condensation on my soda can as I thought about moving Emma. What a pain to change stables when I had a happy horse and an attentive barn manager. Mathilda was part of the family, Gussey's attitude made me laugh and Emma had her horse friends, especially Spunky, the quirky little pony. I picked up the phone and dialed Carol's number muttering into space, "Why can't the footing be improved? We're all happy."

"How does Emma feel about moving?" I asked Carol as soon as we got past the opening greetings.

"Just a minute." The phone receiver clanged against something hard and then the sound of running water stopped.

"Okay, I'm ready now," Carol said. Slow, even breaths told me she was preparing to clear her mind and concentrate. "Emma doesn't want to move. She wants you to know that she doesn't deal well with change."

"Change can be stressful." I agreed. That was one way Emma and I were different. I thrived on change and the possibility of something fresh and exciting.

"She says that horses count on their routine," Carol said. "They don't appreciate their feed being changed. A difference in the way their water tastes disturbs them. They want to know who cleans their stalls and when things are going to happen. They like the predictable."

"I'm sorry Emma." I felt an anxious knot grow in my stomach. "I wish there was another way. I understand this will be hard for you. I'm going to miss Mathilda and Sally."

"I know we have to move," Carol translated using a reassuring tone. "My feet are really sore and I don't want that. Even if my feet didn't hurt, I can't concentrate when the footing keeps changing. It disrupts my rhythm. It's important to me to do well in my career."

"The plan is to move next weekend," I said, thinking that the sooner we moved the sooner Emma's feet could heal.

"Leaving Spunky behind is going to be really hard," Carol translated, putting dejection in her voice.

"Emma, can't you talk to him telepathically?" I said, hoping she could continue her friendship with the happy-go-lucky little pony.

"It's not the same," Carol explained. "It would be similar to talking to former roommates over the phone a couple of times a week instead of living with them."

"Speaking of leaving friends behind, I'd like to talk to Mathilda," I said, wishing I had a better offering for the goose.

"Give me a minute." Carol's breathing got deeper. "She's joined us."

"Mathilda, there is a creek at the new place, but no pond." I held my breath.

"No pond?" Carol translated for Mathilda.

I listened to Carol's steady breathing while I waited for her to go on.

"I need a pond," Carol continued, translating for Mathilda in a sad tone.

"I'm so sorry," I said, massaging my forehead with my fingertips. "The creek is small and it isn't very deep. There would be no where to swim and I don't think it would have the kind of greens you prefer to eat."

"That won't work," Carol translated for Mathilda.

"I wish I could have found a place with a pond," I said, feeling inept and powerless all at once. I also wished I won the lottery. Then I could have my own place and make it so everyone could be happy. "It's hard enough finding a place to meet Emma's needs," I continued. "If I put the requirement of a pond into the equation, I'd end up God knows where. My life and job are here." I felt a pang. I had a hard time imagining a barn without Mathilda.

The first day Emma was in her new residence the morning dawned with a gentle sun and I believed it meant the promise of a better day. To stock up I detoured to the feed store and arrived at the barn with a trunk full of fifty pound bags of grain. On my way to the grain room I saw a cloud of dust billowing in the area of Emma's paddock. She probably was having a good roll.

After I deposited the grain in my bins, I walked over to Emma's stall - my mouth dropped open. Neck raised high and the whites of her eyes showing, Emma paced along one side of the pipe fence. Pounding hooves on the hard, compacted ground pulverized the dirt into whirling puffs that dusted her legs and flank. Grabbing her halter, I dashed into her paddock and matched her stride trying to get her halter on. On the third attempt I managed to slip it on and got control of her head. She looked past me and struggled to get free. I maneuvered her into the barn aisle and led her to the grooming area. No amount of a soothing voice or calming hand brought her relief. Discouraged and feeling helpless, I led her back to her stall.

"Emma, what are you doing to yourself?" I said, shaking my head. "I wish I could help."

Over the next week what had been a slight bobbing of her head escalated into a more pronounced limp. "Emma, we came here to improve the soreness in your feet," I said, leaning over the top pipe rail of her paddock. "You're destroying yourself with quick turns and treading back and forth. Please, can't you relax?"

Boarders whose horses were stabled near Emma's stall told me that she spent most of her time walking the fence line. By the end of the second week her distress appeared worse. She now audibly telegraphed her emotional distress. With each turn in her paddock, she let out a plaintive moan that made the hairs on the back of my neck stiffen. I could hardly stand it. How Joan and the neighbors could cope was hard to understand. Maybe the kids screaming in the community pool next door had habituated them to noise.

Emma barely touched her hay and only gave her grain a cursory taste, grabbing one bite and then hurrying outside to resume her mindless grind, leaving the rest of the bucket untouched. During the third week, her ribs started to show. Emma was right about not adapting to change well.

After checking with Carol and talking to Emma, we decided a trip back to Clear Creek where Emma had happier days might help calm her down. Sally thought it was a great idea and told me to bring Emma over anytime. I made arrangements for the following weekend.

As soon as I stepped out of the truck cab in Clear Creek's parking lot, Mathilda came running and honking. I was covered in a blast of cushiony, golden puffs of love. She chattered and squawked as she paddled around me. Once she settled down, I bent over and petted her back. What a greeting. The love that this goose projected could light up an entire town. I was deep into losing myself in Mathilda's aura when I heard Emma paw the floor boards of the trailer.

"Oops, Mathilda, I need to go," I said, turning back to the rig. "Emma has been having a hard time adjusting to her new home."

Mathilda followed me to the rear of the trailer, inspecting all of my movements. I loved that goose. What a friend.

The pins slipped out easily and the back ramp swung down. Emma didn't need any encouragement to back out. She checked out the environs and then pulled me in the direction of the barn. I jumped ahead of her and led her to the back where the paddocks were located. I heard Spunky's nicker. He had been moved to the end stall near the parking lot. As soon as Emma neared his paddock, he came trotting out and walked up to where she stood. He lowered his head and eyed her through the pipe fence. They both stood side by side, nosing the ground for at least twenty minutes. Quick glances at each other punctuated their exchange. The meeting of the two friends was heart warming and although I couldn't hear it, I could feel their conversation. The dwarf-sized pony and the elegant long-limbed thoroughbred.

Mathilda, snacking on the loose alfalfa leaves on the ground near the hay barn, kept us in view the entire time of the visit. When it was time to leave, I waved good bye and blew her a kiss. She responded with another blast of love. As my eyes took a last sweep of the barnyard, I spotted Gussey ducking into the barn at full speed.

I checked on Emma through the side window of the trailer. She stood more visibly relaxed than when we came. What a relief. I couldn't stand much more of her endless tramping. I put the truck into gear and took her back to Sweet Mountain.

At last Emma's emotions settled down and my highest priority became reducing the pain in her front feet. After a couple of weeks of hand walking in the cushy sand, her lameness didn't seem to lessen. Her relentless pacing must have further compromised her already sore feet. That worried me. I knew what it was like to have sore feet.

A visit from Dr. Andrews was to be followed by a call to let me know the results of the X-rays he took. I was sitting at my kitchen table waggling the tea bag up and down and taking long, slow breaths to inhale the sweet aroma of the jasmine when the phone rang.

"The films show she has a condition called pedal osteitis," Dr. Andrews said, his voice sounding flat. "It's an inflammation in a bone of the feet."

The tea bag dropped with a splat on the kitchen table. I held the phone close to my ear so I could be sure and catch what he was about to say. The sound of the diagnosis made my jaw tight.

"Previous injuries to the feet," he explained, "like the one you described when she was a foal, can be a precondition to this problem. They disrupt the blood flow which can then compromise the joint of the bone. That is the source of the pain she's experiencing."

Listening to the vet's explanation made me ache with a deep despondency. Thoughtless treatment of Emma as a foal had set her up for more suffering as an adult. If people only knew how much pain they caused animals, they might be more careful. I glanced at the bunion poking through the sock on my right foot.

"So what do I do?" I asked.

"The best course of action is to replace your mare's steel shoes with sneakers," he said.

"What are sneakers and how would I keep them on?" I said, checking out the narrow laces on my tennis shoes sprawled at the front door.

"Horse shoes manufactured of hard rubber or plastic about three quarters of an inch thick," he explained. "They cushion the concussion and raise the sole of the foot well above rock or gravel or other inconsistencies on the ground. They're a little harder to keep on because the black smith has to guess where to drive the nails. With these shoes, Emma might recover well enough to resume her work."

"Might recover?" I managed to squeak. What did he mean might recover? Did that mean she might NOT recover? Might be permanently lame?

"There aren't any guarantees. Her bones have been affected," he replied. "These shoes might make her comfortable. I've had good success with them on my other clients' horses."

I hung up the phone and my breath caught. Emma might not be a riding horse. I stared out the bay window motionless, annoyed by the caw of a crow proclaiming its presence in the sycamore across the street. The tears dropped one at a time and then flowed. I fought for control of my emotions and lost.

With tears spent, I clung to the possibility that the vet offered. Emma might get better and with that thought I assuaged my dark thoughts. This wasn't a diagnosis of navicular or ringbone. Hope insinuated a lighter element into my brain as I dialed the phone for the blacksmith.

Emma's bright red sneakers gave her immediate relief. After a month of hand-walking and regular treatments with isoxsuprine to improve the circulation in the feet, Emma trotted out sound. I was ecstatic. Within a couple of more weeks I was back on her, starting with a few minutes at the walk. I increased Emma's work very slowly so I didn't create any more pain in her feet. A little bit of work was needed to increase the circulation in the feet and promote healing. Too much work would reinjure her feet and postpone her recovery. Erring on the conservative side was the way to go. In another couple of months Emma would be ready to start conditioning work and resume her dressage career.

Always the professional, Emma did her work, thoroughly enjoying the mental and physical challenges of the schooling. What I didn't understand was why she continued to mope around her stall. She didn't seem to be returning to the happy disposition she had at Clear

Creek. One evening when I was home in my den, I called Carol to find out what was up.

"Emma, why do you look a little punk?" I asked, settling into my chair. "You still aren't as happy as you used to be at Clear Creek."

"I'm sad and miss my friends," Carol translated. "It's hard for me to make new friends. The horses here don't recognize that I'm intelligent and wise. In every new place, I have to start at the bottom and have to work at being appreciated. It's frustrating."

"I'm so sorry." I knew exactly that feeling. "What do you think about the idea of going to visit Spunky and your other friends at Clear Creek again?"

"Great idea," Carol translated. "I would love to visit Spunky. He knows how to calm me down and make me feel okay with myself."

"We'll go next weekend," I reassured her.

"Can you feel what Emma is sending?" Carol asked.

"No," I said, "when I'm emotionally involved I can't always feel what she sends." I looked at the picture of Emma I kept on the table next to my chair. The white star in the middle of her forehead augmented by the reflective qualities of the glass covering the photo sparkled and seemed alive.

"She's feeling relieved and is sending huge waves of appreciation and thankfulness," Carol said. "I wish you could feel how different she is from when we began our conversation."

"I'm glad she's happier," I said. "We're so connected that it's hard for me to feel zone A when she isn't up to par."

I contacted Sally at Clear Creek who immediately agreed to let Emma come back and visit Spunky. I made plans to trailer Emma there on the weekend. Having something tangible to do that would make Emma feel better made me feel better too.

I maneuvered the truck down the bumpy driveway and got a chill when we passed by the back door of the barn where I had gotten stuck in the mud. A quick shake of my shoulders dispelled the feeling. Mathilda didn't greet me when I drove into the parking lot. Perhaps she was up at her pond or off flying somewhere. Not having her greet me made me realize how much I'd gotten from our joyful reunions. That kind of love is uncommon.

I unloaded Emma and ambled with her over to Spunky's paddock. The little dun pony with the Trojan horse mane jogged out to greet her. Within minutes I could see Emma relax. She lowered her neck and started nibbling the dried grasses next to the pipe fence. Spunky dropped his head as well and nosed the hard packed clay as if he, too, were able to join her in grazing. Anyone who knew horses would get that they were talking to each other. The expressions on their faces changed and their bodies stood angled so they could see each other. It felt as if they were having a sweet interchange. After about half an hour, Emma raised her head and walked off towards the trailer.

A softening in Emma's eyes made her look happier. She stepped with more confidence into the trailer and stood quietly while I secured the back doors.

As long as I was there, I thought it might be fun to catch up on the news around the barn. I looked around for Sally and saw her repairing a fence. I couldn't help but notice an unsettled feeling and wondered what it was about.

"I saw your horse in the front field," I said, pointing to the pasture next to the driveway. "He looks great."

"His hoof is healing and the layoff has given him time to pack on the pounds," Sally said, dropping four-inch nails into a bucket of loose metal.

"By the way, do you know where Mathilda is?" I asked, still wondering why I hadn't spotted her.

Sally didn't answer. She stood up and put the hammer down in her tool box. Her face was blank and devoid of its usual sparkle.

"I don't know where Mathilda is." Sally scuffed her boot in the dirt. "I haven't seen here for at least a couple of weeks."

"Do you think she flew off?" I asked, wondering if she had gone back to migrating with her flock.

"I really don't know what happened to her," Sally said, her eyes squinting against the sun when she looked over at me.

Sally looked down at her boots again and then reached down to pick up her little dog who had been prancing around her feet, demanding attention. She stroked his ears and rubbed his neck. She held him tight as though she needed some reassurance and looked up at me.

"I'm sorry to have to tell you. We found a pile of feathers in the front pasture," she said. "I suspect it might have been either a fox or the Rottweiler next door. I don't know. I can't be sure it was Mathilda."

I felt as if I'd taken a punch to my gut. "Mathilda, gone?" I muttered. No wonder I got a strange feeling when I drove down the driveway. Sally didn't know for sure but somehow I did. It was Mathilda.

"Sorry," Sally said, leaning over to ease her dog to the ground.

I turned and hid my tears until I got back into my truck. I didn't lose good friends easily.

The deep loss I'd felt from learning of Mathilda's passing took a few weeks to dissipate. I was determined to forget my mourning and be fully present to enjoy my ride and connection with Emma.

As soon as I left the freeway and headed down the narrow asphalt road to Sweet Mountain, I opened the car windows letting the pure summer air roll in over me. The breeze carried the remnants of cooling refreshment generated from the fog whose wisps retreated over the foothills to the west and back to the bay. The breeze off of the foothills to the east was filled with the earthy scent of dried grasses and adobe soil as the warmth from the advancing sun released the aromas locked within. I turned my face to the east and let the sun rays stroke my cheeks. The morning was still early enough to be devoid of the midday flies. The delicious heat that I loved would come later in the day. While most others complained about the boiling rays of the sun, I opened my arms and let the superheated air wash over me. This was the only time of year I felt warm. My eyes swept over the rolling hills. The blonde grasses glistened wherever the sun's bounty tickled the dew. I anticipated my trail ride into those golden foothills.

By summer, surface moisture had evaporated from the ground and the resulting cracks, some as wide as your foot, created uneven and dangerous footing for a horse. What looked like inviting grassy hills, were pock marked and booby trapped with fissures. The hills were unsafe, but we were fortunate that they were crisscrossed with plowed, dirt fire roads. I turned off the car engine.

A couple of lizards scattered as I got out of my car and a family of ground squirrels cavorted from burrow to burrow in an adjoining field. Everything was as it should be.

Emma's stall was on the end of the barn nearest the parking lot. As I approached, I didn't hear her nicker for me. She stood in her outdoor paddock on stiff legs as though she was rooted to the ground. That was odd.

I detached her halter from the rack on the door and strode through her stall to the adjoining paddock, keeping my eyes on Emma the whole time. She didn't acknowledge me with eye contact or even an ear flick. That was peculiar. Her stance appeared wooden. I looked her over and didn't see any wounds. My hands ran over her body to squelch any fear that there might be any hot spots or swellings. I put on her halter and led her a few steps to see if she favored a leg. Although reluctant, she took two good steps that were enough to convince me she was sound. I pulled on the lead rope to guide her out of her paddock and through her stall to the grooming area. She pulled back to the rear of her paddock and anchored her feet into the dirt. I took a firm grip of the lead rope and gave a determined tug to encourage her forward. She dragged her feet through the dirt leaving a trail of fine dust swirling in the air.

As soon as I got her into the aisle, she turned around the first chance she got and tried to go back to her stall. I settled my weight into the earth and pulled her head around or she would have succeeded. Not sure what was going on, I responded the way I did to most things – I kept moving.

At the grooming area, I resorted to my usual regimen of brushing her, hoping that the familiarity of our daily routine might help settle her down. Her agitation escalated. She thrust forward and hit the end of the cross ties and then reversed as far as the slack permitted. I had to rock back and forth alongside of her with the brush in hand. She threw her head into the air and I saw the whites of her eyes. She shifted her weight to her hind end as if she were preparing to rear. This behavior was scary. I threw the brush down and unbuckled her from the cross ties. She muscled towards her stall dragging me in her wake. At her door, she rushed past, knocking me with her shoulder as she darted inside.

I rubbed my upper arm where the point of her shoulder had stuck it. That was strange. Emma took care not to bang into anyone or inadvertently hurt them. During a conversation with Carol, Emma had warned me that when playing with her in a turnout paddock not to get too close when she was rearing. She didn't have good vision of where I might be standing and wouldn't know where to land. Emma was always concerned with my and other humans' safety.

Once when I was jumping her over a low fence she made a sloppy attempt, dangled her knees and hit the top rail. She fell forward with her front legs pointing backward. Usually when that happened horses crumbled to the ground on their shoulders throwing their riders over their head. Instead Emma used her nose as a fifth wheel and a plow. She left a furrow in the dirt as she tumbled forward trying to organize her legs underneath herself. She bruised her gums and mouth and scraped her nose to keep me from falling. She often reminded me how puny humans were in comparison to a horse. I had a history of knowing what Emma would do to protect me.

Back in her stall, I took off the halter and let my eyes scan her body, wondering what could be wrong. She didn't move. It was if she were posing for a still life. My mind couldn't offer up any reason for this new behavior. Although it took a few months, the sneakers had given Emma the best possible outcome. She had been working well and I had pulled out the show calendar again hoping that we would only miss a year's showing. Surely we could make a late summer or early fall show. For today, I abandoned any hope of a ride.

Driving away from the barn, I was disappointed in not spending this lovely morning the way I had planned. My fingers drummed the steering wheel. Yet another day I couldn't ride my horse. Every time Emma and I seemed to get some traction on dressage training, something happened. I was getting tired and annoyed with these interruptions. It seemed when she was well, I was sick and when I was well there was some reason why she couldn't perform. Was I ever going to school piaffe or passage?

I'd call Carol as soon as I got home.

The stuffed chair in my den welcomed me. I plopped down on the soft cushions and took a deep breath. It was still early in the day. I would rather be riding my horse and benefitting from the psychological and physical healing that being around my horse gave me. But I knew I shouldn't be moaning. My health was so much better and my job was a huge improvement over the last one.

My new boss, although emotionally cool, did not take drugs, was supportive and treated me with respect. The responsibilities of the job were demanding with several direct mail campaigns going on simultaneously. Although I was only experiencing the normal kind of stresses associated with the marketing and product development profession, I still needed my decompress time. And now something was going on with Emma. I picked up the phone to call Carol.

"Calm down, there's always a reason," Carol reassured me.

"That's the problem," I said. "Too many reasons keep me from riding my horse. I don't have a horse as an ornament."

"I understand," Carol said. "Give me a minute." Her breathing slowed. "I have to sweep out my mind."

"I appreciate you're making yourself available," I said, feeling the eddy of my emotions calming from a tsunami to more of ripple. Deep breathing helped me too. Carol didn't have to keep taking my calls. She had a busy and full life, sometimes working long or double shifts. Life as a trauma care nurse had its challenges for her.

"Waves of anger are ripping through my body," Carol translated for Emma. "The rage is so strong that I'm worried I won't be able to control my behavior. I can't predict when it will happen so I'm concerned that I might hurt someone."

Why didn't I guess that? Emma had done a lot of her grief work from her early life experiences of abandonment and abuse. That she would need to process her anger next made sense. Poor thing. I was embarrassed by my impatient ranting.

"Emma, experiencing anger is another step in the recovery process," I said, remembering how many times I had beat my fists against the pillows on my living room couch to help release all of the frustrations, disappointments and other feelings that had been stuffed and repressed during my early years. "Letting go of anger is a good thing. You need to do it to release the influences of what has happened in the past. What can we do to make you less anxious about this process and to support you through it?"

"I need to bite," Carol translated. "I need to bite hard."

"What about getting you something that you can sink your teeth into and putting it in your paddock?" I asked.

"Yes, but please warn the people who work around me," Carol translated. "I'm not sure I'll be able to control these attacks. I don't know when they'll happen. Don't ride me either. I'd be horrified if I did anything to hurt anyone."

"I'm sorry you have to go through this," I replied. "I had to do it too. My bottled up anger was released through getting physical. I dug fence posts and pummeled cushions. I totally understand. The one thing I know is that it will pass. You can get through this."

I felt empathy for Emma. The recovery process was hard work. Anyone who had done any part of it had my respect and admiration for their courage. Reliving the pain stored in the memories was nearly as bad as the first time around.

Although I couldn't tell the clerks what I was shopping for, a few passes up and down the aisles of the local mega toy store yielded a thin bicycle tire and boxing gloves. Over the next few weeks these articles took a beating. The boxing gloves stayed tied to the pipe fence, but the bike tire got thrown around and sometimes ended up in an adjoining paddock. None of us ever saw Emma do anything to her bite toys, but the dents and scars suggested she was attacking them. I knew she warned me that she might hurt someone, but I couldn't visualize that ever happening. Emma always did her best to be kind. She was a class act.

Then one day Emma's ordeal seemed to end. Her body appeared relaxed and fluid rather than stiff and controlled. The soft, liquid brown of her expressive eyes told me that it was time to get back to riding.

Chapter 16

I hated backtracking, but during the two months it took for Emma to process her anger, she had lost a lot of muscle tone. I didn't want to strain her muscles or ligaments by asking for collection too soon. And then there was always the question of the soundness of her feet to consider. If only twenty meter circles weren't so boring. I was beginning to wonder if I would ever achieve my goals.

I was grateful that Emma enjoyed the discipline and focus required for the sport. Her joy was one of my rewards. Dressage horses gained confidence and pride the more competent they became. It was a fun process to watch. I wasn't so foolish as to forget what I had to be thankful for. Emma was at least sound, for now. I was relieved that her feet seemed to be holding up. The sneakers were staying on. I relaxed my guard and hope tiptoed into my mind, bringing in its wake the hint of happy dreams for the future of our dressage pursuits. I pulled out my AHSA show schedule and circled the dates of local shows. Even though we were getting a late start on our show career, with Emma's athleticism and intelligence we could progress quickly. If she stayed sound and could concentrate.

A couple of times a week, I took a break from schooling in the arena. To relax and kick back I would go out on trail rides with one of the boarders. Sweet Mountain was next to the Sugarloaf open space which connected to the Mt. Diablo State Park trail system via paths that wended their way between housing developments. Emma and I enjoyed riding in the foothills and usually went out with a trail buddy. With fire roads wide enough for two horses to walk abreast, riders could easily carry on a conversation.

Trail riding provided an opportunity to socialize and catch up with my barn friends. The horses had to watch where to put their feet, but I could chat away and bask in the panorama that danced 360 degrees around us. Everything seemed alive. Chipmunks with striped faces and backs scampered across fallen logs, cattle grazed on the matted dried grasses covering the slopes, lizards skedaddled into crevices and hawks circled on the rising thermals. The wind-sculpted sandstone rock formations changed colors with the movement of the sun and offered up a changing pattern of puzzle pieces. At dusk I sometimes saw a swarm of bats leave their cave for twilight foraging. I couldn't resist the call of the hills. Other folks could plop in front of the television. Nature was my spectator sport.

On one such occasion a friend and fellow boarder, Betty, and I went out for a two-hour trail ride. Betty rode her fifteen-hand quarter horse bay mare decked out with all the western accoutrement. She wore a cream-colored western-style hat, plaid snap-buttoned shirt and leather chaps with fringe. Heavy tooling covered her saddle and embossed silver conchos punctuated her bridle and the top of the saddle horn. Emma, on the other hand, sported a black dressage saddle with a white quilted saddle pad trimmed with black piping, white polo wraps on her legs and white raised-leather brow band on her black bridle. The two horses made an odd pair.

We enjoyed making our excursions in a circle instead of just going out and coming back on the same trail. We planned a loop towards Shell Ridge that provided more shade than the other trails and avoided some of the steepest hills. The afternoon sun was warm and Betty wanted the cooler route. On the way home we cut over a hill following a single track, a narrow footpath wide enough for one horse and flanked by a steep drop-off on one side and jagged boulders on the other.

At the top of the hill, two bicyclists came peddling towards us. The trail did not allow enough room for them to pass safely. Betty, who was in the lead, explained politely that the regional parks didn't permit bicycles on single tracks and that they needed to turn around from where they came. She suggested that they needed to stay on the fire roads or other dirt roads that were wider.

The bicyclists didn't respond well to the idea of turning back down the hill. After some unpleasant words were exchanged, the bicyclists charged forward, scraped by Betty's horse and came barreling towards Emma and me. We were standing on an even narrower part of the trail. I panicked. There was a gorge on one side and knee-high rocks on the upward side of the hill. Emma made a quick decision, turned and leaped amidst a jumble of boulders to get out of the way. Without pausing to see what happened, the bicyclists continued hurtling down the hill at speed. Emma scrambled to get her footing and managed to stay upright. I clung to her mane, knowing that I couldn't provide any help. She reared and pivoted to face the trail and then lunged among the rocks to try and get back to the path. She stumbled and regained her balance. My heart pounded. She was a horse, not a goat. I clung to her neck, not wanting to interfere with her balance. Several lunges got her back to the path. I was grateful that she was on all four feet.

Leaning over to get a better view, my eyes roamed over Emma's legs. She seemed unharmed except for an abrasion above the polo wrap on her front left cannon bone. Blood was oozing out, but not running down. Her escape maneuver could easily have broken a bone.

"Are both of you all right?" Betty yelled out.

"What a relief that Emma is standing on all legs," I said, putting my hand over my heart. "I'll be okay when my pulse rate calms down. Emma has a scratch, maybe some bruises, but it doesn't seem serious."

"I wish bicyclists had license plates so that I could report them," Betty said, seething with irritation. "Those people were totally insensitive. Both you and Emma could have been seriously hurt. She did acrobatics to stay on her feet."

"I was lucky," I said, stroking Emma's neck. "You're right. It could have been different. Did you hear about what happened to Carolyn? A group of bicyclists sped around a blind corner and spooked her horse. They both fell over a cliff and were seriously injured."

At the bottom of the incline the narrow path ended on a fire road and we abandoned our single file to ride next to each other and discuss the problems of mixed-use trails. When we approached one of the semicircular swing gates that were designed to give equestrians passage without dismounting, Betty jogged ahead to open it. She maneuvered her horse up to the gate and held it to one side, motioning for me to go through first.

On the other side of the gate, Emma planted her feet. A strange feeling telegraphed it's presence through the saddle. I felt tremendous pressure building up from the very center of Emma's gut. She started to shake and then her muscles jerked. The release of energy caused her to bolt forward. I snatched up the slack in the reins and pulled on the left rein to force her into a circle. She crashed through the underbrush with no regard to the footing underneath or the brambles that were pricking her hide. When we got to a clearing I pulled the rein tighter forcing her into a spin. She continued spinning for several minutes, trampling the grasses into a crop circle. When she finally stopped, she spread her legs and her head sunk as if she were dazed or dizzy.

Sitting up in the saddle I loosened the reins and looked over to Betty. Her lips pursed as she blew out air.

"What in the world was that?" Betty called out, pushing her hat up higher on her head.

"I have no idea," I answered back. "I'm not sure it's over."

"What do you mean?" Betty asked, turning her horse to face me.

"I'm feeling a lot of tension through her back," I said, pulling my baseball cap down farther on my head.

"Let's get home as fast as we can," Betty said, turning her horse toward the barn.

The pressure of my calves told Emma to move forward. She took a few hesitant steps. Within a few yards, I could feel the pressure building. Just as the force was about to erupt, I pulled her head to one side to avoid her bolting forward. She went into another feverish spin, her feet thrashing on the ground. Again, as soon as the eruption exhausted itself she stood still panting. After just a few short moments of quiet, I felt another eruption coming. This time I spun her the other way. I wondered if I would be fast enough to keep her from going completely out of control.

We didn't progress home more than a few yards at a time. My anxiety grew with each episode. Walk a few steps, feel the pressure mount, stop, spin, wait until the dizziness stopped and walk a few more steps. I wasn't sure that I would be able to keep either Emma or myself safe all of the way back.

After the fifth episode, Emma put herself into a spin when the pressure got too great. I didn't have to pull the reins to the side. I could use both hands to grip her mane and hang on. It was clear that she was doing her best to keep me from getting hurt. Distressed horses generally tried to run from things that they didn't like or scared them with little regard for anything else. That Emma was controlling her bizarre behavior to keep me safe was beyond amazing. Betty couldn't believe what she was seeing.

I was grateful that Betty's horse remained quiet and calm. Horses tended to pick up the stress of another. As flight animals, they had sensitive antennae that urged them to flee when in doubt. Each time I spun around I could see Betty sitting on her horse quietly watching us. With all of the stops for spinning, what should have taken fifteen minutes took over an hour to get home. I had never been so happy to see the outline of the parking lot.

The sight of the barn calmed me enough to realize that I was emotionally and physically shot. In the parking lot, I hopped off Emma before she had another fit. I took a good look at her. Her entire body was completely drenched and her neck and chest were covered in white foam. When we entered the barn, Emma shook her body as if she had just had a good roll and sighed. I took that as a sign that the explosions were over.

Other boarders who happened to be at the barn came over to see the exhausted horse and rider. Bringing a horse home in Emma's condition was unusual. The sweat ran off of her in rivulets, leaving a trail of water drops wherever she walked. Her belly was tucked in and I was concerned she might be dehydrated.

After Betty put up her horse, she joined me while I hand walked Emma to cool her out. The experience was so difficult, I was out of words. Betty pulled her hair back behind her ears and stared at me with a wondering expression.

"I'm stunned," she said, walking beside me. "In all my years with horses I've never witnessed a horse act that way. I've trained a lot of young horses and horses that have been abused, but this has me baffled."

"I can't explain it either," I said. "It felt as if earthquakes came straight from Emma's very core. She quivered a little at first and then the power of the shaking escalated. It was as if she had to discharge the energy."

Driving home, I wondered if these attacks were another form of processing rage. Perhaps the incident with the bicyclists triggered a reaction. Both Betty and I were furious at their behavior. Did Emma absorb our feelings? But what Emma did didn't feel identical to rage. Her spins felt like a surging of powerful energy. Raw energy. I needed to talk to Emma.

My house tried to lighten my heart with its cheery buttercream yellow exterior and beckoned me with promise of refuge as I drove into the driveway. I made my way to the embracing arms of my den and sank into my easy chair to call Carol.

"Hey Carol, it's me again," I said.

"Well just color me surprised," she said, laughing. "You are my best customer. What's Emma up to now?"

"She had some kind of fit during our trail ride this afternoon and I want to know why," I asked, impatient to get to the answer.

"Wow, Emma is coming through loud and clear," Carol said. "I didn't even need to clear my mind and focus. Emma wants to talk about it too." Carol's breathing slowed. "She says she doesn't know what it's about."

"Was there a trigger?" I asked thinking of the bicyclists.

"I don't think so," Carol translated. "Nothing that I know of."

"How did it feel?" I asked.

"Horrible," Carol translated, putting enough emphasis in her voice to make chills run up my back.

"Can you describe the feeling?" I asked. "Was it pain, anger, stress?"

"No," Carol translated. "It was horrible. I can't stand it. My reaction really scared me."

"Is there anything that you can tell us that will help us understand what happened?" I asked.

"No," Carol translated.

"For goodness sakes," I burst out in frustration. "We aren't getting anywhere."

"Sorry," Carol said. "I'm just the translator."

"Maybe it won't happen again," I said, wishing that it might be true.

A week later I took Emma for a ride into the hills. As soon as I headed home minor versions of her eruptions began. Fortunately I was close to the barn. The following week a short trail ride was fine, but that turned out to be the exception. Although her fits were never as bad as the first time, it still took all of my skill to negotiate a safe trip home. Trail rides were no longer fun. I didn't need to be roaming the hills on a horse who had a sensitive fuse that detonated explosions inexplicably and repeatedly.

Right. More anxiety. Emma's bouts reminded me of my father's rages. I could feel the pressure building inside of him before he let loose on whoever was closest. The release of energy was followed by a short period of calm. Unfortunately the trickle-down effect ensured that my mother or sister continued the disgorgement of negativity on the littlest one. I was the littlest one.

The loss of trail rides was deeply disappointing and not an insignificant sacrifice to give up. We both missed going out on the trails with its formerly stress-free kick-back time. Despite how much I loved dressage even I got bored when staying in an arena basically doing some version of a circle.

Ring work every day was not the optimum way to train a horse, so I gave Emma more days off with hand walking around the barn. I didn't want to sour either her or my disposition with endless repetition.

One day I turned Emma out in an outdoor paddock to enjoy the extra room and sunshine. If I couldn't take her on trails at least she could enjoy a change in scene and hang out just being a horse. As soon as I slipped her halter off, she trotted away, stopped and stared straight at Mt. Diablo with a wild look in her eye. She threw her head up, shot her ears forward and leaned back on her haunches as if she was startled by something. Something had cranked her energy button up to the maximum. I scanned the eastern horizon to identify what had grabbed her focus. Nothing unusual was there.

Continuing to face east, Emma let out a loud call which more closely resembled a scream. She pivoted off her hind legs and hurled back and forth as if she were looking for a way to get out of the paddock. Her restlessness escalated and was interrupted by sudden pauses, with her fixating on something to the east. What in the world was in that direction?

Emma's high-pitched whinnies increased in volume. She ripped back and forth in extreme agitation and whenever she stopped she pushed against the fence with such force that the boards bent. She reminded me of the velociraptors in *Jurassic Park*, looking for the weak link in their enclosure. The fence held. My nerves were going nuts. I snatched her halter and jumped into the paddock. I stood in her path to slow her but she blasted past me as though I weren't there. Her shoulder brushed my shirt. I couldn't catch her and I couldn't stop her. I felt helpless.

After twenty minutes, Emma's frenzy abated and she calmed herself by weaving – rocking back and forth on her front feet. I hated to see weaving. That was the behavior of neurotic zoo animals who were bored out of their skulls, having been kept in tiny enclosures for too many years with no stimulation. Although Emma had explained on several previous occasions that weaving and pacing created endorphins which gave her relief from her emotions, I cringed whenever I saw her doing it. I was grateful she didn't do it very often. Sick of watching her weave, I haltered her and led her back to her stall.

Driving home, I went over in my mind what happened with Emma. I needed to know what was causing her to experience so much distress. I called Carol as soon as I got in the door. I sighed with relief when she, not her answering machine, picked up.

"Emma, what caught your attention in such a neurotic way when I turned you out?" I asked, hoping I would get a better response than I got when I asked her about her explosions on our trail ride with Betty.

"I don't know," Carol translated. "It scares me."

"Why were you looking off to the east?" I asked. "What scares you?"

"I don't know," Carol translated. "I can't control my emotions. I have to run and weave to try and stop the feelings."

"If it was scaring you, why did you try and go in that direction, keep facing it?" I asked.

"I don't know," Carol translated.

"Emma, your life is getting too restricted," I said in exasperation. "I can't take you on trails and I can't turn you out to run and play. What kind of life is that?"

"She doesn't want to be that way," Carol said. "She is so sorry."

"Maybe it will get better in time," I said, offering up another prayer.

After I hung up the phone with Carol, I sat staring at the wall. The sun crawled toward the horizon and shadows lengthened around the chair in my den. I knew I had spaced out when I discovered myself sitting in the dark. Too much emotional pain. Something would have to give.

Sometimes people who made their living from the care of horses had a sense that vets just didn't have, so I consulted with older, more experienced horse trainers. They were all as perplexed as I was about Emma's behavior and had no suggestions to alleviate her symptoms. I didn't know what to do or where to turn for help. Emma was suffering from uncontrolled emotions and I didn't have any way to ease her misery. All I could do was hope that whatever she was going through would resolve in time.

Just when I thought that I could manage Emma's attacks by staying off the trails and not turning her out in a paddock, she started having them when she was in her stall. One minute she would be standing still happily munching on her hay and then the next minute her head would shoot straight up and she would start pacing. The first time I saw it, I went straight home and cried. The inability to bring relief to someone in your care is an ultimate frustration.

Every time I thought Emma's condition couldn't get any worse, it did. Not only was she having her attacks more often, but the severity had increased. She began weaving more often and her weaving escalated into her hurling her body violently back and forth. She reared and plunged on one foot and then reared and plunged on the other foot. This exaggerated weave was body abuse. Her feet were taking a beating on the hard packed dirt as all her weight came smashing down on one hoof at a time. A sound horse wouldn't stay sound long with that treatment and Emma wasn't exactly a sound horse. My hope that her behavior would resolve itself wasn't coming to pass.

Some of my friends told me to get over it, Emma was only a horse. My close friends knew better. They knew my life was inextricably linked to my riding and my horse. From television interviews I knew that athletes were out of sorts when they couldn't exercise their passion for their sport. I was like them. What was worse was that my apparatus wasn't a baseball bat, tennis racket or running shoes. I needed a living, breathing partner. Maybe ballroom dancers knew how I felt.

One day Emma added otherworldly screaming to the plunging back and forth in her paddock. Not a high-pitched whinny, but something you might imagine coming from a medieval torture chamber. It was the kind of sound that made you want to run and hide from the horror that was being unleashed on some hapless creature. I stood in her paddock, my entire body shriveling from the sound. I tried to distract her with a slice of a Fuji apple. She didn't even glance at what I held in my hand. I slunk home and substituted a glass of red wine for the usual soda, needing something stronger before I called Carol with yet another attempt to understand how I might relieve Emma's emotional pain. As soon as I was in my stuffed chair in the den, I collapsed and dialed the phone.

"I didn't think Emma's behavior could get any worse," I complained. "Now she's destroying her front end with constant concussion to her front legs. Her weaves and pacing have escalated to rears. And she's adding screaming that is the eeriest thing that I've ever heard."

"I'm so sorry to hear this," Carol said. "Give me a minute. I just walked in the door."

The refrigerator door opened. Plastic rustled and drawers clunked shut. Paper bags crinkled. Carol must have been grocery shopping on her way home from work. I was pretty demanding. I didn't even give her a chance to take off her work clothes.

"I'm tuned in now," Carol said. "She's feeling anxiety and then terror. I can feel it throughout my body. It's very strong."

"Terror? What causes it?" I asked, wracking my brain to picture what beast was lurking undetected in the barn.

"My feelings come out of nowhere and randomly," Carol translated for Emma, putting stress into her voice. "I'm anxious all of the time, but the attacks are unbearable. They are so bad I lose control. That makes me even more scared because I might hurt someone. Please do something to make it stop."

"What's going on with her?" I asked, looking up to the ceiling, clearing my mind and waiting for an answer.

"I think I understand what's happening," Carol said. "She's much clearer this time about what strong emotion she's feeling. She's experiencing an extreme fear response. It may be a classic case of panic attack."

"What's a panic attack?" I asked. I had plenty of my own anxiety, but I didn't go running around my bedroom destroying my feet.

"Panic attacks can come out of nowhere," Carol said. "The heart races, the breathing rate increases and the person experiences exaggerated terror. It's an extreme flight or fight reaction. Even though nothing may be going on around them, the person or animal feels as if they are under a life or death threat. It's real to them. Some people have to go to the hospital to resolve a panic attack."

Carol's experience as a nurse exposed her to all kinds of medical maladies. I respected her opinion. She had been helpful in the past with many issues. She may not have been familiar with horses, but she knew about human physiology and a lot of it translated to horses.

"Emma, I'm so sorry you have to do more processing," I said. "I know about anxiety and terror, but I've never had a panic attack so I didn't know what was happening. This must have been what you were experiencing during that trail ride with Betty."

"It's awful," Carol translated. "I'm really terrified when it happens."

"Now that we know what's causing her episodes, I'm calling the vet," I said, the flame of hope sputtered alive in my heart. "There has to be some medication to relieve horses of panic attacks."

"There is for people," Carol said.

"I am so happy to hear that," I said, expecting that science had a magic pill to make Emma better. "I'll sleep better tonight."

"Do you feel the love she's sending you?" Carol asked. "I'm completely bathed in it. She is grateful for everything you're doing for her."

"Yes, I can feel it. What an awesome feeling, but I can't immerse and get lost in it right now. My mind is whirring," I said, my creative juices flowing. "I have an idea that may work in the mean time. Remember how Emma sent Spunky the benefit of my massaging her legs when he needed it more than she did?"

"Sure, of course I do," Carol said. "Her behavior was unusual and so generous."

"Well, if Emma can somehow send through space the benefit of my massaging her to Spunky, why can't Emma send her panic attacks to me?" I asked.

"You have a point," Carol said. "Animals often take on the processing of their persons, so I suppose you could take on her processing, her panic attacks."

"It's the human's turn to do something for the companion animal," I said, rather proud of having thought of it.

"Emma is stunned that you would do that," Carol said.

"Emma, I mean it," I declared, punctuating every word. "Humans have more ways to deal with it than you do. I can do self talk, I can take a tranquilizer or I can go to the pantry and pour myself a drink. I have options that you don't."

"Still, she can't believe you're willing to do that for her," Carol said.

"Emma, I would be more than happy to try and alleviate your suffering, if I can," I said, knowing I wasn't exactly sure what I was taking on. But one thing I knew. Emma's suffering was mine. Why not take on some of her problems if it made her better?

"Speaking of things to be afraid of, did they ever catch the burglars plundering your neighborhood?" Carol asked.

"No, but it concerns me to keep my windows open at night," I said. "They have been invading homes while people are asleep. Just what I need is more anxiety – now my home isn't even inviolable. So many of my psychological issues originated in not feeling safe."

The next day I called the vet for an appointment for the following week when he would be back in town. Meanwhile I kept myself busy at work with the latest campaign and at home with some long overdue projects such as cleaning out my gutters. I didn't want to think too much about Emma's problems. Besides making me sad, I needed a break. A couple of movies and dinner out with Elaine and Tom helped. I didn't feel guilty about the diversion because I couldn't do much for Emma until the vet came out. I wished they had urgent care for horses the way they did for people and I could get a same day appointment.

One night after a particularly long day at work and dinner out with Elaine, I drove home counting the blessings I had in friends. Elaine knew exactly what to say to be supportive and was just plain fun. I always felt good and came away with a sense of wellbeing. The evening was warm and I couldn't resist leaving several windows open to catch a gentle breeze. The star jasmine outside my windows permeated the air with its rich, perfumed scent. As soon as I lay down, I fell into a deep sleep. The kind of sleep that evokes vivid dreams. How sweet it would be, if it were dreams. In my case, my nighttime sojourns were more often realistic nightmares where I was being threatened, beaten, tortured or killed. My therapist had made a lot of progress with me so the number of nightmares and the terrors they evoked had diminished but not disappeared.

Sometime in the middle of the night, I woke up with a start, my muscles froze in a lock-tight spasm. I sensed someone was in my bedroom with malevolent intent. I couldn't breathe. I felt as if I was being suffocated. With life-preserving reflexes I jolted upright. My heart raced and sweat broke out all over my body. I wished I had a weapon under my pillow. The fear was so intense I couldn't scream. Light from the street lamp outside my window illuminated the room and cast hard-edged shadows across the walls. The blackness of the shadows formed sinister patterns, but I saw nothing move. My body was racing out of control from the menace that was in my home. I listened for the footsteps of someone who might be running away.

Then the realization popped into my brain. I somehow knew it was Emma's emotions, not mine. I turned on the light and sat back against my pillow. I took several deep breaths counting to eight for both the inhale and exhale. My thudding heart eased a notch and the terror took a short step back as I repeated to myself, "I am safe."

My heartbeat slowed and I got up and walked the inside perimeter of my home, turning on all of the lights and shutting the windows as I went. In the kitchen I located an opened bottle of wine in the back of the refrigerator. The alcohol, landing in an empty stomach, buzzed to my head and began its lovely work of dulling my senses. Knowing that what I felt was Emma's terror, I sent her my love and envisioned her wrapped in the safety of white light. A body totally absorbed in life-threatening fear is a body out of control. No wonder Emma ran in terror with glazed-over eyes, immune to what lay in her path. Another half-glass of red wine further did its work of resetting my physiology.

I had never experienced anxiety as intense. I would have sworn I was about to die. This was ghastly. It took a good half hour before I felt that I could go back to bed.

The next evening after work, I called Carol and asked her to verify if my understanding of my nightmare was correct.

"Yes, I sent you my panic attack," Carol translated for Emma.

"I wish you could feel how grateful Emma is," Carol said. "She cannot imagine anyone taking that on for anyone else."

"Did you receive the white light I sent you?" I asked.

"Yes, It helped me feel safe, thank you," Carol translated.

"Keep sending me your panic attacks," I said, hoping that this would be the end of her episodes. "It wasn't fun, but I could calm myself down and go back to sleep. When I'm awake in broad daylight, it should be even easier to calm myself down."

"It only works when you're asleep," Carol translated.

"What?" I moaned. "But I'm not riding you when I'm asleep. Why can't you send me the panic attacks whenever they happen?"

"It doesn't work that way," Carol translated. "I'm grateful that you will take them from me at night. Night is even scarier, but they don't happen very often at night."

"I have much more empathy for you, Emma," I said. "That experience has forever recalibrated my estimation of terror. Was I naïve? I thought I knew terror."

"It sounds like the 'good news is' and the 'bad news is' kind of thing," Carol said, commiserating. "Maybe it is just as well that you won't have to go through that very often."

"The vet will be out in a couple of days and he should have some ideas," I said, envisioning the pill that would fix everything, but knowing at another level that my life didn't tend to have easy solutions.

I decided that the vet's visit was going to be met with a happy and optimistic mindset. Why shouldn't I expect modern science to have a medication to fix Emma's behavior problems? It did for humans. I met him in the parking lot and escorted him to the front of Emma's stall. He looked her over. Words describing Emma's behavior spewed out of my mouth like boulders rocketing out of a volcano. My fingers lit on his arm and I stared at him to hold his gaze. My eyes conveyed how badly I needed his help.

Dr. Andrew was short on words. Wasting his or anybody's time was not to his liking. Nevertheless, he listened politely, rubbing his hand over the top of his balding head from time to time.

"I hear what you're saying," he said, looking directly back at me. "I don't know what I can do to help."

"What?" I asked. "There are all kinds of meds for people who have panic attacks."

"To my knowledge panic attacks have never been diagnosed in horses," he said, shrugging his shoulders.

"How can that be?" My gut wrenched in distress.

"If a horse is uncontrollable, he usually ends up at the slaughter-house," he said flatly.

"I can't believe this," I said, my voice carrying a few too many shrill overtones. "What about all the advances in medicine I read about?"

"All right, all right," he said in exasperation. "All I can offer is a Hail Mary."

"What do you mean?" I said, my outlook brightening a nanometer.

"I don't think they'll be able to help you," he said, scribbling in his notepad, "but I'll refer you to the University of California veterinary school at Davis. The school is well respected and someone up there may know of this condition. I'll call ahead to make the referral. You'll need to call and set up a time for an appointment."

"What a great idea," I said, my frown trying to find its way out.

"I wouldn't expect too much," he said, turning to leave. "I mean that."

I had started the day happy then slipped into desperation and now was trying to crawl back out onto the fragile wings of hope. I returned to my house feeling as though I had been whipsawed. So here I was again. No resolution. My frustration, broken free of its shackles, ranted at the unfairness of it all. Somehow I always came back to the same place. Emma's and my history and personalities were so similar that whatever I did to or for her I did to or for myself. Whatever happened to her happened to me. We were so close that we wrote with indelible ink on each other's hearts.

Maybe the vet school would have an answer and give us both peace. I let hope set a bud.

Chapter 17

Elaine and I sat down at our favorite table at a local Mexican restaurant. Emma was tucked away in her stall and we needed to have dinner after our trip to the UC Davis vet school. Elaine ordered up a big meal with all of the extras and wine. I ordered a child's plate.

"Well that trip was a bust," I said, drumming my fingers on the table. "With all of those vets, you would think that someone had come across this problem before. They had no helpful suggestions. They tested her for EPM (equine protozoal myeloencephalitis) but that came back negative. The highlight of the day was watching you bat your eyelashes at the cute vets. Fun for Elaine, no help for Emma."

As usual, Elaine looked stunning. Her make-up was artfully applied, her clothes looked as if they were freshly pressed and with her warm, engaging smile she was the complete picture of approachable elegance. She wore neutral colors appropriate for the dirt that one invariably encounters around horses. Her designer silk scarf was tucked under the collar of her blouse where it was protected from the vagrant swish of a tail.

If Elaine were not such an incredibly nice person, I often conjectured that more women would find it easy to dislike her. It didn't help she was a glamorous fashion model. One time I overheard a conversation between two boarders at the barn. One said to the other, "I hope her horse doesn't sneeze snot all over her perfect clothes," sounding exactly as though that was what she was wishing. I had laughed to myself and felt sorry they were immune to Elaine's other charms.

"Diana, you'll love this," Elaine said, unabashedly changing the topic. "Tom has added another horse to his lineup."

"Another one?" I asked, bewildered. "How does he support them all?"

"He occasionally manages to sell one here or there so he can pay for the upkeep of the rest," Elaine said.

"How is your lease arrangement going?" I asked.

"It gives me the opportunity to ride more often," Elaine said. "I only pay Tom for the board expenses, not vet or shoes. I'm determined to really improve my seat. I have to say that I'm growing fond of this horse."

"Here's hoping that he may melt your heart and turn you into a horse owner," I said, a subdued smile emerging across my face. I resisted the "I told you so" smile.

"Well I have grown attached to him," she said, raising her glass of wine. "I think I'm starting to know what you mean about getting close to one horse."

Despite Elaine's attempts to change the subject, I couldn't stop thinking about our trip with Emma.

"UC Davis is one of the best vet schools in the country and they couldn't offer my horse any help," I said, determined to vent my feelings once again. "We can put men on the moon, but science can't help my horse. Is Emma going to live her whole life in misery? What else was going to happen to her?"

"Did you ever think of getting another horse besides Emma?" Elaine offered, settling against the back of her chair.

"I can't afford it," I said, my mood crashing further. "Emma's special needs require a lot of money and energy. Her sneakers, feed supplements, chiropractor visits, acupuncture treatments to name a few. I can't imagine taking care of another horse while I take care of Emma. My chronic fatigue is better right now, but I never know when another attack is going to happen."

"You're such a talented rider, it seems a shame that you can't do everything that you want to," Elaine said, motioning the waitress for another glass of wine.

"Thanks for the compliment," I said. "You're right. I feel thwarted in my attempt to move up the levels. No trail riding either."

"I still think you would be better off with a man," Elaine said, her eyes twinkling.

Elaine felt that a man in a woman's life was the solution to most emotional needs. As a member of Sufism Reoriented I had to abide by a few simple rules. No lying, live to your highest knowing, no mind altering drugs and no sex outside of marriage. Try and explain all of that to a dating prospect. And it would be a slim chance to find anyone who could tolerate my idiosyncrasies. It was easier not to date at all. Besides, I didn't particularly feel the need to have a man in my life. Teaching had shown me how much I could love children but I had no need for my own. I didn't need to be attached to someone to love. Besides, I don't think that Elaine understood how seriously I took my commitment to a spiritual path. She loved and loved fully – a full blooded Italian woman.

"No comment." My fingers tapped out a quick rhythm on the table.

When dinner was over, I hugged Elaine and thanked her for coming with me.

Safely in my home, my feelings, set loose, rushed out in a torrent of tears. I had done everything possible to make Emma happy and I still didn't have a horse that would help me realize my dreams. The trip to Davis was the last option in providing a solution. More time, more money. Sometimes I felt that having a horse was a sink hole for financial and emotional resources. As I crawled into bed I thought that perhaps I was being too stubborn. As I slipped off to sleep a wisp of a thought flitted through my brain, "Maybe it's time to give up Emma."

The next morning, my temper was short and reactive despite the beautiful sunny day. The trip to Davis had left me depressed. I didn't want to take my disappointment out on Emma so I did my best to improve my negative disposition before I headed out to Sweet Mountain.

I had to do a lot of self talk to make that happen. Each time I tried to stay positive, an unpleasant thought crept into my brain. This horse is costing me a lot of money. Her anxiety is stressing me out. She doesn't want any more stress in her life and I know I don't either. The prospect of being greeted by a wild eyed and unrideable horse didn't help the situation. This wasn't the picture of why I had a horse.

I slammed the car door shut with such force the car rocked. I turned to head to the barn and heard Emma nicker. A nicker? Not a scream? My heart leapt. A quicker beat to my pulse. One of sweet anticipation.

Emma stood in her stall waiting for me at her door. Her eyes were bright and soft. Her expression was present and intelligent.

"Emma, you're back."

What a relief to have my horse as I knew she was meant to be. I wasn't going to let this opportunity pass. These periods of respite usually lasted a week or so. I tacked Emma up and headed to the outdoor arena.

I held the buckle of the reins and let her stretch her neck down and out. What a great feeling to be back on my horse. A placid, tranquil horse. She picked up the trot and her back swung freely. She floated across the ground with long strides.

Near the northwest quadrant of the arena, Emma suddenly swerved and refused to go on. I turned her around and approached the same spot, thinking that she had been startled by something in the trees on the other side of the fence. Again she suddenly veered to one side and stopped abruptly. The behavior seemed to be a bit strange. She wasn't anxious. This didn't feel the same as one of her attacks. She wasn't holding any tension. I urged her back up to the trot and found that we could go around the spot if we stayed very close to the fence. That meant that it couldn't be something in the trees that was spooking her since the trees were on the other side of the fence.

I reversed direction and went back. It was worth the test since horses sometimes exhibit behavior only on one side of their body. When we came to the problem area, she pivoted right and stopped. Puzzled I proceeded to the interior of the arena and trotted away.

Then I got the idea to zigzag the area. After several zigzags I could map the size of the "no go" zone. It was about fifteen feet across, about ten feet from the fence and seemed to be circular. There was absolutely nothing that I could see that would keep us from traveling into that space. Emma would not respond to any degree of coaxing. The best I could do that day was to use other parts of the arena. If I had to avoid a small area in the arena it was an insignificant sacrifice if I could ride my horse in peace. Not being able to ride at all had taught me to not sweat the small stuff.

My curiosity got the better of me. I had learned by now that whenever Emma did something, she always had a reason for it. Sometimes her answers were surprising or charming or in many cases, heart warming. In the evening, I called Carol to find out what Emma was avoiding.

"Emma's isn't having an attack," I said, reassuring Carol that this time all was well. "She's doing something she's never done before. It's strange."

"Before I start translating," Carol said, "I want to tell you how sorry I am that your trip to UC Davis didn't yield better results. I feel for both of you."

"I appreciate that," I said, swallowing hard. "You are one of the few people who understand what we've been going through. You've been with us through every challenge. But today is a good day, Emma was herself and I got to ride. Only Emma wouldn't go into one part of the arena. Why?"

"Emma says there's a swirling force field in the part of the arena where she won't go," Carol said. "She calls it a 'stopping vortex.'"

What in the world was a stopping vortex? One more example to remind me that Emma's world was much more complicated than I could ever imagine. I never had a problem strolling through a space. Granted, some places gave me creepy feelings, but that didn't stop me.

"Why wouldn't you pass through it?" I asked.

"The energy is very strong and my body automatically puts on the brakes whenever I go near it," Carol translated for Emma. "I can't help it. The energy churns around with such tremendous power that I can't push myself through it."

"Carol, I think that Emma just sent me the feeling," I said.

"What does it feel like?" Carol asked. "She's not sending it to me."

"You know how the repelling force grows stronger the closer you try to bring the ends of two magnets together? That's how it feels. By moving the magnets around each other you can detect the force field, but can't see it. The closer Emma gets to the spot, the more she is pushed away. No wonder she can't go there."

"The force field doesn't stay in one place," Carol translated.

"Where does it go?" I asked.

"I don't know, but it will be moving out of the arena shortly." Carol translated.

"Emma, how do you know it will be exiting soon?" I asked.

"I just know," Carol translated.

How does Emma know these things? Where does that kind of knowledge come from? I wish she could tell me more.

"You know, it helps explain why riders often accuse their horses of spooking at nothing," I said, feeling guilty for all of the times I got irritated at my horses for responding to what appeared to be empty space.

"They see things we don't," Carol reminded me. "Rather, Emma, in particular, sees more and experiences things more deeply."

I intended to take advantage of Emma's stability of emotions and headed out to the barn the next day with high hopes of another good ride. I was rewarded with another gentle nicker and soft eye. I rushed through grooming and tacking up. Leading Emma into the arena, I wondered whether or not we were going to encounter the vortex. As Emma had predicted, it was gone and we were able to work uninterrupted in the entire arena. What a joyful day.

A couple of days later when I was working Emma, she refused to go into the northeast corner of the arena. Instead of a sudden halt or swerve she eased into a stop. I couldn't quite put what I felt into words, but it was different from before. She didn't balk abruptly the way she had with the vortex. This felt more like an avoidance without clear boundaries. I couldn't imagine what was happening now. My horse was rideable and instead of a blissful ride of schooling dressage, we seemed to run into an invisible wall of some kind. What was going on now?

Once again I decided to map the "no go" zone and found that it occupied the entire corner including the area along the fence. Because it occupied a major portion of the arena, we were confined to a small area where Emma would move freely. I almost found the place in my heart that would allow laughter over this ridiculous situation.

We had a stopping vortex a few days before. I wondered what else could be populating Emma's world. Or perhaps the vortex was dispersing into a billowy dust devil. My imagination had fun coming up with explanations for our new "no go" zone. That evening I plunked down on my chair and called Carol to find out what other things might exist in the world that I didn't know about.

"Emma, why are you avoiding going to that corner of the arena?" I asked, once Carol was ready to talk to Emma. "Is it a reincarnation of the vortex? A bigger, but gentler version?"

"Emma's not afraid, she isn't being repelled," Carol translated. "She just doesn't want to go there."

"Why, what's different?" I asked. "You always have a reason for what you do."

I heard an interruption in Carol's breathing. She was taking longer than usual to respond. Her pause made me a little nervous.

"Emma says there are Native American spirits there," Carol said, her voice raised in pitch. "They've set up camp. You know, I haven't ever heard of anything similar to this."

"You haven't?" I asked with surprise. "Aren't you the one that had me pretending to be a light house? Emma, what is it with these Native American spirits? Why are they still hanging around and not reincarnating in their next human body? What are they doing here?"

"They are migrating and won't be here for very long," Carol translated. "It's a family group that's temporarily living near the creek. I don't want to intrude on their camp."

"Emma, do the other horses see them?" I asked, remembering that other riders in the ring were using that space.

"To some degree," Carol translated.

"So, why are they unaffected?" I asked. "They don't even seem to slow down in that part of the ring."

"Emma says that the other horses don't care," Carol said. "She's being respectful of the spirits."

I sighed. I was delighted that my horse was being respectful. I was even pleased that Emma could tell us about worlds that I didn't know existed. That was all fine and dandy, but I wanted to ride my horse.

"Emma, why not ask the spirits if it would be all right to use that part of the arena," I suggested, pleased that I might have come up with a solution. I couldn't help but take pause to acknowledge to myself that I had come a long way. Here I was asking my horse to communicate with beings not of this world as if it were an ordinary request, part of typical human behavior.

"I never thought of that," Carol translated.

"Native Americans are very aware of the needs of animals," I said, lapsing into teacher mode. "They know that horses need to use their muscles. Keeping you at one end of the arena in small circles is not good for your body. It's hard on your joints. They would understand this."

"Emma is just repeating that she never thought of that," Carol said.

"When I go out there, I will take you over by them and you can talk to them," I said, formulating a plan in my head.

"Oh no, you talk to them," Carol translated, making the statement a protest.

"Why? I can't even see them," I reasoned. "You are the one who sees them."

"I don't want to talk to them, you do it," Carol translated. "Diana, she's emphatic about this."

"But, why?" I asked, beginning to wonder about the safety of this idea. "They can't hurt you, can they?"

"Please, you talk to them," Carol translated, pleading with the tone of her voice. "I don't feel comfortable addressing the disembodied human spirits."

I laughed out loud. As if it would be any easier for me to talk to disembodied spirits I couldn't see. My skin crawled. Maybe Emma thought if I was courageous enough to take on her panic attacks, I would be courageous on other fronts as well. This was something very different. Then I surprised myself. In many ways I thought of Emma as my child. The mother protector in me rose out of that primal place that gives mothers extraordinary strength when faced with rescuing their babies.

"Okay," I relented. "But you will have to let me know what they say. Remember I don't see them."

Before I even finished that sentence, my mind was taken over by a vision. I had had enough experiences with Emma sending me images that I knew not to be frightened and not to worry that I was losing my mind when the world appeared to be going out of control.

"You're awfully quiet," Carol said.

"Emma is sending me a picture of the group of Indians encamped in the north end of the arena," I responded.

"What do you see?" Carol asked.

"I see them as beings of light," I said, entranced by what was playing out in my mind. "Their bodies, their clothes, their implements, and their belongings are made of translucent, muted light. It's as if an artist has used drawing pencils made of filtered light and softly sketched their outlines with some minimal shading. Everything and everyone in the camp glows in soft, pale luminescent colors of yellow, blue and pink."

"How cool is that?" Carol said.

"If I look very closely, I can just make out their facial features," I said, straining to see as much detail as I could and totally absorbed in the images vividly appearing in my mind. I was like a kid watching a 3D action movie. "They are going about their daily chores and their movements are in keeping with what I'd expect from a living group."

The richness of the experience caught me by surprise. I was watching what appeared to be living, breathing humans. I thought the experience with the whales was an extraordinary occurrence, never to be repeated. Usually when Emma shared visions with me, they tended to be more mundane. Once when she injured her pastern, she sent me pictures of her bandaged leg after the vet had visited. I knew that Emma entered people's dreams to work with them – to help heal them, to open their hearts. Sometimes she entered my dreams and I would wake remembering vague images of us playing together or hanging out in a grassy field.

This felt entirely different. Watching the Indians made me feel like a voyeur. My discomfort rooted me to my chair and I couldn't do anything but sit, squirm and watch this phenomenon. The more I watched the more ill at ease I became. I felt as if I were trespassing on a world that might have consequences out of my control. My stomach tightened and my jaw jammed shut. I was not looking forward to this contact. Then a thought whizzed through my head. Maybe, when I went out to the barn the whole thing might have disappeared the way the "stopping vortex" had. Grabbing hold of that thought provided some relief.

I ended the conversation by saying. "All right Emma, we have a plan. I guess tomorrow I'll find out what's going to happen when I talk to these spirits." I gulped and hung up the phone.

The next day as I drove to the barn I found myself anticipating an encounter of a very weird kind. My tendency in my Mustang was to rush to the speed limit and tear around corners. Each set of tires did well to clock 17,000 miles before I had them worn out. This day I drove well below the speed limit and found the trip to the barn far too short. I hesitated before I stepped out of the car.

Although it was a clear, sunny day, the cold, biting wind penetrated my jacket and made me shudder whenever the strong gusts hit. But then again, it may not have been the wind. Speaking to the departed was out of my realm of experience or understanding. What if I would be contacting something sinister and open some wormhole into an alternate universe of perversity? I tried to ground myself and harness my imagination.

Standing outside Emma's stall, I saw bright eyes and a perky expression waiting for me. No panic attack today to keep her from being ridden. That didn't seem fair. A postponement to a powwow with the disincarnate Indians would have been my preference. I spent more than the usual amount of time grooming. My dawdling ended when Emma's coat glistened and I couldn't find even the tiniest speck of dust to brush off. I saddled her up. On one hand I wanted to postpone this experience as I had no idea what was going to happen. On the other hand I wanted it over with as soon as possible, so the nervousness in my stomach would go away.

On our way to the arena, I let Emma grab any blade of grass lining the path and wishing there was more to detain us. I carefully secured the arena gate behind us and took a few deep breaths. The arena was empty, very empty, having been vacated by a couple of girls riding out to the trails on their ponies. Ponies who moments before had been nonchalantly walking through the north end of the arena. I wondered how it would be to live a simpler life.

"Okay Emma, you'll have to take me to them," I said, resigning myself to my fate.

Emma lowered her head, poked out her nose and with a determined stride headed in a straight line to the north east corner. I lagged back by her shoulder, playing out the reins so she could get ahead of me. About half way across the arena, she shortened her footfall and stopped. She stared straight ahead. Every muscle was in readiness. Her sensory cells seemed as if they were tingling and quivering in wait. That she showed no fear comforted and strengthened me.

I stared in the same direction as Emma, seeing nothing but the ground, wood fence and trees beyond. Without warning, my mind lit up. Emma sent me the picture of the Native American light beings. I studied them for a few minutes as they quietly moved among themselves in their campground. They were engrossed in their activities. I took a breath to ready myself.

"We have come to talk to you," I said, my voice wavering.

The Indians appeared startled and seemed surprised to have a living being address them. The women stopped preparing food and spun their heads to look at me. They remained squatting next to their bowls. The men, however, jumped up, stepped closer, and faced me at full attention. They squared their shoulders and took a wide stance. Their arms were held away from their bodies. They seemed in readiness to fight or perhaps, I hoped, simply on guard to take defensive actions.

I felt my heart race and my palms get sticky. I swallowed hard.

"It would be great to use this part of the arena so that my horse can get her exercise," I said, wondering if further speech might inflame them. "But we don't want to do anything that would be disrespectful." I held my breath and readied to flee.

The Indians stared at me with intensity as if I had interrupted a sacred rite. In a heart beat my dread escalated to fright. Their look felt threatening. I didn't know what they might do. Perhaps I'd better explain myself.

"We have much to learn from you," I said, my voice breaking. "The white people didn't understand what you had to teach them. They didn't understand how well you know how to live with the land, to honor the land, and to live with the earth in harmony. Only with your permission will we use this part of the arena and only if it is not any kind of imposition." I took a gulp of air and a step back.

The men stood without moving as if listening to what I had to say. Their shoulders seemed to soften. Their arms appeared to drop a tiny bit closer to their bodies. But I wasn't sure. A thought raced across my mind. I don't know where it came from. The energy it brought was powerful and I had no choice but to give it voice.

"If it's all right to pass through this space, when we do pass through it, I will open my heart should you choose to help me understand how it is to be in harmony with the earth." I felt as if I became one with the words, the Indians and the experience. I had no idea from where those words emanated.

They stared back in stillness and silence.

"I would be grateful for anything that you would teach me," I said, the words rushing out from somewhere inside me.

The men held my gaze and maintained their posture of heightened alertness. Nothing from their body language indicated whether we would be welcome to use their space. I waited. No one moved. What a standoff.

Not knowing what else to do, I turned Emma around and headed back to the mounting block by the entrance gate. I put one foot on the first step. Then the other foot on the next step. I stood at the top and looked over to the north. The corner had returned to my usual reality. No Indians were to be seen. I picked up the reins and swung my leg over the saddle.

I walked Emma in a small circle near the entrance gate for a few minutes. I eased her into a trot and took a couple of warm-up circles. With a deep, quivering breath, I headed to the encampment. My heart thumped in anticipation of what might happen. Would Emma stop or would she continue on? What would happen to us? We neared the boundary of the camp. Emma continued to trot forward without slowing down or changing her rhythm. I immediately noticed that the way she put down each leg changed. Each footfall became a caress, a kiss and a sacred connection to the Earth. The air seemed alive and to be vibrating in some indescribable harmonic.

I was beyond myself at the divinity of the moment. The quality of the earth underfoot changed. It became alive and connected to us in living energy. I felt as if I had been transported into some alternate reality. Even the wood fence posts seemed to be connected to a living wave of some cosmic rhythm. Everything was moving and vibrating as if a magical conductor was directing the various waves and pulses in a symphony of interweaving themes.

As we moved out of the encampment, the experience stopped as abruptly as it began and I was back in the world as I knew it. My heart, however, did not stop its quickened beat with all of the adrenaline that was rushing through my system. I decided to continue on a large circle and approach the encampment again. As soon as we arrived at the camp boundary the world immediately shifted. It was as if we had entered a temple which was infused with sacred and divine energy. We were given the gift of understanding that everything has consciousness and that all forms are connected. Even the sand was moving and pulsing in a vibrant rhythm.

I knew that there was sound that I could not hear. My body resonated with an enchanting melody that was just out of reach of my ears. The gusts of the wind were gone and the temperature was warm. It was as if we were moving through a soft liquid medium somewhere between the viscosity of air and water. You could see vibrations in the air similar to the ripples and gentle waves on the surface of a pond only these were in three dimensions.

Emma's movement had transformed into a glide with her feet barely touching the ground. It was difficult for me to absorb all of the changes I was seeing. I was in awe of this new vision of relationship to matter. This encounter of "oneness" with all matter and that all matter was alive was a big concept to experience. Once again when we moved out of the encampment everything changed back to what I knew as normal.

As I continued the circle, I approached the entrance gate intending to enter the encampment again. At the gate, a boarder who was standing on the other side of the fence, called out to me. I reined Emma to a stop,

"Yo, Diana, what do you think about the new shipment of hay?" she asked.

I breathed out and felt grateful for the interruption. I wasn't sure that my heart could hold any more of the gifts like the ones I had just been given.

No more than three weeks after coming back from UC Davis and two weeks after the experience with the Native Americans, Emma had one of her attacks. Not on the trail, not in a turnout paddock, not in her stall. It happened in the riding arena while I was schooling her.

She didn't seem to be reacting to anything. The vortex was gone and the Native Americans had decamped after my first encounter with them. The symptoms were her classic panic attack. The whites of her eyes bulged, her body stiffened and she picked up speed. I leapt off her back and managed to land on my feet, grabbing the reins. Pushing and shoving I kept her from knocking me down until I got her back into her stall, slipped off her bridle, dropped her saddle to the shavings and let her loose. I was shattered. Riding on the stable property had seemed to be a place safe from her attacks.

That night, nothing I did, red wine, Cheetos or a distracting television program ameliorated my dejection. Every time I thought I had negotiated a workable solution, Emma's behavior escalated. I felt as if I had explored every possibility to bring Emma relief. Not knowing what else to do, I decided that life must go on and I would simply have to accommodate to her behavior. That meant I would have to be vigilant when I rode, hypersensitive to her emotions at all times, so that I could anticipate an attack. Fortunately, Emma's attacks manifested symptoms a couple of seconds before she became nearly uncontrollable. With the first hint, I learned to dismount as quickly as possible and maneuver Emma back to her stall where she could move around at will, work it off and be safe.

As her attacks grew more severe, my dismounts took the form of a vault while maintaining a death grip on the reins. Although I was never trained, anyone watching might have thought I was a well schooled gymnast by the way I made these hasty departures at all speeds and angles of trajectory. After launching through the air, I always managed to land on my feet. I also learned how to remove Emma's tack on the fly while she dragged me back to her stall. By the time she reached her stall door I had the stirrups up and the bridle unbuckled.

"This isn't right," Betty said one day when she saw me racing down the barn aisle next to Emma, fumbling with my fingers to unbuckle her flash noseband.

"I don't know what else to do," I yelled over my shoulder, as I disappeared into Emma's stall. "I want to ride her. Sometimes riding her seems to mitigate her attacks."

"She didn't use to have them when you rode her in the arena," Betty reminded me.

"I know. For sure, they're getting worse," I admitted. "Emma told the animal communicator that dressage sometimes gives her a reprieve from her anxiety by requiring her to focus on her work." I dropped the saddle to the stall floor.

"Are you waiting for the day that one of you is going to get hurt?" Betty asked, spreading her feet wide and crossing her arms as she stood in the doorway.

"I can jump off of her okay, can't I?" I slid the crown piece of Emma's bridle over her ears freeing her to run out into her paddock and to pace the fence line. Turning to face Betty, I was surprised. I felt as if I had encountered a wall.

"You need to see what you're doing from my viewpoint." Betty's gaze was steady. "It seems every time I'm out here, the picture looks worse. You have to step back and try and see yourself. If Emma were to get loose and run back to her stall she could hurt someone."

My head jerked up and I shifted my weight to my heels. My mind whirred as I tried to imagine what I looked like to others. I couldn't. I imagined how other riders would appear if I saw them flying through the air off a careening horse with wild eyes. My stomach sunk as soon as I got it. I would look pretty stupid and irresponsible. I pictured Emma running over some little kid at the barn. Shame spread across my face with sticky fingers. I realized how unheeding and thoughtless I had become in my efforts to keep Emma as a riding horse.

"I'm not a very good role model for the children who come to the barn, am I?" I asked, sinking deeper in my shame. Embarrassment enveloped me in thick muck. "And you're right. If Emma got away from me, someone could get hurt."

"You have to stop this," Betty said. "It's time to put the horse down. She's a danger to you and herself."

"I don't understand why it's happening. She can have a panic attack while she's just standing in her stall," I said, digging my boot into the sawdust in Emma's stall. "One minute she's fine and then the next minute her misery is at full speed. I don't get it. I've consulted everyone I know. Emma doesn't know what triggers the panic attacks."

"I've seen what she does her in her stall," Betty said, dropping her voice and placing her hand lightly on my shoulder. "It's time to do something,"

"I know saying this was difficult for you," I said, looking at her belt buckle. "I know how hard it was for me to hear. Thank you. I think I needed the wakeup call. I don't ever want to hurt anyone."

Betty opened her arms and encircled me in a hug. I felt the warmth of her body against my belly. My chest heaved with a gut-wrenching sob. Her arms responded by encircling me tighter. We rocked together until she released me and walked back to her horse.

Betty's words repeated in my mind when I was alone in Emma's stall. I fell back against the wall, my shoulders released in surrender and tears poured from my eyes as I watched Emma run back and forth in her paddock. I called her name. Her glassy eyes looked past me as if I weren't there.

Chapter 18

I woke up to a damp pillow the next morning. Swollen eyes and a stuffed nose were the vestiges of the night that had been filled with nightmares, one morphing into another with images of despair, terror and loss. My body felt as if I had been running for my life all night. I shook my head, but I couldn't get rid of the cloud of gloom that encased me.

Thoughts that had plagued me the night before remained ensconced, brooding and unresolved. Betty's words circulated in my mind in an endless loop. She had forced me to get perspective, to understand the ramifications of what I was doing.

The realization of truth hurt. I knew how to live in denial. I did it for most of my early life. I didn't know what to do with Emma, so I ignored how dangerous the situation had become. Each time she got worse, I learned to accommodate. The increments weren't that small so I didn't have much of an excuse other than my own denial. As I looked back now, I realized I never took stock of what was going on. I detached from my own terror. My childhood had taught me how to do that. I had spent years in therapy to stop doing that. An out-of-control Emma was a dangerous Emma. Someone could get seriously injured. I had to get real.

Despite all of my investigations no answers manifested. No one I consulted knew what to do. My dream horse wasn't safe. The horse I had fallen in love with was breaking my heart. The horse that taught me all animals have complex feelings and their own distinct voice. The horse that shared whale energy with me. The horse that connected me to the teachings of the Native Americans. The horse that knew me better than myself. How many people experience these kinds of gifts?

I couldn't put Emma down unless she wanted me to. Murder was not in my make-up. Other people thought nothing of putting a horse down when their serviceable years had passed. Even riders who had their own property and could afford to pasture their horse preferred to destroy their animal when it no longer could perform to their standard.

How could I? How could I look Emma in the eye and say I've decided you're a burden and am going to end your life. Even the thought made me feel sick. It would feel as if I were committing suicide or killing a human.

She wasn't saleable. Besides it would feel like selling a part of me. We were so close I couldn't separate our thoughts. I couldn't ride her and I couldn't afford another horse. How could I give up riding? It was my passion. Riding horses fueled my existence. I saw no way out.

Emma's uncontrolled behaviors had gotten the attention of my horse friends. Having to make difficult decisions themselves for unrideable horses, they came up with several helpful alternatives where horses could be donated for another use. One friend knew of a facility that would accept horses who could be used as blood donors. They took blood on some safe rotation schedule. The horse wouldn't be ridden and would only be handled periodically. There were similar places that I could find where Emma would be treated well. Maybe not well in the way I would want. She would be fed and her health needs would be taken care of. She wouldn't be anyone's pet, but she would have pasture friends and still live out her life.

I sank back in my bed engulfed in despair.

My jaw was set as I drove out to the barn. The early hour ensured that I would see Emma and still get to work on time. Besides, I wanted to be at the barn before anyone got there. What I had to do, I wanted to do alone.

The sun, streaming the occasional beam of light through the morning mist, snuck a glance over the ridge of the foothills. My boots scuffed the gravel as I walked across the parking lot. The crunch of rock broke against my ears and pulled me back to why I was there. The muscles of my diaphragm heaved up, expelled the air from my lungs and collided with my stomach. Nausea claimed victory. I gasped for air and the smell of moist earth, clean and fresh, helped ground me. The early morning fog crept by me and latched its sticky fingers onto the front of my sweater and frizzed my hair. Beads of sweat rolled down the small of my back. My walk slowed to a shuffle, not unlike the gait of a sour horse leaving the barn.

My head oriented to a stomp from the barn. Probably a horse stamping his foot to dislodge a fly. My palms grabbed the metal entry door at the main entrance and I leaned against it, weighted with a decade of reluctance. Emma's stall was the first one on the right.

"I must tell Emma." My vow reasserted itself in an odious expulsion from my lungs.

I forced myself forward and slid open Emma's stall door. The rollers creaked on the metal rails. The fluffy pine shavings in her stall welcomed my feet. Emma turned and looked at me with her soft, brown eyes. She sidled up to me and nuzzled my chest. I gulped and reached deep to where my resolve had retreated. I needed to do this. I needed to tell her I couldn't keep a dangerous horse anymore.

She raised her neck and arched it from her poll to her withers. Her eyes blazed with affection and caring. It was almost as if I could see the golden puffs of her energy envelop my body. I felt weightless and my muscles lost their tension. The liquid brown of her eyes reflected flecks of gold. Another blast of energy intoxicated my brain. I was so consumed with the feeling it was as if the rest of the earth had retreated from view. All I could do was experience the joy of the moment. I felt incredible peace. I was okay with everything in my life and in the world.

My shoulder rested against Emma's neck. No mind-altering drug could possibly give this kind of high. Out of habit I turned to shut her stall door. I couldn't pull away. It was as if gravity pulled me back to Emma's touch. The pull was so strong that my feet wouldn't move. The energy Emma was sharing made me giddy and I wanted more.

Emma was sharing love. My heart was an empty sponge for it. Why would I want to turn away from it? Why would I part with her? What had I been thinking? Isn't it a gift from the Divine? This kind of love was transformational.

Thoughts erupted in my brain. I can sell my house and buy horse property. Maybe my commute will be longer, but I can have a small pasture where Emma can live and have room to self-exercise. Where she can't hurt anyone. I don't HAVE to ride her.

I threw my arms around her shoulders and pressed my chest into hers. She wrapped her neck around me. The warmth of her body soothed me. Tears of joy washed out the muck of anguish and hopelessness.

"Emma, you are my best friend. How could I entrust your happiness to someone else? I can lease someone else's horse. I can school other people's horses if I absolutely have to ride. What you give me is bigger and more important than breath. That you are, that you love, that you make me feel this way…"

I cried with joy as relief romped through my body. My heart opened to receive what poured through me. Hot tears warmed my cold cheeks and a rush of emotion radiated out from my heart to Emma. This epiphany would change my life. I had dropped my guard to intimacy. I got close to something that mattered. And in loving me, Emma had taught me to surrender to love.

The morning sun streamed through the bay window in my kitchen warming the room with its happy light. For the first time in months I had slept well. No longer was I going to agonize over what to do with Emma. I had made a decision and would follow through on implementing my idea of purchasing horse property. Emma was my best friend. She had shown me worlds that I would have never imagined. This relationship was to be prized.

I could no longer look at animals the same way. Several sparrows lighted on a branch in the tulip tree in my front yard. I could imagine the conversation that they were having. And more importantly I now knew that they were capable of rich and complex communications.

A couple of flies darted against the window. And I spoke to them. "How is your day? Are you enjoying the sunshine as much as I am? Have you found love and acceptance in your world? Are you happy and satisfied?"

They landed on the window pane. I could swear that they heard me and were acknowledging my questions.

A squirrel bolted across the street. It perched in a large sycamore tree and seemed to stare at my neighbor who was busy washing his car. His wife had left him and his depression showed in his listless movements. He was doing his best to raise his son. Another squirrel bounced over and joined his friend, sitting on the branch. A bell in my head sounded a ting.

I dashed to my office and pulled out a book of poems that I had recently read and came back to the kitchen. Thumbing through the pages, I found what I was looking for.

Imagine that. In the fourteenth century the Sufi poet Hafiz wrote: "Squirrels and birds sense your sadness
And call an important conference in a tall tree.
They decide which secret code to chant
To help your mind and soul."

(Hafiz poem translated by Daniel Ladinsky.

Published in *I Heard God Laughing*, pg. 81)

I used to think that Hafiz was writing fantasy.

The sun on my sweatshirt, the steam from my tea cup and the bath of love that I felt made me tipsy with joy.

Emma, my world will never be the same. You have expanded my understanding of life. Thank you for all of your gifts.

Epilogue

The impetus that drove me to write *Emma Speaks* was to move the reader farther down the path of respect and regard for all animals, and to gain appreciation for the depth of their involvement in our lives, not just our companion animals who share our homes, but all animals who inhabit this planet Earth with us.

The next book in this series, which I am currently writing, continues that goal with chronicles of my continued search for happiness for both Emma and me. In our journey together Emma continues to surprise me with wonderful adventures and worlds that exist beyond our ordinary senses.

If you are interested in contacting the telepathic animal communicator, Griffin Kanter, who Carol consulted when Emma was lost in the Sierra foothills, please visit: http://www.talkwiththeanimals.com/

Carol is living a private life and did not want to open her practice.

If you would like more information please go to my website. http://www.dianastjames.org

Glossary

At A, enter working trot sitting…	Often the first movement in a lower level dressage test.
bars	A structure on the bottom of the foot of the horse.
cannon bone	In the front leg, the bone connecting the horses fetlock to knee.
cheek pieces	The small leather straps that connect the bit to the headstall of the bridle.
collect, collection	The horse shifts weight to the hindquarters and lightens the front end resulting in being more agile.
colt	Young male horse. Filly is the young female. Foal is the very young horse and not gender specific.

curb bit	Along with the bridoon the curb is the second bit in the horse's mouth when riding upper level dressage.
dock	The base of the tail.
dressage	A classical equestrian sport where the rider and horse perform predetermined movements. The training develops the athleticism of the horse.
dualie	A truck with two sets of tires on the rear axle.
enterolith	A hard lump of mineral salts that sometimes forms in the gut of the horse.
eventing	See three-day event.
FEI level movements	FEI is the international governing body for the highest levels of dressage. The passage and piaffe are movements at this level.
fetlock	The joint above the pastern and hoof of the horse.
flake	Bales of hay are divided into sections called flakes.

flexion	Can be either longitudinal - the horse rounds from nose to tail with the back coming up and the hind quarters stepping further under the horse, or lateral - on a circle the horse curves around the rider's inside leg bending the neck and back on the arc of the circle.
frog	The central part of the horse's hoof that is elastic and cushions the foot when it hits the ground.
girth leathers	The straps of leather under the skirts of the saddle to which the girth attaches.
half-pass	Done in any gait, the horse moves laterally while bent in the direction of travel.
haunches-in	On the rail the horse's haunches leave the rail and track to the inside with a bend throughout the body.
headstall	The part of a bridle that goes over the horse's poll and holds up the cheek pieces which attach to the bit.
hock	The hind end joint above the fetlock.
impulsion	The energy that the horse uses to thrust off the ground with her hind legs.

in frame	Putting the horse on the bit, connecting the horse from back to front.
isoxsuprine	Prescribed drug that helps improve circulation in the feet of horses.
jig	A rapid, nervous, short-stepped trot or jog.
lateral movements	Shoulder-in, haunches-in or half-pass.
Logan	A horse trailer manufacturer.
longe	Using a long rope or tape connected to the horse, the handler exercises the horse in a circle.
Miley	A horse trailer manufacturer.
navicular disease	A disease of the navicular bone that causes lameness in horses and is sometimes difficult to treat.
passage	A movement in the highest levels of dressage. A slow trot with maximum suspension.
pastern	The area of the horse's leg between the hoof and the fetlock.
piaffe	A movement in the highest levels of dressage. The horse lowers the haunches and trots in place.

poll	The top of the horse's head between the ears.
ringbone	Excessive bone growth on the pastern of the horse sometimes causing pain.
seat	Refers to the balance of the rider. How well they are positioned on the saddle and in harmony with the horse's movement.
shoulder-in	On the rail the horse's shoulders leave the rail and track to the inside with a bend throughout the body.
snaffle bit	A bit with a hinge in the center. Considered to be gentler than a straight bar bit with a port.
three-day event	An equestrian sport that combines dressage, cross country jumping and stadium jumping.
warmblood	Often a horse of European ancestry with a combination of the heavier draft breeds and lighter "hot" breeds such as the thoroughbred or Arabian. Many show horses or sporthorses are warmbloods.
way of going	Refers to the way a horse moves, both natural and improved with training.

Made in the USA
San Bernardino, CA
23 November 2013